How Can Man
Die Better

Dedication

*To the young men of the Royal Regiment of Wales
who went on ahead.*

How Can Man Die Better

The Secrets of Isandlwana Revealed

Lieutenant Colonel Mike Snook

Foreword by

Brigadier David Keenan

Frontline Books,
London

First published in Great Britain in 2005
by Greenhill Books, Lionel Leventhal Limited
www.greenhillbooks.com

Republished in this format in 2010
and reprinted in 2014, 2016 by
FRONTLINE BOOKS
An imprint of
Pen & Sword Books Ltd
47 Church Street
Barnsley, South Yorkshire
S70 2AS

ISBN 978 1 84832 581 4

Printed and bound in England
By CPI Group (UK) Ltd, Croydon, CR0 4YY

Pen & Sword Books Ltd incorporates the Imprints of Aviation, Atlas,
Family History, Fiction, Maritime, Military, Discovery, Politics, History,
Archaeology, Select, Wharncliffe Local History, Wharncliffe True Crime,
Military Classics, Wharncliffe Transport, Leo Cooper, The Praetorian Press,
Remember When, Seaforth Publishing and Frontline Publishing.

For a complete list of Pen & Sword titles please contact
PEN & SWORD BOOKS LIMITED
47 Church Street, Barnsley, South Yorkshire, S70 2AS, England
E-mail: enquiries@pen-and-sword.co.uk
Website: www.pen-and-sword.co.uk

Notes on Measures of Distance
In the interests of historical authenticity yards have been
preferred within the text as the unit of measure for weapon ranges
and small arms or artillery engagements. Otherwise, when
considering distance from point to point, metric measurement
has been preferred. All distances cited in the text have been
accurately measured by the Author.

Contents

Foreword

I first read of Isandlwana as a boy. Even at so tender an age, the story grabbed my imagination and fired an ambition to be able, one day, to visit the setting of this extraordinary epic tale. I first made it to Zululand in 1994. I was struck at once, I suspect like many before me, by the dramatic beauty and the mystical ambience of the Isandlwana battlefield. The strangely Sphinx-shaped mountain, at the foot of which the battle reached its bloody climax, has, at certain times of day, a strange, sad and desolate air about it. I have been fortunate enough to have returned there many times since, but I never cease to be awed by the place.

I was serving as the Defence Adviser at the British High Commission in Pretoria when I first met Mike Snook. As a member of our military advisory team in South Africa, he came under my command with the 125th Anniversary of Isandlwana and Rorke's Drift looming. It was a particular bonus to have a well-connected subject matter expert at my disposal. I at once appointed him as my agent in Zululand, the man who could organise and orchestrate British diplomatic and military involvement in the forth-coming commemoration. Working in concert with Zulu representatives, the tourist industry and Amafa, the KwaZulu-Natal heritage body, he was instrumental in ensuring that the UK was well represented at a series of memorable and moving ceremonies. More than once I saw grown men cry that weekend. When he was not working alongside the South African military, Mike was most commonly to be found indulging his passion for travelling in Zululand. Already he had been studying Isandlwana for more than twenty years. Now he really went to town: he walked the ground in every direction, repeatedly, in a determined attempt to get to the bottom of what actually happened in this great clash of arms. He made copious notes, sketched maps and diagrams, and discussed his theories with fellow historians, soldiers and enthusiasts. During his many visits and walkabouts, he met and made friends with a great many members of the Zulu nation. He developed a strong empathy for Zulu culture and society, and an abiding affection for the people. They, in turn, welcomed him warmly and some enduring friendships sprang up. Lone white men are not often seen so far from the beaten trail in South Africa these days. But Mike is very much at home with black Africans and they with him. He often guided other British officers and soldiers around the battlefields, many of whom had little or no knowledge of the Anglo-Zulu War: it was astonishing how many of them returned home as enthused converts eager for yet more AZW history. In essence, Mike Snook is a dedicated and experienced officer, who has immense pride in his Regiment, a passion for military history and an in-depth knowledge of his profession. Importantly he has first-class eye for ground and a keen analytical mind.

When Mike asked me to write the foreword to this book, I hesitated at first. I feared that since so much had already been written on the subject of Isandlwana, that it would prove impossible for somebody to take an entirely fresh look at this well documented piece of history. Any doubts in my mind were quickly dispelled, as I came to realise that *How Can Man Die Better* had by no means set out to follow a well-trodden path: there is a great deal of originality here. I have had the opportunity to read the book several times and to discuss it at length with the author. With his instinctive grasp of military matters, and his distinctive style and innovative approach, he has succeeded in telling this story in an entirely new and refreshing way. Importantly, he has set out to fill in many of the significant gaps in our knowledge: probably only a professional soldier could have done this. The book really brings the high drama of Isandlwana to life; I found I could smell the gunsmoke hanging over the battlefield as I read. There is absorbing human interest too, a glimpse of the pride and the passion of life in the British Army of 1879. I found myself actively disliking some of the characters we encounter, whilst greatly admiring others, and I very much sense that Mike has got them right. His narrative also conveys particularly well, the respect that is the rightful due of the determined and tenacious Zulu fighters of 1879.

It is not my intention in this brief foreword to outline the technicalities of the author's arguments or his findings. Suffice it to say, there are two key areas which are particularly noteworthy. Firstly, through careful analysis of time and space he develops an entirely new explanation of the Zulu preliminary moves in advance of the heavy fighting. This aspect alone directly challenges the orthodox interpretation of the battle. But there are many other thought-provoking ideas within these pages. The second point of note is the author's vivid insight into the character, the tactics and the fighting skills, of the immensely tough and highly experienced 24th Regiment. It fought an intense but orderly fighting withdrawal from extended defensive positions, through to a final stand at the foot of Isandlwana. This particular phase of the battle is most often glossed over quickly as, conventionally, historians have had next to nothing to draw on. In this account, the author displays a well-founded confidence in the natural doggedness and willpower of the British regular soldier, who, amidst the fear and chaos of battle, has so often had to rely upon pride in his regiment to overcome numerically superior foes. He goes on to explain in thought-provoking detail what might have been in the minds of the officers and soldiers as they fought, the tactics they employed as they struggled for survival, and finally how those last dreadful moments of a very fine battalion were played out.

I have thoroughly enjoyed getting to know the Isandlwana battlefield well over the last few years, and the particular advantage that having an advanced copy of this book to hand, has conveyed in getting to grips with the subject. *How Can Man Die Better* is a terrific read and makes for a fine debut by a man who promises to be one of our most readable military historians. *Like Wolves on the Fold*, his account of the Defence of Rorke's Drift follows shortly, and will no doubt offer many new insights into that equally intriguing and most famous of actions.

DAVID KEENAN

Preface

To the First Edition

Something kept calling me back. The more time I spent at Isandlwana, the less convinced I became that the historians had mastered the great battle. There were dimensions of time and space that just did not add up. There were major Zulu troop movements that nobody had explained, but which simply had to have a cause or a reason behind them. The destruction of the 24th Regiment was, it seemed, altogether too difficult to piece together. But, if ever a tale cried out to be told well, it is the story of this supremely dramatic confrontation; this much we owe to those who fell. About ten years ago I set out to unravel the mysteries for myself: the parts of the story that could not be found in the history books; the parts that had been glossed over for an apparent want of evidence. I found that, as a professional soldier, I could sometimes see things on the ground or in the sources which had somehow evaded the historians. Now, whenever I went back to Isandlwana, I went with a specific purpose. Gradually I developed my theories. It took a long, long time. Every so often some new piece of evidence would come to my attention and my ideas would come tumbling down around me. I have scrupulously avoided pushing on with favoured theories against the weight of the evidence, unfortunately, it seems, a common failing in much of today's Isandlwana scholarship. I went back to the drawing board more times than I care to remember. But it was fascinating stuff, much in the nature of a mystery, and I persevered.

In writing up my thoughts for publication, I set out to leave no unanswered questions. The result is a reconstruction of Isandlwana written in perhaps unprecedented depth. In places there are contentions which I cannot substantiate to an evidential standard, but where this is the case I have tried to demonstrate the lines of thought leading to my conclusions. The primary sources available to us are like an incomplete jigsaw; undoubtedly they leave yawning gaps in our knowledge. I have attempted to employ alternative tools, such as military logic and a professional soldier's eye for ground, to fill in the missing pieces. Some of the sources contain half-truths or obscuration which has not always been that easy to detect, but which for the most part I believe I have now run to ground. My account of the battle is unlikely to be a perfect reconstruction, but I hope it will be recognised as about as close as we can possibly get.

This is a military history and is written very much from an anglocentric viewpoint. For the newcomer to the subject who might subsequently wish to examine events from the other side of the fence, I can do no better than to refer them to the work of Ian Knight and John Laband. In order to give *How Can Man Die Better* its particular emphasis on the fortnight of the Isandlwana campaign, and to do the subject justice within the constraints of space, I hope I may be forgiven for taking much as read, and for opening my account as late as the week before the invasion of Zululand, with Lord Chelmsford's army in the final stages of concentration. Many other books cover colonial South Africa and the wider context of the Anglo-Zulu War admirably; there seems little point in going over such familiar territory one more time.

In war the ground is everything. At Isandlwana it is particularly complex. In analysing the battle I have attempted to inter-relate manoeuvre and ground closely. It may be helpful to the reader to photocopy the maps before starting to read, in order to follow the course of events better. Hopefully the annotated terrain photographs will also be a useful visual aid. I have made particular efforts to get 'time and space' right – to recount things in the order that they occurred. Hence there is a certain amount of hopping about in the narrative, for which I apologise in advance, but ultimately it should help in comprehending the true course of the battle.

How Can Man Die Better deals exclusively with the Battle of Isandlwana. The dramatic events played out just a few miles away at Rorke's Drift, and the subsequent course of the war, will be covered in a companion volume entitled *Like Wolves on the Fold*.

I am most grateful to Her Majesty The Queen for her kind permission to publish a number of photographs from the Royal Collection. I am indebted, too, to Major Martin Everett and Mrs Celia Green at the 24th Museum in Brecon for their kind assistance: in particular many of the illustrations were provided by the Regiment. I am also grateful to Mr Ron Sheeley, who has so generously made his private photographic collection available, and similarly to Ms Frances Dimond at Windsor Castle. The talented South African artist,

Mr Jason Askew, kindly allowed me to use a number of his excellent AZW paintings as illustrations across both books; his website can readily be located on the internet. David and Nikky Rattray at Fugitives' Drift Lodge, and Pat Stubbs, Rob Gerrard and Lindizwe Ngobese at Isandlwana Lodge, were kind and thoughtful hosts, and helped make my trips to the battlefields memorable and pleasurable experiences. Lieutenant Colonel William Marshall of the South African Infantry, with whom I shared an office in Pretoria as a UK military adviser to the South African National Defence Force, was a great friend to a curious foreigner, as was Colonel Dudley Wall, a frequent visitor to our office, who, as luck would have it turned out to be one of the South African Army's expert guides on his country's battlefields. For the muster rolls at the appendices of both of my books, I have drawn extensively on the painstaking research of the late Norman Holme, and on the equally meticulous and admirable *England's Sons* by Julian Whybra. Any errors in the acute detail will be of my own making not theirs. Ian Knight, Ron Lock, Peter Quantrill, David Rattray, Julian Whybra and Rob Gerrard are amongst the most expert contemporary authorities with whom I have had the pleasure to discuss the Zulu War, but there were countless others too. I was lucky enough to be tutored in military history in a golden age at the Royal Military Academy Sandhurst by such eminent figures as John Keegan, Richard Holmes and the late David Chandler, and later, at the Army Staff College, by Brian Holden-Reid. The depth of their knowledge of the art of war was, for me, inspirational: I hope that the maestros will not be embarrassed by the efforts of a mere pupil. I am grateful of course to Lionel Leventhal and his team at Greenhill Books, not least David Watkins and Rob Gardiner, both of whom provided much excellent help and advice. The maps were drawn by John Richards. I would also like to thank Colonel John Wilson, the editor of the *British Army Review*, and his readership, whose generous reception of some of my writing on the AZW tempted me to make this much more significant foray into the field.

There are other reasons, too, why I have been tempted into print – not least amongst them a recent spate of books in this field, which have been irksome for their many errors of fact, their sometimes eccentric interpretations, and, particularly, the deeply unpleasant vein of cynicism which runs through them. I am far from being alone in my annoyance with the genre. There are, for example, writers who seem to suggest that Melvill and Coghill died not in an attempt to save the Queen's Colour of their regiment, but their own skins, a cheap slur on two men, who, as if any reminder were necessary, are holders of their nation's highest award 'For Valour'. Fortunately, in this country, it is the sovereign, on the advice of the senior military professionals of the day, who decides such matters, and it does not fall to any of us to gainsay such judgements from a range of 125 years. Only the availability of compelling new evidence could justify or excuse such arrogant revisionism. Needless to say, in the case of Melvill and Coghill no such evidence has come to light. The fact of the matter is that they died and were buried as heroes, and even in this cynical modern age there is absolutely nothing wrong in remembering them in exactly the same way.

Similarly, the revisionists would have us believe that the Defence of Rorke's Drift was not really that big a deal, that the officers who led it were congenital idiots, and the award of eleven Victoria Crosses was a put-up job to deflect attention from the disaster that preceded it, none of which, funnily enough, happens to be true. Such controversial contentions are arrived at by magnifying and trumpeting grains of half-truth or subjective contemporaneous opinion, until they have been elevated above their rightful place as mere footnotes in history, and begin to subvert the main gist of the history itself. If *How Can Man Die Better* succeeds in alerting its readers to the existence of this deeply unsatisfactory genre, and can play a part in deflecting its destructive influence, it will have served a worthwhile purpose. It is to be hoped that we can arrest the decline and move instead to preserve, rather than to destroy, the great stories of the Anglo-Zulu War; for they are magnificent and compelling tales, though of course an undercurrent of tragedy runs through them all.

Before moving on with our story, there are two important groups of people I must single out for particular thanks, as both have helped me in indirect ways to gain a better comprehension of their forbears. I am grateful to the local community at Isandlwana, who have been kind enough to tolerate my endless roaming of their kraals and pasture, and who are responsible in large part for the huge esteem in which I hold the Zulu people. Finally, I must express my undying admiration for 'my boys' as we Sandhurst men say – the young British officers and soldiers I have had the privilege to lead, who in far-flung corners of the world never once flagged or failed. They sacrificed so much; please appreciate them.

MIKE SNOOK

Preface

To the 2010 Edition

More than five years have passed since *How Can Man Die Better* was first published. For me, the long hot hours spent pondering, reasoning, ruling-in, ruling-out and head-scratching atop the many commanding vantage points dotted across the Isandlwana landscape have been more than amply rewarded by the kind reception afforded to the book by the reading public. As the original 2005 preface explains, any historian looking at Isandlwana in any detail has no alternative but to rely on hypothesis to address some of the issues surrounding the blood-chilling climax of this great battle. Some hard-core history purists disapprove of such an approach, but it was not for their benefit that this book was written. I was much more interested in bringing this epic battle to life for the thousands of people who find it so intriguing, and who seek a deeper understanding of how, in military terms, the fight was actually played out. I am satisfied that the broad thrust of my arguments has survived contact with an extremely knowledgeable body of AZW historians and enthusiasts.

I have, therefore, made only a few amendments to this edition, in order to accommodate one or two new points of emphasis. For example, those venerable AZW scholars Peter Quantrill and Keith Smith have managed to convince me that Lieutenant Charlie Raw may not have gazed down at the main impi from Mabaso Ridge, as the conventional version of the moment of discovery would have it. His account, I agree, is not consistent with his having gained the crest. Even so, I have not fallen in with their wider hypothesis that the impi was already out of the Ngwebeni Valley at the moment of discovery. I judge that the clearcut accounts of Sergeant Major Nyanda and Commissary James Hamer, the inter-visibility from Mkwene Hill (an occupied British outpost), and the certain presence of a patrol of Natal Carbineers above the escarpment conspire to preclude this possibility. It seems to me, therefore, that while some, perhaps even most, of Raw's amaNgwane troopers did get to the crest in company with Nyanda, Hamer and Captain George Shepstone, Raw himself must have been lagging behind. This could have occurred for any number of reasons, as the NNMC troops were scattered into small details operating across the width of the plateau. So Charlie Raw himself has been written out of the precise moment of discovery, though he was certainly close at hand, rallied his men at the foot of Mabaso, engaged the onset of the impi and commanded the troop's withdrawal across the plateau.

A second significant change of emphasis occurs around the vexed issue of command of the camp. The simplicity of the issue has been long-clouded by the controversy surrounding Colonel John North Crealock's inaccurate (and possibly disingenuous) assertion that Colonel Durnford had been specifically ordered to assume command of the camp. Emphatically this was not so, as the later recovery of Durnford's orders was to prove. Whilst this is an issue of real importance in the context of Lord Chelmsford's efforts to evade personal culpability, it is substantially irrelevant to the personal interaction between Durnford and Pulleine on the morning of the battle. The straightforward military fact of life was that one was senior to the other, and it was this that governed their interaction. There is clearcut source evidence that Pulleine deferred to his senior from the outset. At its simplest, Durnford was in command.

Colonel Durnford spent the best part of an hour and a half in Pulleine's company, before deciding to mount his foray into the plain. It seems clear then that the conversation reported by Lieutenant Cochrane covered the initial exchange between the two colonels, but not what passed between them subsequently. Contrary to the longstanding 'urban legend', if I may coin that phrase, which would have it that the camp was surprised, all the evidence would suggest that, by mid-morning, the garrison was positively expecting to be attacked. If Durnford arrived believing that the general required his services upcountry, then it seems clear that he was eventually disabused of the notion by Pulleine's briefing and the absence of any supplementary orders to that effect. Over the next hour and a half, though, the threat to the camp appeared to be receding. People took false comfort from the enemy's apparent reluctance to 'come on'. It was at around 11.30 a.m. that Lieutenant Higginson tendered the crucial report that the Zulus above the escarpment were 'retiring everywhere'. Durnford had been content to remain at the camp so long as it was to be the focus of the enemy's attention, but Higginson's report changed everything. It was this that triggered the lapse of judgement that those who knew Durnford best had always feared. He now took the offensive: where simple reconnaissance would have been justified, full-scale offensive action emphatically was not.

Durnford remains a controversial figure. Even now he has an ardent fan club, the members of which have not relished my interpretation of his competence as a commander, his temperamental nature, or his inner motivations – much of which I cover in the companion volume Like Wolves on the Fold. It is intriguing that many modern Natalians have adopted the Durnford of legend as a local hero, for the historical Durnford was emphatically not a local but a British imperial officer through and through, and, with the exception of a small, very British, liberal clique in Pietermaritzburg, had earned the positive disapprobation of most contemporary Natalians. Since writing How Can Man Die Better, I have come across a substantial journal entry by Garnet Wolseley, a harsh judge of men admittedly, which records his mid-decade impression of Durnford. Far from shaking my faith in my interpretation, Wolseley's journal has served only to vindicate it. I make no apology, therefore, for a broadly unflattering portrayal that I have no doubt some people will feel is overly harsh. But I have no doubt that this is where history, rather than myth, leads us. I intend no offence to Colonel Durnford's descendants and, notwithstanding his perceived failings, once again draw attention to the colonel's undoubted, entirely admirable physical courage. For all his faults, he died a soldier's death.

And this much too should be plain. It is the nature of the ground at Isandlwana, in my view, that a minimum of ten companies of British regular infantry would have been required for the all-round defence of the camp. Where once there had been twelve, there were now, at the very moment of decision, only six. This was nothing whatsoever to do with Colonel A. W. Durnford. Rather, it was entirely the GOC's doing. What the colonel did wrong was to turn a very high probability of a crippling reverse, into an absolutely certain battle of annihilation. This he did by precluding any possibility of his NNMC troopers covering the British rear – even this would have offered only an outside chance at best., But it would have at least been a chance. Ultimately, therefore, the blame for the Isandlwana disaster must rest in by far the greater proportion with Lord

Chelmsford. Sadly he never came to terms with his own culpability, and his attempts to suggest that the fault was exclusively that of the late Colonel Durnford were neither appropriate nor militarily sustainable.

As will be well known to almost all readers, on 26 January 2007, in between the publication of the first and second editions of this book, KwaZulu-Natal was cruelly deprived of the great historian and raconteur, David Rattray, who did so much to popularize the story of the Anglo-Zulu War and to boost the South African tourist industry. Sadly I have not been able to get to Fugitive's Drift Lodge since David's death, but feel sure that when, once again, I wend my way down the hill towards the final resting place of Lieutenants Melvill and Coghill, I will sense the near presence of the great praise-singer himself. After all is not the whole point of the Isandlwana-Rorke's Drift saga that while mere men can die in Africa, an African legend can live forever.

MIKE SNOOK
Pretoria
2010

Prologue

'And how can man die better,
Than facing fearful odds,
For the ashes of his fathers,
And the temples of his Gods.'

Horatius, Lord Macaulay

Over the course of the long and distinguished history of the British Army, there have been many occasions when infantry battalions have found themselves in serious trouble. None has ever found itself in quite such dire straits as the 1st Battalion, The 24th Regiment of Foot, on the afternoon of Wednesday 22 January 1879. There was never a stage at which the Battle of Isandlwana was going well, but there had at least been a period of illusion when it had the appearance of doing so.

The illusion was exposed for what it was by Colonel Anthony Durnford's withdrawal from the Nyogane Donga. At the very moment his miscellany of troopers turned to snatch their reins from the horse-holders arrayed behind them, the destruction of at least one infantry company was assured. The right flank had been turned. In that instant, retreat, flight, even mere survival, all became impossible for the men of Lieutenant Charlie Pope's G Company. For a while hope lived on; perhaps their imminent sacrifice would buy time for the other companies to change front and re-form. The Zulu trump card, the turning of the left flank to complete a crushing double envelopment, would dispel even this remote prospect only minutes later.

Freed of the heavy suppressive fire which had thus far kept them in check, the warriors of the uVe and iNgobamakhosi regiments surged up the long slope to their front, making for the ordered rows of tents and wagons at the foot of the 'Sphinx'. As the majority of Durnford's riders galloped in a disorderly rout towards the camp, firing the odd wild shot from their carbines as they went, a handful of brave-hearts at the rear checked their horses and continued to present a bold front. As these troopers fumbled cartridges from bandolier to breech, their mounts pranced excitedly just ahead of a by now maddened enemy. Some men drew their revolvers and blazed away until the hammer clicked repeatedly on empty chambers. Although a few more Zulus tumbled into the long grass, such bold defiance was plainly futile. Even the brave-hearts were forced to turn their horses and race for the saddle between the Sphinx and the stony koppie to its south. Two of their number were shot and fell at the feet of the iNgobamakhosi, 'the Humblers of Kings'. If the troopers were alive when they hit the ground, only a few more seconds of life remained to them. Then the great host fell upon the hapless G Company.

In the next few minutes, every man who was fated to survive the coming massacre would fly the battlefield. Destiny, luck and horsemanship would decide who would live and who would die. Yet, as the last of the lucky riders spurred away down the 'Fugitives' Trail', several hundred men on foot were still alive and fighting hard. With few notable exceptions, historians have done these men a disservice. In the telling of their tale, the scholars have killed them off easily and precipitately in front of the camp. The clear-cut hopelessness of the situation, the overpowering odds they faced, the renowned martial skill and ferocity of their opponents – all the first glance factors – have driven the historians to their inevitable conclusion: whole companies were slaughtered in a few short seconds. Yet, in truth, it is clear that the Battle of Isandlwana raged long and hard after the flight of the lucky ones.

No white man who fought in the final phase of the battle would live to tell the tale of the desperate stand made by these few hundred stalwarts. Clustered around their officers and sergeants, the men of the 24th Regiment were the backbone of a heroic resistance. Through a succession of largely defective interpretations of the evidence, the story of the last stand of the 24th has almost been lost to history but, for those with the eyes to see, it survives yet. By the application of a little military common sense it can be reasonably accurately reconstructed. When the Zulu main bodies reached the tents, the great majority of the 600 redcoats in the field that day were still alive. They were not scattered over the open veldt before the camp, as many would have us believe. They were formed in close order, they were resolute and they were skilfully led. They were grim, frightened, and knew that they were doomed to die. Above all else though, with the stubborn arrogance that has typified the British infantry over the centuries, they were determined to sell their lives dearly. It was to be a fight to the finish with no quarter asked or given, and these men would take some killing; a lesser foe might not have achieved it. This is the story of those men and of the brave warriors who killed them. By any standard it is a tale of extraordinary high drama.

This is a story of Briton and Zulu, two peoples who fought each other with such remarkable courage that, even before the last shots of 1879 had been fired, it had forged a mutual respect so profound that it would blossom in next to no time into a strong friendship, a relationship that survives to this day and continues to flourish. With the sweeping away of apartheid and the normalisation of Anglo–South African relations, members of the modern regiment are now frequent visitors to Zululand. In our train have come more and more tourists, keen to experience the renowned beauty of the countryside and to pay homage on the great battlefields. Whatever small part we in the Royal Regiment of Wales have been able to play in further cementing the friendship of the British and Zulu peoples we are inordinately proud of, for the man lucky enough to call a Zulu his friend will come to know something of the nobility and majesty of old Africa. And so long as courage and self-sacrifice are held in high regard, men will tell this story.

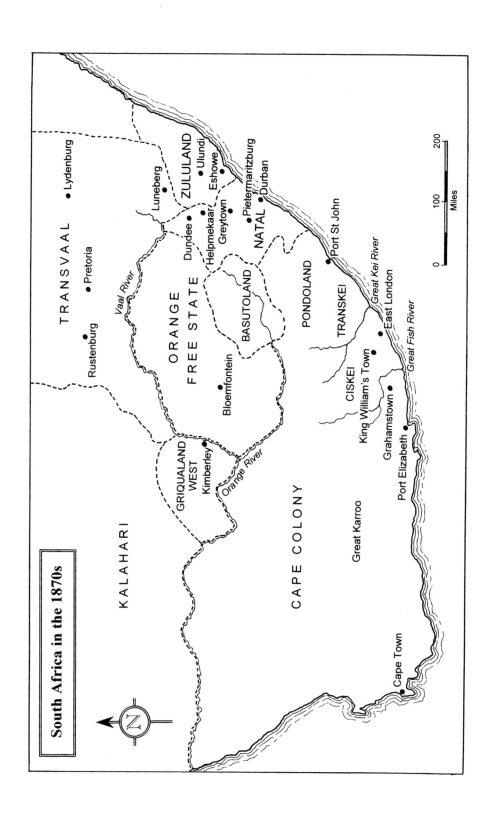

South Africa in the 1870s

KALAHARI

TRANSVAAL

• Lydenburg
• Pretoria
• Rustenburg

Vaal River

Luneberg •

ZULULAND
• Ulundi
Eshowe •
Dundee •
Helpmekaar •
Greytown •
• Pietermaritzburg
• Durban

NATAL

ORANGE FREE STATE

• Bloemfontein

BASUTOLAND

GRIQUALAND WEST
• Kimberley

Orange River

PONDOLAND

Port St John •

TRANSKEI

Great Kei River

CISKEI
King William's Town •
East London

Grahamstown •

CAPE COLONY

Great Karroo

Great Fish River

Port Elizabeth •

Cape Town •

0   100   200
Miles

Part One

Gathering Storm

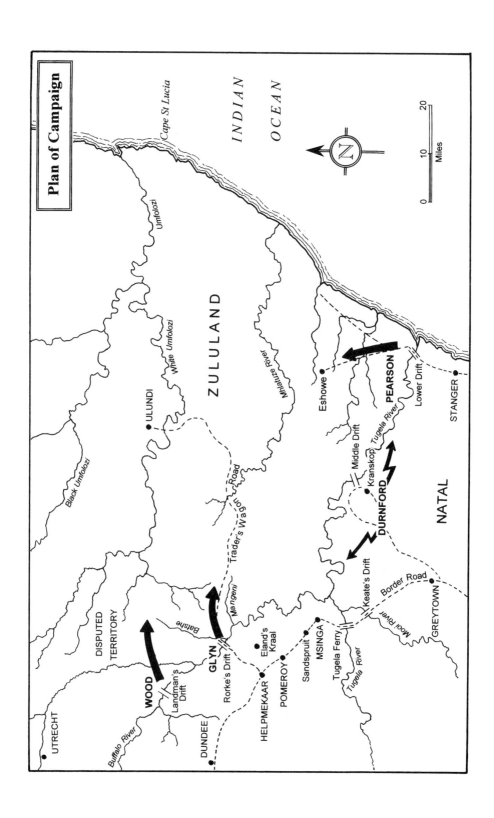

Plan of Campaign

Chapter 1

Better Luck This Time

In the Concentration Area

Even by the standards of an imperial age, this was far from being a just war. From Whitehall there appeared to be no discernible reason to bring down the Zulu. The liberal establishment would never wear an unprovoked war; there would be an outcry. Had not Sir Theophilus Shepstone* himself crowned King Cetshwayo? Was not the admittedly powerful potentate, already a client-king of the British Empire? So much for officialdom in distant London, but to the 5,000 citizens of colonial Pietermaritzburg things looked markedly different. The thought of native insurrection amongst even the militarily weak clans of Natal was worrying enough.[†] The prospect of the mighty Zulu descending on the colony was a nightmare of wholly different proportions. Put at its simplest, Cetshwayo's crime was to be an autonomous black ruler with an army.

Sir Bartle Frere, Governor of the Cape and High Commissioner for Southern Africa, was only too keenly aware that the king of the Zulus could field close to 40,000 fighting men. Frere had been largely left to his own devices after Lord Carnarvon's resignation from the Colonial Office. The Colonial Secretary's big idea for Africa, a confederation of the continent's disparate southern territories, quickly fell out of fashion in Whitehall, but in Frere and Shepstone it still had enthusiastic and powerful advocates on the ground. The High Commissioner could take anti-Zulu sentiment for granted in vulnerable Natal, but London would be trickier. In the meantime, Lieutenant-General Lord Chelmsford could begin preparing for the war Frere was determined to provoke. In the event, a positive

---

* Natal's Secretary of Native Affairs, 1856–76. Responsible in 1877 for implementing the British annexation of the Transvaal.

† The total black population of Natal in 1879 was close to a quarter of a million people. The European population was about 25,000.

prohibition of the war by the new Colonial Secretary would arrive at the Cape far too late to impinge upon the now inexorable course of South African history.

Plan of Campaign

By January 1879 Chelmsford's army was assembled along the Zulu frontier, waiting for the expiry of the period of grace allowed by the High Commissioner's eleven-point ultimatum. Some demands were cleverly designed to justify hostilities to the London government, still oblivious to the imminence of the invasion, but others were intentionally insurmountable conditions, terms that everybody in Natal knew King Cetshwayo could never accept. The die was cast; the war would begin on 11 January 1879.

Mindful of the infinitely superior mobility of the Zulu *amabutho* and the resultant necessity to prevent a counter-invasion of Natal, Chelmsford divided his limited military resources between no fewer than five columns. Three of these were main force invasion columns, whose task was to strike across the major river crossings and converge on the royal kraals at Ulundi, in order to bring the campaign to some kind of credible military denouement. Two reserve columns had been assigned to the defence of the border settlements in Natal and the southern Transvaal.

The main force columns had been entrusted to the three senior regimental commanders in South Africa: in the north, Colonel Evelyn Wood, VC, of the 90th Light Infantry; in the centre, Colonel Richard Glyn, CB, of the 24th Regiment of Foot; and on the coast, Colonel Charles Pearson of the Buffs. Each had been assigned two battalions of regular infantry, a battery of guns, a couple of thousand levied black auxiliaries, and a few hundred white mounted troops, many of them from police or part-time citizen units. Chelmsford and the army staff would accompany the central column, Number 3 Column, under Glyn.

Operating defensively along the stretch of frontier between Glyn and Pearson would be No. 2 Column under Lieutenant-Colonel Anthony Durnford, RE,* which alone of the five columns consisted entirely of black

---

* Durnford was gazetted full colonel in December 1878 but Lord Chelmsford's correspondence indicates that news of the promotion had not reached South Africa by the time of Isandlwana.

troops. In a slightly patronising way, the army staff said knowingly that Durnford was 'good with the natives'. By and large the citizens of Pietermaritzburg did not much care for the quirky sapper colonel. In Natal, Durnford had baggage.

Number 3 Column

No. 3 Column assembled at Helpmekaar on the Biggarsberg Plateau, high above the Buffalo River Valley. Afrikaans speakers had given the tiny hamlet a place-name, perhaps in anticipation of great things to come, but even today Helpmekaar scarcely warrants the privilege. Literally translated the name meant 'help one another', a reference to the necessity for trekkers and traders to double up their teams, if they were to get their ox-wagons up and down the berg safely. It was a bleak and windswept spot, marked only by a couple of rough and ready domestic dwellings, one of which served as a post office, and now, in January 1879, by a pair of corrugated iron sheds erected by the commissary officers to house their perishable stores. One by one, over Christmas and the New Year, the units assigned to No. 3 Column came marching up the Greytown Road, until at length there was a veritable city of canvas on the plateau. When all the troops were up and the ultimatum was within a few days of expiry, it would be time to move down from the Biggarsberg to the river crossing at nearby Rorke's Drift. In the meantime, it was largely a matter of keeping dry. The drought of the past few years had broken dramatically; every afternoon there were heavy and protracted downpours. The officers on the transport staff monitored ground conditions like umpires at a cricket match.

Each new contingent was accompanied by the inevitable train of lumbering ox-wagons, a supremely impractical means of transporting large quantities of stores. Impractical or not, on the Natal frontier it was the only way. Ox-wagons were slow, difficult to manoeuvre and would stick every time when confronted with heavy mud. Usually they were pulled by sixteen head of oxen, inspanned in eight pairs, so that even relatively small convoys could stretch back over miles of road. A general shortage of transport meant that the commissaries often overloaded the wagons they did have available. In difficult going, on steep slopes, or at river drifts such heavily laden vehicles could require the pulling power of double the usual number of oxen, and the ability to drive thirty-two independent-minded animals to a common purpose was a rare gift indeed. The most common outcome was a time consuming snarl-up halfway across the obstacle. The animals themselves were sensitive, easily fatigued, and needed to spend half a day grazing over good grass, or failing that on fodder carried aboard the wagon. In order to leave any room for travelling military stores, it would be necessary to establish major logistic stockpiles at regular intervals and to shuttle convoys of wagons back and forth between them. It could take weeks for a substantial military force to get anywhere, and if the commissaries had not done their sums properly, it could be a case of three steps forward to four back. Wagons, teams, conductors and *voorloopers* were expensive to own, expensive to run and, in time of war, as Lord Chelmsford had now discovered, even more expensive to hire. If nothing else, settler society was determined to cash in on the impending overthrow of its Zulu neighbours.

Colonel Glyn had been assigned both battalions of his own regiment, the 24th Regiment of Foot, which in theory at least, according to the provisions of the newly adopted 'Cardwell System', should not both have been overseas at the same time. The outbreak of yet another frontier war with the Xhosa had brought Lieutenant-Colonel Henry Degacher and the 2nd/24th dashing out to South Africa a little over a year earlier.*

Glyn's 1st Battalion had been out since 1875 and was by now widely acknowledged as the best unit in the colony. Already it had two notable victories in the Transkei to its credit. On 13 January 1878, Glyn had attacked and defeated a strong Xhosa army at Nyumaga with a mixed force which included A and F Companies of his own battalion. Less than a month later, Captain Russell Upcher received intelligence that his camp at Centane Hill would be attacked within the next few days. He threw up an earthwork redoubt on top of the hill, laagered his wagons alongside it, and then dug rifle-pits around the edge of the high ground. He was attacked out of a morning mist on 7 February 1878 by 4,500 men of the Gcaleka clan, but was able, by dint of his thorough defensive preparations and the rolling musketry of F and G Companies, to hold his ground with ease. The moment they wavered the Gcalekas were attacked and scattered by the mounted troops. Whilst the infantry were preparing a hearty breakfast to celebrate their victory, a force of around 1,500 Ngqika Xhosa suddenly

* Degacher knew South Africa already; prior to assuming command of the 2nd Battalion he had been the senior major in the 1st/24th.

came up. Upcher attacked immediately and, although a number of the mounted troops got into a scrape with some well concealed bodies of warriors, Lieutenant Charles Atkinson quickly turned the tide with a flank attack and a few hard-hitting volleys. The Xhosa may have taken as many as 700–800 casualties at Centane; certainly at least 260 dead were left on the field. In stark contrast the 24th had lost not a single man; two black auxiliaries were the only fatal casualties. It was the first real indication that, in the Martini-Henry rifle, the British infantry was now equipped with a force-multiplier of unprecedented potency. After Centane there no longer seemed much reason to fear the armies of black Africa.

The 1st/24th arrived at Helpmekaar before its sister battalion, though for the time being it could field only four companies. Three more were marching rapidly along the lines of communication to join the column, but Captain Henry Harrison's B Company had been left far behind in the distant Transkei on detached garrison duties, and was thus destined never to see service against the Zulu. As was traditional, when the 2nd/24th came marching up from Greytown, the band of the 1st/24th turned out to play the new arrivals into camp.

No. 3 Column's artillery component was N Battery, 5th Brigade, Royal Artillery, under Brevet Lieutenant-Colonel Arthur Harness,* consisting of around 130 officers and men, and six horse-drawn 7-pounder RMLs (rifled muzzle-loaders). The 7-pounder was a short-barrelled mountain gun, mounted for South African service on locally manufactured 'Kaffrarian' gun carriages. From a distance the carriages gave the weapon the appearance of a field-gun, but the 7-pounder's firepower was nothing like as potent.

The battery had forged a strong bond with the 2nd/24th during the past year's campaign in the Amatola Mountains. In the Ciskei, the Xhosa had fought a guerrilla campaign from their traditional mountain refuges. There had been nothing akin to the major field actions fought by the 1st/24th in the Transkei. Conditions had been tough, and such fighting as there was had been distinctly nerve-wracking work for the infantry; most commonly they were compelled to flush densely wooded kloofs, in search of an elusive and cunning enemy. But N Battery had not been the only gunners in the Amatolas. Such was the shortage of artillery in South Africa in those troubled times that the band of the 1st/24th had been pressed into service

* Harness received the new of his brevet promotion as recently as Christmas Eve, 1878.

as two *ad hoc* gun-crews. They too had done sterling service alongside the 2nd/24th, but were now back in their more customary roles as full-time musicians and part-time stretcher-bearers. All in all, the regular army elements of No. 3 Column, infantry and artillery alike, had every right to think of themselves as seasoned African campaigners. It was a good start in assembling a fighting force fit to meet the Zulu.

Infantry, gunners, transport; all Glyn needed now was some cavalry – the all important eyes and ears of an army, and its mobile striking force. As usual there was not a single regular cavalryman to be had in Southern Africa, where expensive Irish horseflesh invariably went into prompt terminal decline. Instead, No. 3 Column's 'cavalry' arm was improvised from various mounted units which, since they carried neither lance nor sabre, should technically speaking be categorised as mounted infantry. The cavalry lines contained a miscellany of such units, operating in three squadron-sized bodies. First, there was No. 1 Squadron of the Imperial Mounted Infantry (IMI), 120 infantry soldiers who claimed to be able to ride, drawn in four regimental detachments each about thirty strong, from the 2nd/3rd Buffs, 1st/13th Light Infantry, the 1st/24th and the 80th Regiment. A second cavalry squadron was found by the colony's full-time constabulary, the Natal Mounted Police (NMP), a quasi-military force of around 130 men under the command of an ex-regular officer called Major John Dartnell.

The colony's part-time volunteer units, too small to act independently of one another, were grouped into a third composite squadron. The largest contingent was found by the Natal Carbineers, a fashionable Pietermaritzburg-based unit with a strength of about sixty men. Captain Theophilus Shepstone Jnr., 'Offy' for short, was the unit's senior officer. (Sir Theophilus's other son, George, was serving in No. 2 Column as a member of Colonel Durnford's staff.) The Newcastle Mounted Rifles (NMR), thirty-five strong, were all citizens of the nearby frontier town of the same name, and were commanded by the extravagantly bewhiskered Captain Robert Bradstreet. The smallest volunteer unit, a mere twenty-five men, was the Buffalo Border Guard (BBG), a group of kindred spirits from the more remote farms and trading posts along the Buffalo River frontier. The late Jim Rorke, for example, the man who had given his name to the most important local river crossing, had been a member of the BBG.

All the volunteers were smartly uniformed in patrol jackets, breeches and the customary blancoed cork sun-helmets. The police and the BBG were turned out in black, the carbineers in navy blue with white facings, and the NMR in a dark rifle-green. All had been equipped at the colony's expense with the latest revolvers and breech-loading carbines. Amateurs they may have been but, like frontiersmen the world over, they were experienced horsemen and they liked to shoot. Importantly they looked the part and, part-timers or not, now that they were mustered for war service, they felt very much like professionals.

The 24th Regiment of Foot

During the last few days at Helpmekaar, the officers of the 1st/24th decided to hold a commemorative dinner to mark the impending thirtieth anniversary of the Battle of Chillianwallah, an action in the Second Sikh War in which their regiment had played a famously heroic part. Naturally, they would invite the officers of the 2nd Battalion as their guests. The invitation was duly extended, remarkably, between two brothers. Since Colonel Glyn's elevation to the post of column commander, the 1st Battalion had been under the temporary command of its senior captain, William Degacher, whose elder brother, Henry, was the commanding officer of the 2nd/24th. Lieutenant-Colonel Henry Pulleine was due to come up from Pietermaritzburg to take over the 1st Battalion, but was not expected to arrive in time for the act of invasion. In the meantime, Glyn had set the younger Degacher above the other captains of the 1st/24th by appointing him to the rank of acting major.

Chillianwallah. It was a famous story in the Victorian era, now sadly all but forgotten, but commemorated at least by the impressive memorial to the fallen which stands in the grounds of the Royal Hospital on the Chelsea Embankment. On 13 January 1849, Sir Hugh Gough's army had come upon a strong Sikh force entrenched along a jungle fringe. Sir Colin Campbell, the 24th's divisional commander, came galloping up to the regiment and ordered the commanding officer to storm the Sikh batteries with the bayonet. There was to be no stopping to fire he insisted. Taking the general at his word, Colonel Pennycuick* had not even instructed his men to load. The regiment attacked bravely, but the Sikh gunners plied their trade well, blowing bloody furrows through the oncoming British ranks.

---

* Pennycuick was also the brigade commander.

On the flanks, the Indian battalions of the brigade hung back; in the centre, the 24th pushed on without regard for its mounting losses, and without heed to its increasingly isolated position. Up and over the earthworks they went, clearing the guns at the point of the bayonet, before then charging on into the masses of Sikh infantry arrayed in depth. Counter-attacked in overwhelming strength, the 24th was slowly driven back in disorder. Colonel Pennycuick was killed near the guns. The eighteen-year-old Ensign Pennycuick, newly arrived from Sandhurst, was cut down defending his father's body.

The regiment had gone into the assault over a thousand strong; it came out of action with a quarter of that number dead and another quarter wounded. Thirteen officers were killed. They were laid out that night on the dining table in the officers' mess tent. Nine more officers were seriously wounded. The plaudits heaped on the regiment by the great men of the old Indian Army were generous, but scant consolation for the carnage. Sir Charles Napier wrote of the 24th, 'Their conduct has never been surpassed by British soldiers on a field of battle.' It conveys much that when, five years later, an onlooker expressed stunned disbelief at the terrible destruction of the Light Brigade, another officer was heard to scoff, 'Pah! It is nothing to Chillianwallah.'

Notwithstanding the rough and ready conditions at Helpmekaar, the Chillianwallah dinner was probably a fine party. The 24th was well known not only for its military proficiency, but also for the gentility of its officers and the good behaviour of its enlisted men. The 1st Battalion had travelled extensively in South Africa since 1875 and was highly regarded in all the major towns of the colony. Cape Town, Kimberley, King William's Town, Pietermaritzburg – all had all been thoroughly charmed by the members of the officers' mess. Sir Bartle Frere thought of himself as a particular friend of the regiment.

William Degacher was typical of the company commanders. Educated at Rugby, he had joined the regiment at the age of eighteen, and had served in Mauritius, Malta, Gibraltar and Brecon. He was now thirty-seven years old. In 1875 he had participated in the Griqualand West expedition, when Colonel Glyn and three companies had marched all the way from Cape Town to the diamond fields to suppress a Fenian-inspired plot amongst the lawless digger population of Kimberley. Fortunately, the impressive bearing of the 24th had allowed the colonial authorities to re-assert themselves without recourse to bloodshed. Not long afterwards Degacher returned to England on long leave. Bored by the absence of active service, he announced he would be leaving the army. The outbreak of the 9th Frontier War brought him hurrying back to South Africa to rejoin his battalion. He had been married to his wife Caroline for less than two years.

After Degacher, the next senior 1st Battalion officer at Helpmekaar was Captain George Wardell, the Officer Commanding H Company. Wardell was the son of a long-service regular officer and had been born in Toronto in February 1840. He had been educated in Canada and London and joined the 2nd/24th at the age of eighteen. He had served in England, Mauritius – where in 1867 he married his wife Lucy – and Burma. In 1870 he exchanged into the 1st Battalion. After a spell in Gibraltar, he returned home in 1873 to undertake a tour of duty at the new regimental depot. Two years later he brought a draft of Brecon-trained recruits out to South Africa. When Glyn was told to provide a company for garrison duty on St Helena, he chose Wardell for the task. At the end of the year-long tour, the governor of the island wrote to Glyn commending the faultless behaviour of the enlisted men, and remarking that, with George Wardell's departure, he was losing a close friend. In the war in the Transkei, Wardell and his company had constructed an earthwork redoubt named Fort Warwick on the Great Kei River frontier. Most local settlers abandoned their farms and sought sanctuary there. The Xhosa kept the post in a state of loose siege for almost four months. In January 1878 they mounted a strong night attack, which Wardell and his men successfully repelled. With food in short supply, it was necessary to send for help and a few days later a relief expedition arrived to extricate the garrison and the refugees. Widely respected and popular with his men, Wardell was strongly built and sported a thick black beard, tinged with a first hint of grey.

At the other end of the spectrum of experience was Second Lieutenant Edwards (*sic*) Dyson, a slightly built, dark-haired, twenty-year-old. Educated on the continent and at Wimbledon School, he had passed out of Sandhurst less than a year earlier, and had been in the 24th for only eight months. By the time he arrived in King William's Town, the operations in the Ciskei and the Transkei were over. As a brand new subaltern yet to win his spurs, he was expected not to pester his elders and betters. Probably the captains had little to do with him. He did not mind unduly; it was the way things were. Perhaps by the time the war against the Zulus had run its course, he would be more readily accepted, if not as an equal, at least as a young officer worth his salt.

By 1879 the 24th was already almost two centuries old. It had accumulated an array of distinguished battle honours, principally from the great European campaigns of Marlborough and Wellington. Indeed, John Churchill, 1st Duke of Marlborough, had been one of the regiment's early colonels. 'Corporal John', as he was affectionately known, was famous as the first senior officer of the standing army to have been genuinely concerned for the well-being of his troops. Not unnaturally, the 24th pioneered many of his enlightened practices and reforms, so that Marlborough's colonelcy left a legacy, which can still be traced down to the modern day regiment, in the paternalism of the officers towards their men, and the strong sense of mutual respect existing between ranks. Appropriately, all four of Marlborough's great continental victories, Blenheim, Ramillies, Oudenarde and Malplaquet, featured amongst the 24th's earliest battle honours.

The regiment also saw distinguished service during the American War of Independence. For his Hudson Valley campaign of 1777, Sir John Burgoyne appointed the regiment's highly capable commanding officer as the brigadier of the elite 'Advanced Corps' of the army. The regiment fought in both battles of Saratoga and, in the second of them, it was Brigadier Simon Fraser and the 24th who covered the retreat of the army, as it routed from the Barber Wheatfield under heavy American attack. Mounted on a white horse, Fraser quickly caught the eye and the admiration of the enemy. Legend has it that he was identified as a target to the long-rifleman who shot him, with the words, 'that officer on the white horse is a host unto himself'. Fraser took a day to die; notoriously, the Americans fired on his funeral service, an act for which they later apologised to Burgoyne.

In the Peninsular War, the 2nd/24th was one of Wellington's most trusted veteran battalions, earning no fewer than nine battle honours in the course of his campaigns. On 28 July 1809, it saved the day at Talavera by standing firm in the centre, when other regiments gave ground and retired. The position was held at the cost of fifty per cent casualties. Busaco, Fuentes d'Onoro, Vittoria and Salamanca were amongst the other Peninsular battle honours.

In more recent times, the 24th had seen service in the Indian Mutiny, and in the Andaman Islands, off the Burmese coast where, in a single action in 1867, five members of the regiment had won the recently instituted Victoria Cross. Even prior to the Zulu War, the 24th had earned a reputation for bad luck with its colours. One set had been burned before the surrender at Saratoga, another set was thrown overboard from a troopship intercepted off Mauritius by French men-of-war in 1810, and only the Regimental Colour had been brought out of action at Chillianwallah. The Queen's Colour was never seen again and is believed to have been buried in a mass grave around the waist of a private soldier, who rescued it after yet another ensign had been shot down by the Sikhs.

Since 1782 the 24th had been nominally connected with the county of Warwickshire, its unabridged title being 'The 24th (2nd Warwickshire) Regiment of Foot'. The regimental numeral was preferred ahead of the county title, to which little recourse was ever made. Under the terms of the Localisation Act, the Cardwell reforms required the regular regiments of infantry to acquire genuine regional or county identities. In the case of the 24th this was to be Welsh. In 1873 the new regimental depot was opened in the mid-Wales town of Brecon. Both town and county immediately took the 24th to heart. Within a year or two the regiment was regarded as an integral and important part of local society. In 1881, in somewhat overdue recognition of its new regional identity, the regiment would be famously re-designated as the South Wales Borderers, under which title it saw distinguished service in both world wars. In 1969 it would change its name again, this time to the Royal Regiment of Wales (24th/41st Foot), when the South Wales Borderers was amalgamated with the Welch Regiment.

By 1879 the percentage of Welshmen in the ranks of both battalions had risen markedly. There was also a good smattering of Irishmen, many of them second-generation immigrants to the burgeoning Welsh mining communities. It is often suggested that the 1st/24th consisted largely of long-service soldiers enlisted under pre-Cardwell terms and conditions of service, and the 2nd/24th of younger men, enlisted under the new short-service system. The same theories would have it that the 2nd Battalion was much more Welsh in character than the 1st Battalion. In fact, the regimental records of this era are insufficiently comprehensive to support such overly dogmatic conclusions and in practice there seems to have been little difference between the two units.

Under the Cardwell system newly trained recruits went straight from the regimental depot to the home-based battalion. In turn, the home battalion was chartered to provide an annual draft to its sister battalion overseas, in order to make up manpower losses arising from battle casualties, disease, retirement, medical discharge, or any one of half a dozen other reasons. The 1st/24th was joined by its first draft of Brecon-trained men in Gibraltar in October 1874, just prior to embarkation for South Africa. Subsequently, there were further annual drafts of eighty men in June 1875, eighty more in June 1876, and sixty-eight in July 1877 so that, by the time of the Zulu War, well over half the other ranks were short-service men trained in Brecon. Many of the others had enlisted under the old terms and conditions of service but were still safely on the right side of thirty. A company photograph taken in the Ciskei, in which the soldiers are sporting only moustaches and not campaign beards, reveals a good deal about the composition of the 1st Battalion. Almost all the men in the back row, amounting to about a quarter of the company, are fresh faced clean-shaven young men, and this at a time when a moustache was compulsory unless specifically excused by virtue of the man's inability to grow one. Clearly many of these soldiers are in or only just out of their teens. Only the sergeants appear to be on the wrong side of thirty. All in all, there are no compelling reasons to infer that the battalions were markedly different in their regional affiliations or their average age.

A battalion of regular infantry was divided into eight companies, a headquarters staff, the band and drums, and the quartermaster's department. The companies were divided into right wing companies (A–D), and left wing companies (E–H). The lieutenant-colonel commanding, who might have been elevated to full colonel during the course of his command tour as was the case with Richard Glyn, was assisted by two majors, who each commanded one of the wings.* One of the 1st/24th's majors was Henry Pulleine, now breveted lieutenant-colonel and about to take command *vice* Glyn. The other substantive major, Logan, was medically unfit and had been left behind on detached duties in Pietermaritzburg. Russell Upcher had been breveted major for Centane, but with two substantive majors above him, remained employed as a company commander. The 2nd/24th's wing commanders were Major William Dunbar and Major Wilsone Black, both of them capable and experienced veterans. Companies were commanded by a

---

* Also referred to as 'half-battalions'.

captain, with two subalterns and a colour-sergeant to assist him. In practice, anything up to half the companies could be in the hands of a senior lieutenant. Internally, companies were sub-divided into four sections each under the command of a sergeant and a corporal. Two sections could operate as a 'half-company' under one of the subalterns. Theoretically around a hundred strong, the actual strength of the 1st/24th companies after their four year stint in Africa was down to somewhere between seventy and eighty men. Those of the 2nd/24th, having been overseas for less than a year, still hovered in the nineties.

Like all regular soldiers in Southern Africa, the men of the 24th were obliged to turn out in their home service uniforms – the same rig they would have worn in winter on Salisbury Plain. The high collared tunic was in an uncomfortably thick scarlet serge, trimmed at the collar and cuffs in the regimental facing colour – in this case 'grass green' – in actuality quite a deep green colour. Officers had the choice of wearing scarlet like the men, or alternatively black-braided navy blue patrol jackets. Trousers were navy blue with a red stripe down the outside seam, and were worn with black ammunition boots and shin length leather gaiters. The one concession to the African sun was the lightweight cork sun-helmet, blancoed white in peacetime, but stained down to a dirty yellow-brown with tea leaves or coffee grounds for operations. In certain orders of dress a navy blue glengarry side-cap could be worn in lieu of the helmet. Equipment was the white leather 1871 'valise pattern', which in the field tended to be stripped down to a light fighting order based on the waist belt and ammunition pouches.

Although this was still a scarlet-clad army and there was much about it that veterans of the Crimea would have been at home with, much more recognisably modern practices were now making their debut. The troops could still drill and fight in close-order lines, columns and squares if necessary, but skirmish tactics were no longer the exclusive preserve of a hand-picked light company. At the beginning of the decade the Franco-Prussian War had revealed the deadly potential of the breech-loading rifle. Extended-order tactics would be the norm from now on, with soldiers making use of any natural cover they could find on a firing line. The men of the 24th were armed with the recently introduced and highly potent 0.45-inch calibre Martini-Henry breech-loader which, although it was a single-shot weapon, was capable of an unprecedented rate of fire – ten rounds a minute with ease. Its muzzle velocity was 1,320 feet per second, and at 200 yards it could penetrate quarter-inch iron plate. It weighed 8 lb 12 oz and was 4 ft 1½ in. long. The rolled brass Boxer cartridge was a big, heavy round, of which only seventy were customarily carried on the person. A further thirty rounds a man were held by the quartermaster as the battalion first line reserve. Thus it was now possible for a soldier to shoot off his entire first line ammunition in little more than ten minutes. But the British Army knew only too well just how protracted colonial engagements could be, and the importance of strict fire control was pre-eminent in the teaching of the musketry instructors. Volleys by companies, sections, or alternate ranks, were the norm; only rarely would the men be given permission to fire at will, and even then the number of rounds they were permitted to fire was specified as part of a fire-control order given by the company or section commander. The rifle was sighted to an extremely optimistic 1,500 yards, but more realistically a close-order native enemy could expect to be first brought under fire at about 800 yards. At 600 yards the slaughter would begin in earnest, whilst at 400 yards the fire could be murderous. Anything less than that and you couldn't miss, insisted musketry-instructor Sergeant George Chambers. In practice, hitting an individual target skirmishing across the veldt required a skilful shot, even at relatively short ranges. Even a 'massed' target was never quite as massed as it seemed.

The Martini-Henry came with a sleek and vicious 22-inch bayonet, known colloquially as the 'lunger'. Colour-sergeants and sergeants carried a different bayonet from the rest of the men. The 1871 pattern sword-bayonet was as long as the lunger, but in some production runs proved much less robust; a decade later it would cost men's lives in the Sudan. Officers were required to fire the annual musketry practices and to be competent with the Martini-Henry, but it was usual for them to arm themselves at private expense with swords and pistols. Whilst there was no standard service revolver at this time, the Adams proved a particularly popular acquisition. The baggage of the officers invariably included a veritable arsenal of sporting guns.

By 1879 it was usual for a battalion to form in three distinct bodies, the skirmishers, supports and the reserve (or main body). Typically companies were divided between these tasks in configurations of 2/4/2 or more typically of 2/2/4. If the battalion was attacked in force, the skirmish line could be thickened up by sending forward sections or whole companies from the supports. If forced to give ground, the forward companies could fall back on the supports and if necessary the main body. In order to maximise its 'close order' firepower, the infantry still placed its reliance on the traditional two-deep 'fighting line'. In extended order, however, the rear rank men stepped forward into the front rank intervals to create a single-rank skirmish line. What we tend to think of as the 20th-century principles of covering movement by fire, and of keeping 'one foot on the ground', were in fact well understood even in these early years of the modern military era. These doctrines demanded that only half of a tactical grouping should manoeuvre at any one time, and that it should do so with the benefit of covering fire from the other half. Although such ideas were relatively innovative in the infantry of the line and were frowned upon by some of the old colonels, there is no evidence to suggest that Richard Glyn was in any way averse to them. Although most of the tactics employed in Africa were improvised to suit local circumstance, and were not to be found in any manual, they were mostly derived from these essential basics.

Native Allies

On the Cape Frontier, the regulars had become well accustomed to the presence in the field of allied black auxiliary troops, often referred to as 'friendlies.' In the Transkei and the Ciskei, large bodies of irregulars were levied from the Mfengu population, an agglomeration of Bantu clans that had fled south at the time of the *mfecane*, the period of inter-tribal turmoil associated with the forging of Shaka's Zulu empire. Commonly referred to as 'Fingoes', they were often settled by the colonial authorities on recently annexed Xhosa territory, and thus could be relied upon as willing allies in times of war. In the 8th Frontier War of 1850–3, the Fingoes had tended to fight under their own leaders, but in the most recent war of 1877–8, it had become increasingly the norm to provide native contingents with European officers drawn from the settler community. One such officer was the 29-year-old Rupert Lonsdale, an ex-regular army subaltern of the 74th Regiment, who had left the service under a cloud and had come out to South Africa to nurse a sick brother. Lonsdale earned a good reputation in the fighting in the Amatolas, and in particular was very highly regarded by Colonel Evelyn Wood, who thought him the best leader of native irregulars he had seen.

The Fingoe homelands lay far to the south, however, and for the campaign against the Zulus Lord Chelmsford would supplement his regular and colonial forces with native contingents levied from the tribes and clans of Natal, many of which were of Zulu extraction. By and large, the clans living under colonial rule had lost any martial prowess they once possessed, and lived in fear and awe of their thoroughbred cousins across the border. The task of raising the Natal Native Contingent (NNC) was entrusted to Lieutenant-Colonel Durnford. In Pietermaritzburg, there had been considerable reticence about raising such a corps, so that the co-operation of the lieutenant-governor and his colonial administration was only secured at the last minute.

Chelmsford directed that the NNC be organised formally into battalions and companies, and trained and drilled in imitation of the regular infantry. It was to prove questionable practice. There were to be seven native infantry battalions, each of ten companies. The 1st Regiment would consist of three battalions and would be the mainstay of Durnford's reserve column. The other two regiments would consist of only two battalions and were assigned to main force invasion columns: 2nd Regiment to Pearson, and 3rd Regiment to Glyn. Evelyn Wood would use Swazi irregulars from the far north, long-standing enemies of the Zulu.

With only a few short weeks of 1878 remaining when the lieutenant-governor finally relented, the raising, training and resourcing of the NNC became a frantic rush for all concerned. Most of the military-minded young men of Natal were already enlisted in the colony's volunteer units, so it became necessary to bring most of the European officers and NCOs up from the Cape. Many former officers of the Fingoe contingents came north, including Rupert Lonsdale, who was appointed as the regimental commandant of 3rd NNC. Lonsdale's 1st Battalion was entrusted to the well-travelled Commandant George 'Maori' Browne,* a veteran of operations in New Zealand and of the recent campaign in the Transkei. The 2nd Battalion went to Commandant Edward Cooper who, like Lonsdale, was an ex-regular. Many members of a white auxiliary unit, raised around King William's Town by Henry Pulleine, also came north to

---

* He is often referred to as Hamilton-Browne, as this was the name under which he published his memoirs. In fact he changed his name later in life; in 1879 he was just plain Browne. He was born Richard Burke in Ireland around 1849. He had in his day been an enlisted man in the Royal Artillery, a sous-lieutenant in the Papal Zouaves and a duellist. He had fought as an irregular against the Maoris, against the Sioux and the Xhosa.

provide the nucleus of the NNC's NCO cadre. At best they were a roughneck bunch, many of them former railway navvies, drifters or barflies. Barely any of them spoke Zulu, the most widely spoken language of Natal, and few were inclined to be tolerant of the blacks in their charge. There were to be three European officers and six NCOs to each hundred-strong company of levies.

As the colonial administration could not bring itself to contemplate the distribution of 7,000 firearms to the black population, Chelmsford ordered that only one man in ten should be armed with a rifle. As a further sop to settler paranoia, each man so armed would be given only five rounds of ammunition. In the NNC, five men per company received a Martini-Henry and five an obsolescent Snider-Enfield. By contrast, all the Europeans were given Martinis and a full-scale issue of seventy rounds of ammunition. Typically then, an NNC company of 109 officers and men could field nineteen firearms, the balance being armed with traditional cowhide shields, assegais and knobkerries.

Conceptually, it was envisaged that the NNC would fulfil similar roles to the Fingoes in the last war: they would man distant outposts to give early warning; they would act as beaters and cut-offs in 'drives' through difficult close terrain; they would act as flank guards and escorts; and they would be launched in pursuit of a broken enemy force retiring from a failed attack. It was not envisaged that they would fight from a line of battle against a set-piece Zulu assault. Bellowed at and brutalised by men they were unable to comprehend, and set to perform complex military manoeuvres which almost invariably went horribly wrong, the levies quickly came to question the advisability of tackling their Zulu cousins in such improbable ways.

In addition to the NNC infantry battalions, Durnford also formed two other native corps. These he singled out for personal attention. Although he was insistent upon on a rigorous training regime, Durnford went out of his way to foster a much higher standard of man-management in these two units. The first was the Natal Native Mounted Contingent (NNMC), sometimes referred to as Durnford's Horse.* This consisted of six fifty-strong troops of irregular horsemen. The first three troops came from the

---

* The NNMC is often erroneously styled the Natal Native Horse (NNH), a name that did not come into use until later in the war.

amaNgwane clan of the chief Zikhali, the fourth from the followers of the Basuto* chief Hlubi, the fifth from the Edendale Mission just outside Pieter-maritzburg, while the sixth was styled Jantze's hors. The men of the Edendale Troop were all devout Christians and in token of their faith held twice daily prayer meetings in the field. All 300 troopers received a modern breech-loading carbine and a bandolier of fifty cartridges. The NNMC were turned out in discarded European clothing and battered hats, but with the exception of the booted and spurred Edendale Troop, preferred to ride barefoot. The only Europeans in the unit were the six troop commanders. In the absence of any formed bodies of Royal Engineers, Durnford also raised a three-company Natal Native Pioneer Corps (NNPC). He singled this unit out as a cut above the rest by issuing the men with white breeches, a smart red tunic and a pillbox hat. Importantly, they also received a Snider-Enfield rifle each. Each of the main-force columns got a company of the pioneers under command.

Command and Staff

The Commander of No. 3 Column, Colonel Richard Thomas Glyn, was in his late forties, had been in the army for almost twenty-five years, and had commanded the 1st/24th for the last seven of them. Now a devoted family man with four young daughters, he had started his military career in the 82nd Regiment, with which he had served in the closing stages of the Crimean War. Glyn's first spell of genuine war service was as a captain in the Indian Mutiny. His majority and later the lieutenant-colonelcy of the 24th were both obtained by purchase, the latter in 1867. Four years later he was promoted to full colonel. Short in stature, greying, and by now carrying a few pounds with the onset of middle age, Glyn had great affection for his men and was a popular and well-regarded commanding officer. He was well known as a fanatical hunting man and had insisted that the officers of the 1st/24th maintained their own pack of foxhounds in the Cape, where the black-backed jackal served as prey. He had been awarded the CB for his services as the military commander of the Transkei in the 9th Cape Frontier War, a campaign in which both the colonel and

---

* Modern usage favours 'Sotho' rather than the nineteenth-century renderings Basuto, Basoto or Basotho. In the interests of historical authenticity, 'Basuto' is preferred throughout the narrative.

his battalion had earned high praise. Glyn and his officers were particularly well acquainted with Sir Bartle Frere, who had lived happily amongst them in their mess at King William's Town throughout the long period of hostilities against the Xhosa.

Glyn's principal staff officer was Major Francis Clery, a fellow infantryman and a former tactics instructor at Sandhurst. Clery's appointment was very recent and the two men were not yet used to each other's ways. By nature Clery was a thruster and somewhat inclined to underestimate Glyn. Amongst the subordinate staff officers were Captain Alan Gardner of the 14th Hussars, Captain Edward Essex of the 75th Regiment, Surgeon-Major Peter Shepherd, the Principal Medical Officer, and Lieutenant Francis McDowel, the colonel's engineer adviser. Glyn had left the post of orderly officer vacant, in response to a request for a place on his staff from Lieutenant Nevill Coghill of the 24th. Coghill, the 26-year-old son of an Anglo-Irish baronet, was Dublin-born and mischievous by disposition. During his tour at the regimental depot in Brecon, he had wagered that he could jump his Spanish pony over the dining room table at the Castle Hotel. Sadly history does not relate the outcome.

In the New Year, the GOC arrived at Helpmekaar at the head of the army staff. Lieutenant-General Lord Chelmsford had come out to the Cape early in 1878 to replace Sir Arthur Cunynghame who, in alliance with Frere, had been in constant conflict with the first self-governing cabinet at the Cape over the conduct of operations on the eastern frontier. The haggling had degenerated into a fully-fledged constitutional crisis, which ended only when Frere dismissed Prime Minister John Molteno to assert the supremacy of the imperial power over its seemingly truculent colonial subordinates.

When Horse Guards cast about for a general officer of a suitably diplomatic disposition to make a fresh start in the Cape, attention fell upon Major-General The Honourable Frederick Thesiger, CB, at the time commanding the 1st Infantry Brigade at Aldershot. The 51-year-old Thesiger was an infantryman and an aristocrat, a former commanding officer of the 95th Regiment of Foot, and heir to the Chelmsford peerage, to which he succeeded only a few months after his arrival in South Africa. He was a veteran of the Mutiny and of Napier's Abyssinian campaign, where he had done sterling work on the staff as a deputy adjutant-general. The Duke of Cambridge, the commander in chief, concluded that his experience of colonial campaigning, and his widely acknowledged charm, would make him the ideal choice for South Africa.

Accompanying the new GOC when he disembarked in the Ciskei were his right-hand men from Aldershot. His former deputy assistant adjutant-general (DAAG), Major John North Crealock, would now act as his military secretary, whilst his former brigade major, Captain Matthew Gosset, would be his principal ADC. Crealock was an old India hand from the general's own regiment. Amongst other things he was a talented watercolour artist, but as a person most people found him sarcastic, superior, and extremely difficult to like; in short, he was objectionable by disposition. By the time of the Zulu War, Crealock had been breveted to lieutenant-colonel, and Gosset to major. Although military secretary was an innocuous sounding title, in the absence of a formally designated chief of staff, it was Crealock who fulfilled this role. Almost immediately Crealock and Clery began to grate against each other. Additional aides on the army staff included Captain Ernest Buller of the Rifle Brigade, and the naval officer Lieutenant Berkeley Milne, RN.

There was considerable friction over the choice of commander for the mounted troops. Chelmsford had laid his hands on a bona fide cavalryman, Captain J. C. Russell of the 12th Lancers. Anxious to make best use of a cavalry professional, Chelmsford had secured him a brevet majority and then granted him local rank as a lieutenant-colonel. 'Colonel' Russell, it was announced, would command the cavalry. There was immediate consternation amongst the police and volunteers who had assumed they would be operating under the command of one of their own – the highly regarded commandant of the NMP. John Dartnell might be an ex-regular, but he was now a son of Natal through and through. Volunteer officers had quiet words with staff officers; there was every danger their men would refuse to serve under Russell, they confided. Precisely as intended, the staff officers went running to the general. Embarrassingly for all concerned, the controversy was reported in the Pietermaritzburg press. Chelmsford quickly came up with a devious compromise; Dartnell was such a good man that he would be quite indispensable as a member of the GOC's personal staff. The staff officers confided this back the other way, where it was swallowed hook, line and sinker by the volunteers. Chelmsford got his way. Russell was appointed to command the cavalry. Anxious to prevent any further difficulty or embarrassment, Dartnell loyally went along with the general's ploy.

As the ultimatum wound down, the army moved up to its forward assembly area. By 10 January, the whole force, some 4,500 men in all, had assembled on the banks of the Buffalo River at Rorke's Drift, where the two thatched buildings of Jim Rorke's old property were now in use as a mission station. Mr Otto Witt was the resident missionary, but for the time being his house and chapel were in the hands of the military as a hospital and storehouse respectively. The river crossing and the mission were nestled beneath a long whale-backed hill known in Zulu as Shiyane, which Mr Witt, a Swede, insisted on calling the Oscarberg, in honour of his king.

The invasion would begin the following morning. There was much last-minute work to do and few officers had reason at this stage to recollect William Degacher's toast at the Chillianwallah dinner of a few days earlier. Within a fortnight though, the memory of that moment would come flooding back to those who had been there. Recollecting events in the Punjab thirty years earlier, and looking forward to the immediate future, Degacher had proposed, 'That we may not get into such a mess – and have better luck this time.' No doubt people laughed aloud.

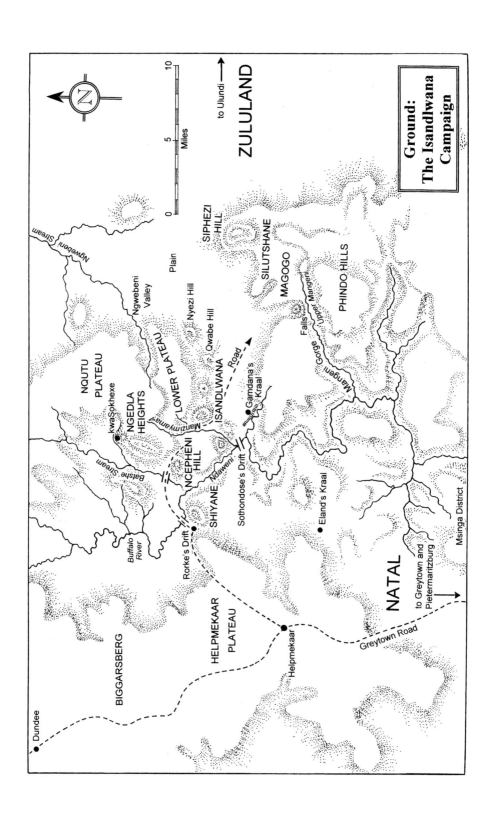

N

10

5

0

Miles

to Ulundi

ZULULAND

Ngwebeni Stream

Plain

SIPHEZI
HILL

SILUTSHANE

Ngwebeni
Valley

Nyezi Hill

MAGOGO

Owabe Hill

NQUTU
PLATEAU

LOWER PLATEAU

Road

PHINDO HILLS

kwaSokhexe

NGEDLA
HEIGHTS

ISANDLWANA

Falls

Upper Mangeni

Batshe Stream

Manzimyama

Gamdana's
Kraal

Mangeni Gorge

NCEPHENI
HILL

Buffalo River

SHIYANE

Ndaweni

Sothondose's Drift

Eland's Kraal

Rorke's Drift

Msinga District

HELPMEKAAR
PLATEAU

NATAL

to Greytown and
Pietermaritzburg

BIGGARSBERG

Helpmekaar

Greytown Road

Dundee

**Ground:
The Isandlwana
Campaign**

Chapter 2

Enemy Territory

No. 3 Column, 10-20 January

During that last afternoon of flurried preparation for war, there was probably little time for the men of No. 3 Column to reflect on how the campaign would unfold. If there had been, few could have imagined that it would entail the most complete military disaster of the colonial era. Few could have conceived that the subjugation of a 'primitive' African nation would take the mighty British Army seven months of hard fighting, that the GOC would face humiliation, that massive reinforcement from home would yet be necessary, that there would be no fewer than seven pitched battles, that guns and colours would be lost, and that, in order to achieve victory, the British would have to kill so many Zulu fighting men that ultimately the war would leave an unpleasant after-taste.

What was the expectation then? Surely it would be a war in which the greatest difficulties would be logistical. As ever such problems would be overcome by sheer hard toil, and the British Army's unparalleled knack for improvisation. The war would be short; the royal kraals at Ulundi lay a mere eighty miles away. Once No. 3 Column was properly into its stride, that sort of distance could easily be covered in a fortnight. Consciences had been salved by Sir Bartle Frere's propaganda campaign: this was a just war; a war to bring enlightenment to one of the darkest corners of a famously dark continent; Cetshwayo held sway by fear alone; his people would be glad to see the back of him. The invasion would probably be the cue for coup and assassination: Cetshwayo would share the fate of Shaka and Dingane. There might not even be any fighting said some cynics. Most of the young officers hoped that such tiresome forecasts would prove wide of the mark.

In the past year almost all the regulars had experienced enemy fire cracking overhead. They had seen the pathetically twisted corpses of dead men, or the horrible suffering of wounded ones. Mostly such casualties of war had been amongst the Xhosa enemy. Yes, one could be maimed or killed fighting in Africa, but as a rule one had to be pretty unlucky. Thus it was perfectly possible to be unconcerned, blasé or even excited about the onset of a new bout of hostilities. Most people expected to get one good fight out of the Zulu. With the notable exception of Centane, the Xhosa had not really 'come on'. It was common talk around the campfires that the Zulu would be different. And their courage would sow the seeds of their destruction; for then they would get their introduction to the Martini-Henry. The clash of empires would be brief and bloody, but for the men now encamped on the Natal bank of the Buffalo, there was little reason for trepidation.

In idle moments in the past twenty-four hours, most of the officers and men of the 24th had found time or reason to saunter down from their tents to the riverbank. Some went to do laundry, some to fill water bottles and some for a stroll with friends. Many went to stare into the water because it was something to do and the drift was a pretty spot. Silhouetted in a gap in the hills on the distant horizon, was a distinctive hill feature with a high southern crag and a long northern slope. Nobody knows who first spotted the resemblance between Isandlwana and the Egyptian Sphinx, but everyone agreed that it was pronounced. The men of the 24th wore a pair of brass Sphinx collar-dogs on their tunics to commemorate the regiment's service in Egypt. Not everybody felt comfortable with the omen. Chelmsford had the landmark in mind as a temporary staging post en route to Siphezi Hill, which had been chosen from the map as the site of the first fortified encampment. To obtain a decent view of the ground along the intended axis of advance, it was necessary to climb to the top of Shiyane, or to ride beyond it to the east. Perhaps because from afar Isandlwana seemed to dominate its surrounds, people insisted on calling it a mountain.

During the course of the afternoon, Lieutenant Coghill rode into Rorke's Drift with his soldier-servant Private Edward Turner, his black groom 'Johnny', and a remount for Colonel Glyn. The ride up from Pieter-maritzburg, where until lately Coghill had been ADC to Frere, had taken the party three days. With operations up-country imminent, Coghill had successfully obtained his release.

Most men in the camp had done all that they could do by late afternoon and ate their suppers over the light-hearted banter so beloved of British soldiers. They were early to bed, for their orders called for a pre-dawn start. Establishing a bridgehead into hostile territory is invariably a high-risk undertaking. In this instance, the planners had been assured by those who claimed to know that the operation was certain to be opposed. Accordingly, the N Battery guns and the 2nd/24th were to cover the crossing from the home bank. The bridgehead would be seized by the 1st/24th, secured on the flanks by the NNC battalions, and then screened by the cavalry. Once the units of the first wave were safely established, the 2nd/24th and the guns could move across to join them. Undoubtedly the biggest challenge of the day would be getting the numerous and cumbersome transport wagons across. Even if the move went like clockwork, it was sure to be a tedious and time-consuming process. A new camp would be established on the far bank during the course of the afternoon.

Whilst the infantry were busy securing the new site and putting up tents, a wing of the cavalry would conduct a reconnaissance in the direction of a kraal called kwaSokhexe, the homestead of the prominent local chieftain, Sihayo. This was located above the Batshe Valley, two ridgelines into Zululand, and was said to be well fortified and strongly held. As a murder at Rorke's Drift, perpetrated at Sihayo's behest, had been one of Frere's major pretexts for war, the early chastisement of his district would represent a salutary lesson for the Zulu and, much more importantly, would send exactly the right message to London: military operations were focussed on the murderous Zulu leadership, not indiscriminately on the people. Political dimensions aside, there were also good military reasons for the reduction of kwaSokhexe. The old traders' wagon road, which was to be Glyn's main supply route, climbed out of the Batshe Valley in the near vicinity of the kraal. Clearly no major enemy strongholds could be left astride it. If the cavalry made a favourable report during the course of the day, an offensive operation could be considered for Sunday morning.

Once the crossing was secure and the tedious administrative work of the day was under way, Chelmsford planned to leave Glyn in charge and ride to a pre-arranged rendezvous with Evelyn Wood some twelve miles to the north. Wood's column was crossing into Zululand that day, twenty-four hours ahead of Glyn, and a day before the expiry of the ultimatum.

Invasion

Reveille was at 3.00 a.m. The morning air was cold and damp. There was a distraction when the men's kit was searched for grog and tobacco, stolen

the previous evening from a sutler called Stewart. Nothing was found and
Stewart was told to be off, before the officers ordered his wagons pitched
into the river. Lieutenant Francis McDowel, RE, was down at the two
hawser-operated ponts early, to ensure that everything was still in good
working order. The main crossing-point was sited on the deep-water pool
just upstream from the concrete road-bridge of today. The ford, Rorke's
Drift proper, was 500 metres downstream of the ponts. The heavy summer
rains had brought the Buffalo well above the level that local people had
become accustomed to; now there was white water breaking noisily over
the big rocks between the ponts and the drift. Even so, there were chest-
deep shallows where the cavalry and the levies should be able to cross
without too much difficulty. A few miles down-river, in the direction of a
seldom-used native crossing known as Sothondose's Drift, the Buffalo
entered a steep-sided gorge. Here the water was now rushing through the
defile with such force that the drift beyond had been rendered impassable.

By 5.00 a.m. it was light. Charles Norris-Newman, the war
correspondent of the *Standard*, known universally as 'Noggs', had hatched
a none too subtle plot to get his scoop: he swam his horse over the river
well ahead of the military, in order to label himself as the first man into
Zululand. His one-man invasion complete, he waited nervously in the mist
for the arrival of the troops. Lieutenant-Colonel Harness trotted his guns
down to the ridge above the ponts and unlimbered facing the river. When
the mist cleared, he would have an excellent field of fire over the Zulu
bank. In the meantime N Battery was pretty much wasting its time. The
2nd/24th marched briskly down to the river and disposed its companies
along the home bank. When Henry Degacher was content, he sent word
to his brother to begin crossing with the 1st Battalion. Captain George
Wardell's H Company was the first to shuffle onto the ponts. Thankfully
there proved to be no Zulu riflemen concealed on the far bank. As soon
as the ponts grounded, H Company doubled ashore and fanned out to
secure a defensible salient. The men of the NNC, meanwhile, were
crossing at the shallows on either side of the ponts, Edward Cooper's
troops upstream to the left, and Maori Browne's at the drift, downstream
to the right. The mounted troops also splashed over at the drift and then
cantered on to the ridge above the river. They did not get across entirely
without mishap: an unhorsed private of the IMI had to be rescued
midstream by Captain Hayes of 1st/3rd NNC. The incident was played out

in front of the GOC himself. Typically, his lordship called at Browne's encampment later in the day to commend Hayes in person. From the ridge above the river, the cavalry could see nothing of the enemy. The two NNC battalions shook themselves out along the ridge on either side of the 1st/24th. Major Degacher was taking no chances in the mist and formed his companies in 'receive cavalry' squares. Content that the crossing was secure, Chelmsford departed for his meeting with Wood.

Gradually the sun burned off the morning mist, and by early afternoon it had become a blazing hot day. Business proceeded much as planned. By mid-morning both regular battalions were across, and in the early afternoon Major John Dartnell rode away with a police patrol to scout kwaSokhexe. A new tented camp quickly sprang up inside a protective screen of vedettes and pickets. Notwithstanding Lord Chelmsford's standing orders for South African campaigning, no instructions were given regarding improvised defences. The transport was every bit as slow as had been anticipated. The oxen were pushed across at the drift, but the wagons themselves had to wait for the ponts. In the event the backlog was such that Harness was forced to abandon any idea of getting his guns over that day.* The ferrying work went on long after dark and would be resumed before dawn. The Zulus remained conspicuous by their absence. By late afternoon, Chelmsford was back from his long ride. He and Wood met not long after 9.00 and then spent over three hours deep in conversation. In the course of the trip, the general's escort had managed to round up 200 head of cattle. Wood's escort had driven a similarly rich haul back northwards.

When he arrived at the site of his new headquarters, Chelmsford found Anthony Durnford waiting for him. The colonel had ridden up from No. 2 Column's encampment at Dalmaine's Farm, near Kranskop, to acquaint the GOC with items of intelligence from across the Tugela River. His most significant piece of news was that all Zulu men of fighting age had just been summoned to Ulundi. No doubt it sounded important, but it did not really tell the GOC anything he could not have guessed at for himself. It may have been a pretext for Durnford to visit so that he could query his most recent orders. There had been significant changes to his part in the plan which were not at all to his liking. Durnford had received his first set

---

* *Narrative of Field Operations.*

of written orders on New Year's Day. At that stage, Chelmsford's idea was that No. 2 Column would be allowed to cross the Tugela at Middle Drift, and from there move on to Entumeni. The move could not take place until Pearson was well into Zululand and pushing for the abandoned mission station at Eshowe. From Entumeni, Durnford was to open a line of communication with No. 3 Column, which by that stage should be near the headwaters of the Mhlatuze River. This original scheme of manoeuvre would have entailed Durnford operating independently inside Zululand, with a brigade-sized force, albeit one composed entirely of native troops.

On 4 January, however, Chelmsford had visited Durnford's encampment, over-nighted there, and unveiled an entirely new plan. Durnford was to detach two of his three NNC battalions to Sandspruit, in order to protect the vulnerable Msinga district against cross-border raids. There was a possibility that the battalions would be tasked to co-operate with Glyn. Durnford, the third battalion, and the NNMC, were to wait at Middle Drift, but would not be allowed to cross into Zululand until Pearson was actually at Eshowe. In other words, No. 2 Column was no longer to be used as a brigade, but by detachments, in largely defensive roles. The move to Sandspruit was to take place on Chelmsford's order. In the meantime, No. 2 Column was to remain concentrated at Kranskop. On 8 January the executive order to move the two battalions to Sandspruit came through. Nothing moved.

By the time the 11 January meeting at Rorke's Drift had broken up, a third plan was in effect. Now only one battalion was to move to Sandspruit. The other two would stay at Kranskop to cover Middle Drift. Few military commanders appreciate being asset-stripped by their higher commander; it seems, then, that Durnford was successful in arguing that the bulk of his force should remain concentrated under his direct command. It would also appear that Chelmsford granted him the tactical discretion to make limited forays across Middle Drift, should he have good reason for doing so.

Not long after the meeting with Durnford ended, Major Dartnell rode in to make his report. The police had heard a war-song on the high ground above the Batshe Stream, but otherwise had been unable to locate the enemy. It seemed certain that kwaSokhexe would be defended, but there were no real pointers to the strength of Sihayo's force. Chelmsford instructed Glyn to put together a strong offensive foray for the following morning and turned his thoughts to supper. As Commandant Rupert Lonsdale was suffering from concussion after a fall from his horse,* Glyn sent for Major Wilsone Black of the 2nd/24th and appointed him as the stand-in commandant of 3rd NNC.

It had just got dark when Glyn's orders went out. Maori Browne was rolling himself into his blankets after a frugal meal of bully beef and biscuits when Lieutenant Coghill arrived with instructions for him to parade eight of his companies at 5.00 a.m. William Degacher's orders were to parade all four of his 1st/24th companies at the same time. Henry Degacher and Edward Cooper were to muster four companies each at 8.00 a.m. and move up to the Batshe Valley behind the two leading battalions. The bulk of the cavalry would leave in the 5.00 a.m. departure. Glyn would be in command but the general and his staff would go along to observe the proceedings. This was to be expected, but it was also the first hint that there might be too many cooks for the central column broth. Relations between the two staffs had become tense in the build up to the invasion; from now on they would go into steep decline. There were two primary causes of the deepening spat. The first was Chelmsford's inability to confine himself to the purely operational level of command – the co-ordination and manoeuvring of his columns. Rather, he also insisted on dabbling in the tactical level business of No. 3 Column. The practice soon bred uncertainty over division of responsibility. The second cause of friction was the mutual loathing of the two chiefs of staff. Both Crealock and Clery were immodest enough to rate themselves highly, and both could be extremely difficult customers. Their antipathy was unlikely to help an already delicate situation.

The Attack on kwaSokhexe

The following morning, the first significant action of the Zulu War was fought in the Batshe Valley. Although the four-kilometre approach march was mostly uphill, the slope was gentle and the going easy. When the

* Remarkably, the incident occurred when Lonsdale was reminded of an imminent inspection of his regiment by the GOC. He had known about it for a number of days, but had told none of his subordinates, and on the morning in question had quite forgotten about it. His fall occurred as he was galloping about trying to rally his companies together for the inspection. He spent the parade unconscious in his tent! One suspects from this and other occurrences, that Wood's assessment of Lonsdale was flawed.

British arrived on the western side of the Batshe Stream, they had the
Masotsheni Ridge behind them and a feature called Ngedla to their front.
With only indifferent maps at their disposal, the officers probably thought
they were looking at a single hill, running north to south for about four
kilometres. In fact this was the western face, not of a single hill, but of a
range of hills known as the Ngedla Heights. These stretched away to the
east for nine kilometres, narrowing progressively as they went. There was
a steep bluff halfway up the western face and some fairly thick scrub at its
base. Far from being a hilltop stronghold, kwaSokhexe turned out to be
located on an easily accessible spur at the north-west corner of the heights,
which for the time being was out of sight to the troops. The old wagon
road, little more than ruts in the grass, lay to the south of the Ngedla high
ground. For about two kilometres it ran steeply uphill from the stream,
before disappearing from sight over a wide saddle between Ngedla and a
rocky crag to the right called Ncepheni Hill. The crest precluded any long-
range view into Zululand. Isandlwana lay just five kilometres ahead but
was not visible from the Batshe Valley.

Glyn's plan was to be executed in two phases. First, the Ngedla high
ground would be cleared, and then there would be a direct assault on
kwaSokhexe. Maori Browne's 1st/3rd NNC was to spearhead the attack on
the heights from the west, and then sweep north across the top of Ngedla
towards the kraal. The 1st/24th would be in support. The cavalry would
ride up to the saddle, gain Ngedla from the south, and then act in concert
with Browne. In the final phase, four companies each of the 2nd/24th and
the 2nd/3rd NNC would swing north up the Batshe Valley, to mount the
attack on the kraal.

When Chelmsford and Glyn were in position to survey the scene, they
could see only small parties of warriors on Ngedla. The sound of a war-
song was again drifting in the air. There appeared to be cattle grazing in
the scrub at the foot of the high ground. It is not entirely clear at whose
order it was, but Coghill was sent back to the camp to hurry out the
8.00 a.m. departures early. Possibly this was Chelmsford fiddling with
Glyn's plan. In the meantime, the cavalry wheeled out to secure the flanks,
and Maori Browne brought up his battalion. He passed Chelmsford on his
way across the valley, and was told to round up the cattle grazing in the
brush, before then pushing his advance up through the bluffs to the
summit. On no account, said his lordship, was Browne to fire first, nor was

any harm to be done to women and children. It was probably a little after 8.00 a.m. when Browne put in his attack.

With the exception of three of his companies, manned by a disaffected Zulu clan called the isiGqoza, Browne had little time for the bulk of the levies under his command. In particular, he found the idea of advancing in front of his native riflemen deeply troubling. To be on the safe side, he gave orders that none of them were to be permitted to fire. He then gave the signal for the already ragged line to advance. The attempts of the European NCOs to keep the levies dressed by the right quickly degenerated into farce. But what their drill was lacking, the levies made up for in apparent ferocity; Browne was convinced they would slaughter all the women and children they came across.

At the foot of Ngedla, a voice from above demanded of the attackers by whose orders they came. One of Browne's officers, the Zulu-speaker Captain Duncombe, gave the famous reply, 'By the orders of the great white queen'. With that there was a volley of shots from the hillside above, and the Anglo-Zulu War began in earnest. Detaching his outermost companies to make flanking moves against a great U-shaped notch in the bluffs, Browne pressed a frontal attack with the remainder. The exuberance of the NNC evaporated with the onset of heavy firing and most of them hung back in the assault. Accompanied only by his faithful isiGqoza, Browne pressed on into the scrub, where there was a brief bout of hand-to-hand fighting with small parties of warriors. Most of the Zulus quickly fell back to the foot of the notch and retired up a narrow footpath. This turned out to be barricaded with rocks and covered by riflemen concealed in nearby caves. A group of Zulu women and children were rounded up in the thickets at the foot of the notch and quickly ushered to the rear.

Seeing the disarray in 1st/3rd NNC, Major Black decided to ride forward and lend moral support to Maori Browne. He was accompanied by Captain (local rank) Henry Harford, a special service subaltern of the 99th Regiment employed as Lonsdale's staff officer. On his way up through the scrub, Harford spotted a Zulu rifleman aiming at Colonel Glyn, as he stood observing events from a nearby patch of open ground. Harford was able to shout a warning just in time. Black was soon riding back and forth amongst the levies, railing against their hesitancy. Harford kept moving forward with a party of men he had rallied to his side. A little further on, a wounded Zulu staggered out of the bush and fell at his feet. The man had a deep assegai wound down his back, which was so horrific that Harford briefly contemplated shooting him dead to end his suffering. In the end he thought better of it, but the man expired anyway. Encouraged by Major Black's furious demeanour, the Europeans drove the levies forward again. The bayonets of the 1st/24th were the strongest incentive of all to resume the advance. Trapped between the regular infantry and the enemy, the rifle-armed levies did exactly what Browne had always feared and opened fire from behind him. The men at the front of the assault quickly took cover in the rocks and thanked their lucky stars that the levies had been issued only five rounds a man. When the short-lived fusillade had petered out, the isiGqoza tried to push forward again, but soon found themselves pinned down by heavy Zulu fire.

Browne thought the attack was at an impasse and decided to halt in cover until his flanking parties had gained the bluffs. Wilsone Black, however, dismounted, came up to the front of the troops, and continued to urge the men forward. He was standing not far from the foot of the bluff, waving his sword around, when a rock thrown from above hit him painfully 'below the belt'. Even the NNC NCOs, men well accustomed to the sporting language of the frontier, were mightily impressed by the stream of Gaelic oaths emanating from the doubled-up major. Black decided to retire for a moment or two to regain his composure, and on falling back through the bush came across Glyn, Clery and Browne, who had been eyewitnesses to his discomfiture. One of them was thoughtful enough to express regret at the major's 'wounding', at which all three collapsed into fits of laughter. Before long the flanking companies had seized the top of the notch, whereupon the fighting on the western bluff began to peter out. Harford had distinguished himself by clearing a cave single-handedly and bringing in four prisoners.

While Browne was in action on the hillside, the cavalry detachment under Russell made its way to the top of Ngedla from the south. Here they surprised a band of fifty or sixty warriors in the open, and in a short, sharp, running fight, killed eighteen of them before the party could scatter into the hills.

The fighting on Ngedla was over by 9.00. Over the next hour the troops marched to the north and took up vantage points above kwaSokhexe. From the high ground they could see that the kraal was undefended. They arrived in good time to watch the advance of the 2nd/24th and 2nd/3rd NNC. Before long the redcoats were skirmishing earnestly towards the kraal, as if expecting to be brought under fire at any moment. From the hillside above, the men of the 1st/24th rained down derision on the efforts of their sister-battalion. Rather self-consciously, the 2nd Battalion broke off their attack and hurled some insults back. Both battalions rather enjoyed the joke. Some old women were found in a nearby cave and revealed that the other residents of the kraal had fled the day before. After firing the huts, the troops began the return march to the Buffalo. Halfway home they were drenched by a sudden downpour. Chelmsford rode back to camp well pleased with the morning's proceedings. Over thirty Zulus had been killed, including one of Sihayo's sons, and there had been a good haul of the chief's livestock, around 400 head of cattle and 550 goats and sheep. The limited British loss fell entirely upon the 1st/3rd NNC: two Europeans and around a dozen levies had been wounded. Of Sihayo himself, there was no news.*

The Durnford Reprimand

For the men of No. 3 Column, Monday 13 January was a day of rest. For the commander of No. 2 Column, it was something of a personal disaster. His command was still intact at Dalmaine's Farm, within easy striking distance of Middle Drift. During the course of the day, Durnford received a letter from Bishop Schreuder, a local missionary known to be well connected on the other side of the river. The bishop's sources had intimated that a raid across Middle Drift was imminent. Durnford took it into his head to move his troops over the border to intercept the enemy. Not unnaturally, he decided to send a note to Lord Chelmsford advising him of his intent. To any impartial judge, the source of Durnford's intelligence was at best questionable. Chelmsford's reaction, though, was furious. Durnford's command paraded in the early hours of the 14th, ready to move off at first light, but before the sun had come up a galloper arrived from Rorke's Drift with a response from the GOC.

> Unless you carry out the instructions I give you, it will be my
> unpleasant duty to remove you from your command and to
> substitute another officer for the command of No. 2 Column. When
> a column is acting separately in an enemy's country I am quite ready

* The chief had gone to the muster of the army at Ulundi.

to give its commander every latitude and would certainly expect him to disobey any orders he might receive from me, if information that he obtained showed that it would be injurious to the interests of the column under his command. Your neglecting to obey the instructions in the present instance is no excuse. You have simply received information in a letter from Bishop Scroeder [*sic*], which may or may not be true, and which you have no means of verifying. If movements ordered are to be delayed because reports hint at a chance of an invasion of Natal, it will be impossible for me to carry out my plan of campaign. I trust you will understand this plain speaking and will not give me any further occasion to write in a style which is distasteful to me.

The note shook Durnford. Captain Dymes of 1st/1st NNC was near him when it arrived: 'I saw a change in his face at once. Suddenly he gave the word to retrace our way to camp and I well remember the look of disgust that crossed his countenance when he read the order.' Chelmsford seldom resorted to such heavy-handedness in his correspondence, or indeed in any of his dealings with his subordinates. This was more than just a rebuke for making a move to protect Middle Drift – after all Chelmsford had already conceded such freedom of action. It seems clear then, that some other factor must also have been in play. The letter seems to be focussed directly on the issue of disobedience, rather than misjudgement. Speculatively, it is possible that Durnford had become recalcitrant and difficult from the moment he was ordered to detach troops to Sandspruit, a task in which, clearly, he saw little merit. He may have argued and lost the point during the general's visit of 4 January. Given that he received an executive order to move two battalions on 8 January, but all three battalions were still at Kranskop on 13 January, then it follows that the executive had still not been implemented by the time of the 11 January meeting at Rorke's Drift. This is certain to have irritated Chelmsford, who quite rightly expected to be obeyed by his senior subordinates.

The letter of 13 January may be couched in quite such strong terms because it had been preceded by a face-to-face reprimand for prevarication two days earlier. Under pressure from the disappointed Durnford at the Rorke's Drift meeting, the general may have agreed a compromise proposal that only one battalion should move to the north. If he had been disappointed and irritated by Durnford's prevarication on 11 January, then he would have been justifiably livid to find on 13 January, that all three battalions were still at Kranskop and that the Msinga area remained defenceless. Whatever had passed between the two men in their conversations of 4 and 11 January, it is clear that Durnford had somehow pushed the GOC's patience to breaking point.

The Long Pause

Reconnaissance into the Batshe Valley had shown that the wagon road was impassable at the point at which it crossed the stream. For the advance to proceed it would be necessary to improve the entry and exit points in the banks of the stream, and to dig two significant ditches to channel the flow of water. In effect the aim was to create a passable causeway through what had become a minor swamp feature in a hollow in the ground. The job was likely to be manpower-intensive, time-consuming and unpopular. It was decided to establish an advanced camp at the site, in order to avoid tiresome daily journeys back and forth. Lieutenant McDowel, RE, would be in charge of the project. Captain Nolan's company of native pioneers and Maori Browne's 1st/3rd NNC would provide the bulk of the unskilled labour. Because such an advanced camp would inevitably be somewhat isolated and vulnerable, Henry Degacher was instructed to provide four companies of the 2nd/24th for its defence. Major Dunbar's left wing companies were duly nominated. Dunbar would be the overall commander of the 1,500 men now detailed to the Batshe Valley.

The road-builders deployed on Tuesday morning. For some reason, the staff had chosen the site of Dunbar's camp for him. The major did not like the position one little bit. It was sited on the eastern side of the Batshe Stream, halfway up the long slope to Ncepheni Hill. There were highly limited fields of view to the east and south, which after dark could allow an enemy force to approach far too close for comfort. It was also within small-arms range of Ncepheni Hill. By contrast, a site on the western side of the valley would have infinitely better fields of fire and would be safely out of range from any commanding high ground.

For Durnford, if Monday brought the GOC's ire, then Tuesday brought his retribution. Chelmsford slept on his subordinate's failings overnight and despatched fresh orders first thing the following morning. The new plan for No. 2 Column entailed the Sandspruit battalion crossing the Buffalo near Eland's Kraal and co-operating with No. 3 Column against the stronghold of the chief Matshana kaMondisa, the next major chieftain along Glyn's axis of advance. Matshana's district ran across the Phindo Hills and down into the rough hill country at the junction of the Mangeni stream and the Buffalo. A second chief Matshana, (kaSitshakuza), lived in roughly the same area. So rudimentary were Chelmsford's arrangements for the management of intelligence that the staff were quite unable to distinguish between them. The name was most commonly rendered as 'Matyana', and the chiefs were invariably referred to as 'the two Matyanas', as if they were a single entity.

The NNC battalion at issue, the 2nd/1st NNC, was under the command of a special service regular, Major Harcourt Bengough. By operating on the east bank of the Buffalo, Bengough would fulfil a dual purpose. First, he would provide a forward line of defence to Msinga District and, second, he would provide some guarantee against a Zulu force concealing itself in the difficult terrain on Glyn's right. This was to be avoided at all costs, as such a force might be able to hit No. 3 Column when it was at its most vulnerable – strung out on the line of march.

The orders for Durnford's other battalions remained unchanged: 3rd/1st NNC under Captain Cherry, and six companies of 1st/1st NNC under Captain Montgomery were to remain at Kranskop to cover Middle Drift. Durnford himself, with five troops of native horse, the three 1st/1st NNC companies still remaining to him, and Major F. B. Russell's rocket battery, was to move up as far as Sandspruit with Bengough and wait for an executive order to come on to Rorke's Drift. For Durnford this was a body blow. In the space of a few short days he had gone from being the commander of an independent brigade-sized force, to being the CO of a regiment of irregular horse operating under the direct supervision of the army commander.

Nothing better illustrates the principal defect in Chelmsford's generalship than his uncertainty over the role of No. 2 Column. It was not that he was unable to make decisions, but rather that he was unable to stick by them. One might have thought that, after the various iterations of the plan up to this point, this really had to be the final version. Yet, later in the week, Chelmsford would change his mind again, when he concluded that Bengough would be at too great a risk east of the Buffalo, and ought instead to come on to Rorke's Drift to marry up with Durnford. Chelmsford had slipped into the bad habit of manoeuvring his units like chess pieces, with very little regard for the practical implications of his rapid changes of heart, and little cognisance of the potential for confusion in the minds of his subordinates.

As there was reason for one of the three 1st/1st NNC company commanders* to stay behind at Kranskop with Montgomery's main body, plans were made to disperse his men between the other two companies of Durnford's much reduced command. Thus, when the time came to move north, D and E Companies under Captains Cracroft Nourse and Walter Stafford respectively, did so at an atypical strength of something in excess of a dozen Europeans and 150 levies each. With Jantze's Horse remaining, the five other troops of native horse amounted to 257 troopers and half a dozen white officers. Brevet Major Francis Russell, RA, had an artillery bombardier and eight misemployed privates of C Company, 1st/24th, to man his three Hale's 9-pounder rocket troughs. It was not much of an army. Inwardly Durnford despaired of ever getting his big opportunity.

Lieutenant-Colonel Russell and the IMI were the only men in No. 3 Column with anything meaningful to do on Wednesday, when they conducted a long patrol to reconnoitre the potential camp sites ahead. First, Russell had a good look at the area of the Sphinx. From the base of Isandlwana, the view to the east encompassed about seventy square miles of open plain. On the horizon was Siphezi Hill, already selected to be the site of No. 3 Column's first properly fortified base camp. Russell rode on towards it, keeping one eye open for the enemy and the other for anything that might delay the advance of the wagons. A number of dongas seamed through the plain at regular intervals. In the barren months of an African winter, such stream beds would dry up completely, but following the recent summer rains each of them now had a few inches of water running along the bottom. The principal problem, however, was their steep sides and the availability of viable entry and exit points. On his return to camp, Russell was closely questioned by the staff on the terrain ahead, but of the enemy he had nothing to report.

Thursday and day three in the Batshe Valley. Dunbar now had two dark and tense nights in the advanced camp behind him. Nobody much cared for the vulnerable position in which they found themselves, and when the general and his staff arrived to see how the causeway was coming on,

---

* Captain Hay.

Dunbar decided to advocate a re-think. As ever, the poisonous Crealock was at Chelmsford's side. Glyn too was in the party. Dunbar greeted them all politely and proceeded to brief the general. He was an experienced soldier of considerable standing, having served in the Crimea and the Mutiny with distinction. He was the sort of man that junior officers looked up to: distinguished in appearance, able, and well known to be as brave as they come. Eventually Dunbar moved the conversation on to the tactical defects of the advanced camp. He concluded by asking permission to move it to the home bank of the Batshe.

Before Chelmsford could respond, Crealock, whom one senses must have sited the position, intervened with words to the effect of, 'If Major Dunbar is afraid to stay here, we could send up someone who is not.' It was a vile and poisonous slight on a fine soldier. Dunbar took mortal offence. Hurling aside his helmet, he roared out his resignation and stormed off. It was a hideously embarrassing moment.* The details of what then ensued are not clear, but Chelmsford and Glyn must both have snarled a fierce rebuke at the insufferable Crealock. Chelmsford himself apologised to Dunbar, and Glyn spent a long time attempting to placate him. By nightfall the story had flown around the officers of the 24th. To insult a man of Dunbar's standing was to insult the regiment itself. From now on, tension and ill-feeling dogged the interaction of the infantry with the army staff. It is not known how long it took Glyn to persuade Dunbar to return to duty, but in the later stages of the stay in the Batshe Valley, it was Black who commanded there. It seems likely then, that the retraction of Dunbar's resignation may have taken Glyn some time to effect.

By Friday 17 January there was some hope that the causeway would be ready for the coming Monday. In preparation for the advance, Chelmsford rode into the hinterland to reconnoitre the ground ahead. During the course of the day, he confirmed that Isandlwana would be the site of the next temporary encampment.

Back at the camp on the river, Henry Pulleine had arrived from Pietermaritzburg. He was a familiar figure to the officers and men of the 1st/24th, but for the first time he had now come amongst them in a quite different capacity – as their commanding officer. The son of a clergyman

---

* Recorded in Captain W. P. Symons's unpublished narrative of the campaign. Royal Regiment of Wales Museum, Brecon.

and the grandson of a colonel in the Scots Greys, Pulleine had been born in Yorkshire and educated at Marlborough. He was now forty years of age and had been in the service since the age of seventeen. He had served in Ireland, Mauritius, Burma, India, Malta and Gibraltar. He was an experienced regimental officer, was an extremely able administrator in an age when most officers were not, and had a quite remarkable knack for making friends. Wherever he went in South Africa, he soon had colonial society eating out of his hand. His popularity had been put to good use by Sir Arthur Cunynghame, Chelmsford's predecessor as GOC, in raising two units of volunteers in the Ciskei. More recently, Chelmsford had appointed him as the Commandant of Pietermaritzburg and had used him to run the remount depot, a crucial administrative task if the army was to be sustained in the field. When Glyn was appointed to command No. 3 Column, Pulleine knew that the 1st/24th was his, and immediately agitated for his release to regimental duty. Chelmsford had written to him asking him to stay on in Pietermaritzburg, where as usual he was proving invaluable, but Pulleine was not to be denied and politely rebuffed the general's flattery. Command of the 1st/24th was now Pulleine's by right and ultimately Chelmsford had no alternative but to agree his release. That afternoon Pulleine caught up on the gossip with the two Degachers, and talked things through with his adjutant, Lieutenant Teignmouth Melvill. Later on he reported formally to Glyn and Chelmsford. Just as No. 3 Column was turning in for the night, Durnford's command was pitching its tents at Vermaak's Farm, near Sandspruit.

On Sunday morning Chelmsford rode out to the Batshe Valley to inspect the new stretch of road. Lieutenant McDowel confirmed that it would definitely be passable by the end of the day. After a week of tiresome inaction, this was welcome news. The column would march for Isandlwana early the next day. There was some discussion with Maori Browne over an intelligence report newly arrived from the north. According to Evelyn Wood, the main *impi* had recently departed Ulundi. Browne asked Crealock for permission to stop work and laager his camp, but the request was refused. When the staff trotted off, Browne downed tools anyway, brought his wagons about, and told off his Europeans and isiGqoza to battle positions. He made no arrangements for his other companies, as he was sure they would bolt at the first sign of trouble. Other parts of the force also took defensive precautions. Black threw up low stone walls to the front and right of the advanced camp, whilst back at the main encampment Glyn had some sangars raised.

Advance to Isandlwana

Down on the Buffalo, spirits soared at the news of the imminent advance. Before long the encampments were a hubbub of activity. Not long after his return, Chelmsford told the staff to send an order to Durnford instructing him to cross the Buffalo at Rorke's Drift on the morrow. He also wrote to the chastened Durnford in person, to keep him abreast of things. In his letter the general announced his intention to advance to Isandlwana the next day, and to move on as rapidly as possible thereafter to harry the local chiefs. 'I shall want you to co-operate against the two Matyanas [*sic*] but will send you fresh instructions on the subject,' he wrote. Amidst all the warlike preparations, Glyn deemed it appropriate to find time for prayer and convened a Sunday afternoon drumhead service. At the appointed hour, the troops assembled in a great hollow square to hear Chaplain George Smith offer up his prayers: for the Queen, for her subjects, for her soldiers, and for victory.

Maori Browne's battalion led the way the next morning. Major Clery and a party of unit representatives overtook them on the road and cantered on to Isandlwana to site and lay out the camp. It would run north–south, 150 metres from Isandlwana's eastern scree slope. As the principal direction of threat was to the half right, the direction of Ulundi, Clery directed that the 1st/24th should pitch its tents just to the right of the wagon road. Immediately to the left of the road would be the cavalry lines. These two locations were on the forward slope of the wide saddle between Isandlwana and the stony koppie known as Mahlabamkhosi to its south. All the other encampments would have the scree slope of the Sphinx directly to their rear. Next to the mounted troops would be the N Battery lines, and beyond that, roughly at the centre point of the mountain, would be the tents of the 2nd/24th. At the far northern end of the scree slope would be the native encampments; Browne's battalion would be next to the 2nd/24th, whilst Cooper's would be on the extreme left, only a few hundred metres from the long escarpment delimiting the northern side of the plain. Unit transport wagons were to be parked neatly behind the rearmost rank of tents. The centralised transport assets would be kept in a wagon park in the saddle. Surgeon-Major Shepherd's hospital tents would be alongside them. The headquarters tents would be pitched at the bottom of the scree slope, just behind the transport lines of the 2nd/24th. The frontage of the camp, from the 1st/24th on the right to 2nd/3rd NNC on the left, was only just under a kilometre. Water would not be a problem. A mile behind the mountain was the Manzimyama Stream, around which the oxen could be left to graze, and there were two dongas in front of the camp. Firewood could be obtained from the scrub on the western slope of the mountain. Clery tasked Inspector Mansel of the NMP to site the outlying cavalry vedettes. Each of the infantry battalions would have to find a picket company, which would mount/dismount from a twenty-four-hour tour of duty at 6.00 a.m. daily. The pickets would be thrown well out by day, but would contract to a much tighter inner ring by night.

Back down the track, No. 3 Column was at last lumbering slowly and noisily forward. The air was filled with the cries and oaths of the wagon drivers and *voorloopers*. Somewhat more melodiously, the band of the 1st/24th struck up a good marching tune from time to time. With over 4,000 men strung out along a five-mile line of march, No. 3 Column was a formidable sight for prying Zulu eyes to contemplate. It was around mid-morning when 1st/3rd NNC marched into the new camp. Before long the first tents had been raised at the foot of the mountain. The main body arrived in the early afternoon, by which time Browne's levies had constructed crude brushwood shelters for themselves. To the rear, the transport was as usual proving problematical. McDowel's causeway partly crumbled before all the wagons had crossed and had to receive running repairs. Then, when the leading wagons reached the stony drift across the Manzimyama Stream, there were yet more difficulties. Two of the NNC officers, Captain Krohn and Lieutenant Vaines, were experienced wagon handlers and broke away from their duties to supervise the crossings.* They performed sterling work all day, frequently driving wagons across the obstacles themselves. Even so, it became clear that not all the wagons would reach the saddle before sunset: around a third of them would have to overnight on the Manzimyama.

It had been around noon when the GOC rode into the camp. He stayed for about an hour, during which time he lent his endorsement to Clery's arrangements. With an eye to future operations, he then rode out across

* Harford.

the plain to scout in the direction of the Phindo Hills and the swathe of territory that the British had christened 'Matyana's Stronghold', some twenty kilometres to the south-east. Whilst Chelmsford, Glyn and the staff were thus preoccupied, the great encampment envisaged by Clery gradually came to fruition.

The Ground at Isandlwana

Since a thorough understanding of the ground is crucial to our comprehension of the coming battle, a detailed description of the terrain around the camp is now called for. The tents looked down from the top of a long glacis-like slope at the foot of Isandlwana, into an inner bowl of around two and a half kilometres in diameter. Because of the elevation at the top of the slope, it was possible to see past the lower-lying outer edge of the bowl to the great plain beyond. As we have already noted, the panorama encompassed some seventy square miles in all, but there were many undulations and blind spots, and on a hot day the heat-haze could obscure much. To the north, or the extreme left of the camp, the outer rim of the bowl was defined, first, by the line of a rocky spur called Tahelane, and then by a long escarpment called the Nyoni Ridge. The spur was linked to the escarpment by a steep uphill gradient of about 1,000 metres in length, culminating at a high point known as Mkwene Hill. Just under three kilometres further along the escarpment there was a 600-metre-wide cleft in the high ground, known today as 'the notch'. Immediately to the right of the notch was a second high point called Itusi Hill. From this point on, the escarpment swung away to the north-east and was in dead ground to the camp. Halfway down the notch, the incline of the escarpment met the lower slopes of a prominent conical koppie to form a low nek. In Zulu the koppie was known as Amatutshane. At about 12 o'clock from the tents, Amatutshane's southern slopes met a low curved ridge of about three kilometres in length known as Nkengeni.

Running through the bowl from left to right were two significant dongas. Closest to the camp was the Mpofane Donga, which scarred through the glacis slope about a third of the way down. The head of the feature was only some 400 metres from the N Battery tents. In its upper reaches it was narrow and over eight feet in depth. It shallowed out and splayed wider as it ran obliquely downhill to the right, so that by the time it crossed the wagon road it was only knee deep and wide enough for a wagon to cross with ease. At that point, it was some 800 metres from the saddle.

The outer rim of the glacis slope was defined by the line of a low ridge strewn with scree-boulders known today as the 'rocky ridge.' At the foot of the rocky ridge, and commanded by it, was the Nyogane Donga, the most significant watercourse in front of the camp. A number of much smaller tributaries flowed down the front face of the escarpment to feed it. The flow of water in these feeder dongas amounted to not much more than a two-inch trickle. The Nyogane itself contained four or five inches of water and arced around the rocky ridge in a three-kilometre crescent downhill to the right, before exiting the Isandlwana bowl between the Nkengeni Ridge and the outermost slopes of Mahlabamkhosi; it crossed the wagon road about 1,700 metres from the saddle. On the far side of the Nyogane, the ground rose at all points: towards the lower slopes of the escarpment on the left, towards Amatutshane in the centre, and towards the Nkengeni Ridge on the centre-right. Because of the recent heavy rain, the entire bowl had a lush covering of grass, which in many places was around three feet high.

Beyond the immediate environs of Isandlwana, an open plain stretched twenty kilometres to the east, where Siphezi Hill and the Phindo range defined the far horizon. Running back from the Phindos at a right angle, and delimiting the southern side of the plain, was a great bastion of high ground. Farthest out was a ten-kilometre-long feature called Hlazakazi, whilst to the south of the camp, echeloned some six kilometres behind the Nkengeni Ridge, was the eye-catching and sheer-sided Malakatha. In fact, Hlazakazi and Malakatha were opposite ends of the same range of high ground, but over the millennia they had been partly divided by a wide drainage cleft in the northern slope. This was the work of the Ndaweni Stream, which swung sharply west at the foot of the high ground, to run down towards the Buffalo. Thus it ran directly across the face of the Malakatha, where it had carved a hidden valley between the bluffs and the plain. A little way short of the Ndaweni Valley was a small ring of beehive huts, the kraal of Sihayo's elder brother, Gamdana, now almost seventy years of age. The chief had been in touch for some time with Henry Fynn, the resident magistrate at Msinga, about coming in to surrender, and was visited by Chelmsford during the course of his reconnaissance. Gamdana was not deemed to pose a military threat and duly received guarantees from the GOC that his kraal would be left alone. To the west of the Malakatha, inside a great loop in the Buffalo, and well to the south of the Isandlwana bowl, there was a jumble of scrub-covered hills and valleys which were next to impossible terrain for formed bodies of troops. Twenty kilometres from the camp, the Mangeni Stream rose in the Phindo Hills, ran down through an upper valley, and then dropped via a high waterfall into a deep gorge behind Hlazakazi: this was the terrain that Chelmsford had come to think of as 'Matyana's Stronghold'. From the head of the gorge, the Mangeni snaked down to the Buffalo behind the Malakatha. This, too, was extremely difficult ground, which importantly was completely blind to Isandlwana.

Similarly, there was also a worrying amount of dead ground on the opposite side of the plain. Out to the north-east, behind the Nyoni Ridge, and also quite invisible from the camp, there was an undulating plateau of between two and four kilometres in width, beyond which rose the line of the Ngedla Heights. These delineated the southern edge of the Nqutu Plateau. To avoid any confusion the Nqutu Plateau will not be mentioned again, and all subsequent references to a plateau should be taken to mean the lower plateau between the escarpment and the Ngedla Heights. At various points along the heights, drainage streams had cut re-entrants down to the plateau. There was a shallow valley between the Ngedla Heights and the Tahelane Spur, along which one such stream descended to join the Manzimyama at the rear of Isandlwana. The plateau came to an abrupt end just over seven kilometres from Mkwene Hill, at a boulder-strewn ridge called Mabaso.

Defensive Arrangements

At about 5.00 p.m., Major Black arrived in the Manzimyama Valley with the rearguard – four companies of the 2nd/24th. He was told to bivouac around the wagons delayed on the west bank of the stream. There was a small abandoned kraal with a drystone wall beside the road,* which Black noted would make a good redoubt in the event of an alarm. Up in the main encampment, as officers strolled about in conversation, or took sun-downers in their messes, or paid social calls on each other's tents, there seems to have been a distinct feeling of unease about the sprawling layout

---

* *Hixtorical Records of the 24th Regiment.*

of the camp and the absence of any improvised strongpoints. Lonsdale had returned to duty that day and called on Browne at his tent. 'My God Maori, what do you think of this camp?' he asked. 'Someone is mad,' Browne replied. In another conversation reported by Browne, Captain Duncombe remarked, 'Do the staff think we are going to meet an army of schoolgirls? Why in the name of all that is holy do we not laager?' Later on, Browne wandered over to the 24th's lines to catch up with some of the regular officers. He met Colonel Glyn on his travels and remarked that the camp looked 'very pretty though rather extended'. In his memoirs Browne wrote that Glyn 'looked hard at me, shook his head and said, "Very."'

There had been some discussion between the column commander and the army commander on the subject of improvised fortifications, but we cannot be sure exactly what passed between them. Glyn knew that the GOC's standing orders, *Regulations for Field Forces in South Africa*, conveyed upon him the duty to 'partially entrench on all sides'. Contrary to popular myth, this document did not contain long passages on the importance of laagering encampments. This came in a second edition, published after the Isandlwana disaster. Nonetheless, it seems that Glyn had every intention of taking the one-line injunction to 'partially entrench on all sides' seriously. Chelmsford, however, remarked that the ground was too stony for shelter trenches. In the aftermath of the coming battle, he stated in his correspondence that such trenches would have served no useful purpose against a Zulu attack. In this he was right: it was not depth underground that was needed but breastworks; obstacles that would stall a fast moving enemy long enough for the Martini-Henry to exact a crippling toll. At this stage in the war, laagering was considered by the regular army professionals to be a dated and parochial Boer ritual, a tactic which was both impractical and unnecessary for a modern army. A wagon laager was useful for preventing wily native opponents from running off livestock after dark, but that was about it. If something went badly wrong, the regular infantry battalions could form 'receive cavalry' squares in next to no time, and a British square was well known to be all but invulnerable. The Martini-Henry would make all the difference and, apart from anything else, the transport wagons would be required to shuttle back and forth on the lines of communication. There was no time to laager on Monday evening, and the first shuttle run back to Rorke's Drift was due on Wednesday morning. Chelmsford's columns were quite strong enough to meet a Zulu army in the open field, provided always that the available combat power was kept concentrated. The right answer for the camp at Isandlwana would have been a number of mutually supporting redoubts at key points on the ground. There were plenty of scree-boulders for the construction of such positions, even though the work would be both backbreaking and time-consuming. Such redoubts would have a permanently assigned garrison, cleared fields of fire and stockpiled reserve ammunition. The British Army of 1879 knew exactly how to do this, and if any one of the company commanders had been left to his own devices in some isolated post, this is precisely what he would have done. At Isandlwana it was a function of complacency at the highest level of command that no such measures were enacted.

Plans for 21 January

The reconnaissance patrol by the staff passed uneventfully for all but one of its participants and had returned to the camp by 6.30 p.m. Back at his tent, Nevill Coghill was obliged to ask his man Turner to help him down from the saddle. With his usual propensity for high jinks, Coghill had given chase to an evasive chicken at an abandoned kraal and had badly aggravated an old knee injury in a fall. Now he was all but immobile.

The camp had been in shadow for a couple of hours by the time the sun finally sank behind Isandlwana. In the deepening twilight, the men of No. 3 Column gossiped over their suppers. Lord Chelmsford's repast was briefly disturbed by Sub-Inspector Phillips of the NMP, who rode in from the vedettes to report that his men had captured an old Zulu. Under questioning the man had intimated that a big *impi* would attack the camp, not from the south-east as the British were now anticipating, but from the north-east. The general thanked Phillips for his report and went on with his meal. After his afternoon ride, however, he remained preoccupied with the ground on the right. The Malakatha/Hlazakazi range, and the Mangeni Gorge beyond, could be concealing any number of Zulus and would need to be cleared before any further advance could be undertaken. As he ate, Chelmsford concocted a plan for a reconnaissance in force the following day. A cavalry detachment under Dartnell would scout across the plain to the head of the Mangeni Gorge, whilst Lonsdale's NNC battalions would clear through the valley to the rear of Hlazakazi and the Malakatha. Warning orders went out before nightfall. And there now occurred a quite extraordinary breakdown in command and control, the significance of which, in terms of personal relationships between the senior officers, has been entirely missed. Lonsdale and Dartnell were summoned to the general's tent to get their orders for the morning – in itself not a technically correct staff procedure, as Chelmsford should have tasked Glyn to organise the operation and to give detailed orders to his own subordinates. To make matters worse, in an example of quite unbelievably bad generalship, Glyn was not invited to attend the orders group, nor was he consulted about the plan, nor was he even advised what was afoot. Clery's correspondence makes it clear that the column commander had no role whatsoever in a hugely significant troop movement, which deployed almost half of his command on an independent, high-risk, operational task: '. . . neither Colonel Glyn nor myself knew in the least where they were being sent to or what they were being sent for.' Not only was this extraordinarily bad soldiering, it was also excessively bad manners, and it must per se have meant that throughout the events of 21/22 January, Richard Glyn must have been incandescent with suppressed rage and, probably, barely on speaking terms with the GOC. Of course other major players in what should have been functioning as an all-informed command team, officers such as Arthur Harness, Henry Degacher and Henry Pulleine, must, by extension, also have been left completely in the dark.

Believing themselves to be the rearmost element of the column, the men of Black's wing were much surprised towards dusk to see another company of their regiment marching downhill towards the Manzimyama to join them. The new arrivals turned out to be F Company of the 1st Battalion, the battle-hardened veterans of Nyumaga and Centane. They had been marching hard from Pietermaritzburg for the past twelve days. 'Thank goodness; here we are at last,' said Captain William Mostyn as he approached the 2nd Battalion officers. As it would soon be dark and the main body of the column was just over the next rise, Mostyn decided to spare his footsore men the long flog uphill and bivouacked alongside Major Black.

Despondency

Ten kilometres back down the road, Durnford's men were pitching their tents on the ground vacated by No. 3 Column that morning. A little later in the evening Durnford found the time to write home to his mother. In the main text of his letter he admitted to feeling 'down'. Perhaps it was understandable. Now forty-eight years of age and coming to the end of an eminently undistinguished career, Durnford had spent his entire service yearning to for a chance to demonstrate the military prowess he so greatly admired in others, including such figures as his own father, a general, and his close friend 'Chinese' Gordon, already a living legend. Everywhere he turned, Durnford met distinguished fighting men. By contrast his own service had been nothing short of dull. Most officers of his generation were veterans of the Crimea and the Mutiny; Durnford had fought in neither. He was a sapper through and through, a builder of roads and bridges; as a soldier he had no broader dimension. For a long time, Anthony Durnford unwittingly despised himself. Then, in South Africa in November 1873, he got his break.

An amaHlubi chieftain called Langalibalele found himself in serious trouble with the colonial authorities over accusations of gun-running. He attempted to flee Natal across the mountain passes of the Drakensberg. Major Durnford was given command of a mixed colonial force, tasked literally with heading the exodus off at the pass. There were twenty-five mounted Basutos acting as guides at the head of his column, but the mainstay of the force was a fifty-strong troop of part-time citizen volunteers – the Natal Carbineers. Durnford had already been badly injured in a fall by the time he caught up with Langalibalele's rearguard at Bushman's River Pass. There was a confrontation. The troops were in a bad position. The warriors started to close in. In accordance with his orders, Durnford instructed the carbineers not to fire the first shot. It did not stop the amaHlubi from doing so. The patrol fled in disarray. In the rout, a black interpreter and three of the carbineers were killed. Durnford himself was stabbed in the left arm so severely that the limb would be left useless for the rest of his life. He had been personally courageous and had shown great determination throughout, but ultimately the affair had been badly mishandled. Worse, during the recriminations that followed, Durnford publicly criticised the carbineers for ill-discipline and cowardice. They never forgave him. Natal never forgave him. People called him 'Don't Shoot Durnford'. Somebody poisoned his dog. He was forced to leave his house in Pietermaritzburg and move into Fort Napier. Five miserable years had gone by since Bushman's River Pass. Durnford knew in his heart of hearts that he had it in him to be a great soldier. Now, in the twilight of his career, there was war against the Zulus. Redemption beckoned.

Durnford put down his pen. Then, for his mother's peace of mind he felt the need to amplify his earlier remark. In a prophetic and ominous postscript he added, 'I am down because I am left behind, but we shall see.'

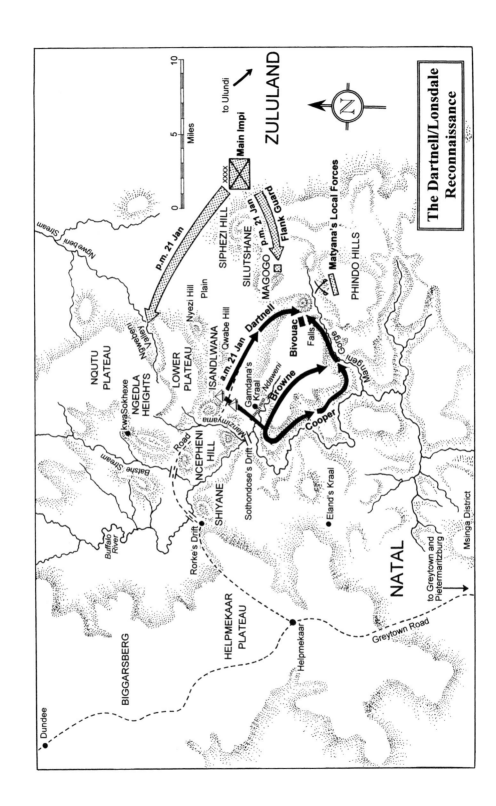

The Dartnell/Lonsdale Reconnaissance

ZULULAND

to Ulundi

Main Impi

p.m. 21 Jan

SIPHEZI HILL

SILUTSHANE
MAGOGO   p.m. 21 Jan
Flank Guard

Matyana's Local Forces

PHINDO HILLS

Ngwebeni Stream

Nyezi Hill
Plain

NQUTU
PLATEAU

Ngwebeni Valley

NGEDLA
HEIGHTS

kwaSokhexe

LOWER
PLATEAU

ISANDLWANA

Qwabe Hill

a.m. 21 Jan

Dartnell

Bivouac

Falls

Browne

Mangeni Gorge

Cooper

Gamdana's
Kraal

Mzinyathi

Ndaweni

Mzinyathi

Road

NCEPHENI
HILL

Batshe Stream

SHIYANE

Sothondose's Drift

Eland's Kraal

Rorke's Drift

Buffalo
River

NATAL

Msinga District

to Greytown and
Pietermaritzburg

BIGGARSBERG

HELPMEKAAR
PLATEAU

Helpmekaar

Greytown Road

Dundee

N

Miles
0   5   10

Chapter 3

Enemy in Sight

Reconnaissance in Force, 21 January

Typically reconnaissance is a task best suited to small, fast-moving patrols whose best defence lies in their mobility. Their business is to move cautiously through the target area, observing all the while, and to report their findings back to the main force in a timely fashion. Such patrols are expressly not in the business of combat, other than for reasons of self-defence; in the event that they do make hostile contact, they will seek to break clean and extricate to safe ground. Yet, on Tuesday 21 January, the task of reconnoitring the Mangeni Valley was given to no fewer than sixteen companies of NNC infantry, some 1,700 men in all. Thus the operation may more aptly be described as a 'reconnaissance in force', an uneasy military expression, which many soldiers would argue is a contradiction in terms.

It is often suggested that Chelmsford launched Dartnell and Lonsdale out of concern that the main *impi* might be concealed in the lower Mangeni Valley, or in some other hiding place in the loop in the Buffalo. Yet this cannot have been what was in his mind when he gave Dartnell and Lonsdale their orders, for this would have been to expose their commands to certain defeat and probable annihilation. Rather his concern was that there might be sufficient warriors mustered locally under the 'two Matyanas' to pose a threat to his right flank and rear during the next stage of his advance – the forward move to establish a fortified camp in the vicinity of Siphezi Hill. Thus the task was much in the nature of a clearing patrol. In other words, Dartnell and Lonsdale were to scour the dead ground, either to establish that it was in fact unoccupied by the enemy, in which case the GOC need have no further concern for his right, or to make contact with the local Zulu force and clear it from the Mangeni Valley by means of offensive action. Although more than enough time had elapsed since Wood's warning for the main *impi* to be in the vicinity, as yet there were no clear-cut indications that a force of such size was at hand.

Both Cooper and Browne took out eight of their ten companies – theoretically 800 levies and seventy Europeans from each battalion. In practice, the number of officers and NCOs left in camp seems to have been disproportionately high, so that there may have been only around a hundred Europeans deployed in the field. The four companies staying behind would find the two battalions' respective picket companies of the day, and their reliefs the following morning. Dartnell's cavalry patrol consisted of around eighty members of the mounted police under Inspector Mansel, twenty men of the NMR under Lieutenant Jones, sixteen men of the BBG under Captain Smith, and twenty-seven Natal Carbineers under Captain Offy Shepstone. The NMP operated as a single troop, whilst the three details of volunteers acted as a composite troop, under the senior volunteer officer, Shepstone.

The levies set off not long after daylight, many of them trotting ahead with their cooking pots in order to gain a big enough lead on their European leaders to finish their breakfasts in peace. Perhaps somewhat charitably, the NNC officers ignored the breach in discipline and put it down to the 'African way'. It was anticipated that everybody would be back at Isandlwana by sunset, so most of the Europeans carried only enough hardtack biscuits to provide for a light mid-day snack. Lonsdale's route lay to the south, past Gamdana's kraal, and on towards the towering Malakatha. By the time the troops were dropping down into the valley of the Ndaweni Stream at the foot of the great bluff beyond, the sun had become uncomfortably hot. In the bottom of the valley Lonsdale divided his command. Cooper's battalion was to bear to the right, follow the Ndaweni downstream, and then round the Malakatha at its western end. Maori Browne's men would proceed directly to the top of Hlazakazi via the cleft. This was a hard slog for an hour or so, but once they were on the summit the going became relatively easy. Cooper's 2nd/3rd NNC had to cling to the difficult western slopes of the Malakatha, until they had rounded the feature to the south and begun to descend into the lower Mangeni Valley. It was a journey of some twelve kilometres through some extremely trying terrain and, together with the remorseless heat, it took a hard physical toll of the white NCOs. Nearly all the officers who left an account of the day remarked on their fatigue. Dartnell and the mounted troops had a much easier part to play. They had merely to ride across the plain to the south-east, take up position in the upper Mangeni Valley, and wait for the NNC to flush the enemy into the open. They could afford to give the NNC a head start and left camp well over an hour later.

For the rest of the column, this was to be the first full day at Isandlwana; no doubt there would be a plethora of tedious administrative tasks to be undertaken under the direction of the quartermasters and commissaries. Lord Chelmsford wrote a long letter to Frere before breakfast and then decided to ride out to see Gamdana. As usual Glyn and the army staff would accompany him, though two of the general's aides, Major Gosset and Captain Buller, were already out with Dartnell, monitoring proceedings at Mangeni. Chelmsford left camp not long after 9.00. He found Gamdana's kraal completely deserted. There was every reason to have anticipated this; doubtless the unheralded early morning approach of two NNC battalions had been deeply alarming to the village. Alerted by their cattle-boys, Gamdana and his clan had fled into the surrounding countryside and even now were watching the general and his staff from places of concealment. Chelmsford decided to ride on and see how Lonsdale was getting on, but by the time he arrived at the edge of the Ndaweni Valley, the NNC had long since disappeared over or around the Malakatha. It looked like being a wasted morning. The general announced that, after resting their horses for a spell, they would return to camp in good time for lunch. As was his wont at such times, Crealock pulled his sketch pad from his saddlebag and sat down to draw the view back in the direction of Isandlwana.

The Sense of Unease Spreads

By lunchtime the sense of unease expressed by the colonial officers the evening before had spread to the regulars. Major Dunbar was the field officer of the day and as such had responsibility for the picketing of the camp. He is reported to have approached an unnamed staff officer to express his disquiet at the absence of a watch over the Manzimyama Valley, at the rear of Isandlwana. The officer is said to have replied, 'Well, sir, if you are nervous, we will put a picket of the pioneers there.' The response suggests that the officer was at least equal in rank to Dunbar and that he had the executive power to order such a measure himself. Since Dunbar was not on speaking terms with Crealock, surely this is the voice of Clery, who as Glyn's chief of staff was the obvious port of call for Dunbar.

Interestingly, Inspector Mansel claimed in the wake of the disaster to have approached Clery about picketing the rear, only to be told that, 'The rear always takes care of itself.' Mansel's correspondence shows him to be deeply inimical to the regulars and given the glib nature of the alleged response, the story is perhaps best treated with a pinch of salt. Lieutenant Melvill, the adjutant of the 1st/24th, an intelligent, energetic and highly regarded officer, was also anxious and irritated by the complacency of the staff. He is said to have approached a field officer, probably Dunbar, and said,

> I know what you are thinking by your face, sir. You are abusing the camp and you are quite right. These Zulus will charge home, and with our small numbers we ought to be in laager, or at any rate, be prepared to stand shoulder-to-shoulder.

All of these conversations were recorded for posterity with the benefit of hindsight and are unlikely to be verbatim renditions of what was actually said. We can, however, safely take it as read that Dunbar and Melvill both gave voice to their concerns that afternoon, and that the over-extended layout of the camp and the absence of improvised fortifications, were the subject of open discussion in the mess tents of both battalions of the 24th.

During lunch Chelmsford's thoughts turned northwards to the Nyoni escarpment. He had taken comprehensive steps to scout to the south-east, but the north-east had so far received scant attention. Lieutenant Edward Browne had taken a small IMI patrol out in the direction of Siphezi Hill first thing that morning, but his report was still awaited. In the meantime, the GOC and the staff would make their second outing of the day and ride along the line of vedettes on the Nyoni escarpment. Just as the party was saddling up, Gamdana and a few of his men arrived under escort. Henry Fynn, the magistrate with whom Gamdana had first opened negotiations, was now up at Isandlwana at Chelmsford's insistence, acting as his interpreter and political adviser. There is a strong possibility that much of Chelmsford's preoccupation with his right flank may have originated with Fynn, as 'Matyana's Stronghold' lay pretty much directly across the river from Fynn's magistracy and the indomitable Mrs Fynn, still defiantly in residence at Msinga. It was probably the swathe of Zulu territory that Fynn was most knowledgeable about and, no doubt, the area about which he worried most. The old chief greeted Fynn and the general, apologised for missing them that morning, and explained that an *impi* was coming from Ulundi to wipe out his clan. He went on to declare that he had brought in some firearms in token of his submission. On inspection, the muskets at issue were found to be notable only for their age and poor state of repair. Fynn quietly explained that the general would require a rather more sincere gesture of disarmament. A protracted *indaba* now began. It ended only when Gamdana reluctantly assented to his men returning the next day with some of his more modern weapons. A party of his retainers did indeed return on Wednesday and were in camp late enough in the morning to have had some brief interaction with Durnford.

By early afternoon, Maori Browne had crossed Hlazakazi and descended into the lower Mangeni Valley where he rendezvoused with Lonsdale and Cooper. During the course of the morning both battalions had discovered a number of small Zulu homesteads dotted about the landscape, but neither had seen a single man of fighting age. Periodically, Browne and Captain Duncombe had rounded up small groups of locals and interrogated them about Zulu military movements. At least two ostensibly unconnected youths said that the arrival of a big *impi* from Ulundi was now imminent, and that it would attack the British at Isandlwana in two days time. For whatever reason, and it may well be because he resorted to brutality to get the information, Browne was now firmly convinced that he was in possession of the Zulu battle plan. It seems improbable that such insignificant figures, in such remote homesteads, could genuinely have been party to the plans of the Zulu high command, but as luck would have it Browne was indeed now fully abreast of Zulu intent. In his own mind he was convinced that the time was right to dash back to Isandlwana, alert the general, and fortify the camp. During the course of the morning about 200 head of cattle had been rounded up and since it would be next to impossible to get them out of the gorge near the waterfall, it was decided to send them back along the approach route. Lonsdale tasked Cooper to provide a company to drove and escort the animals; Captain Orlando Murray's No. 1 Company got the job. In his memoirs Browne states emphatically that two companies were sent back, but no reference can be found in the sources to confirm the presence of a second company at Isandlwana the following day. It seems probable that Browne was mistaken.

After an extended lunch-break to allow the NCOs to regain their strength, Lonsdale led his battalions up the lower valley and into the gorge below the waterfall. On the high ground above, Offy Shepstone and the volunteers were dismounted and snacking on their biscuits. They had left Dartnell and the police troop in the upper valley, scouting in the direction of the Phindo Hills. A few hundred metres to their rear, there was a conical koppie called Mdutshana. Dartnell and the police suddenly appeared from behind it at a canter and rode across to join the volunteers. As they reined in, the police troopers excitedly broke the news that they had just encountered a party of around 300 Zulus further up the valley. A small detachment had been left behind in order to keep the enemy under observation. Having ascertained the position of the volunteers, and watched the NNC flogging up the side of the Mangeni Gorge for the eastern end of Hlazakazi, Dartnell rode off with a small escort to find out what the latest situation was. Before long a galloper came flying back again, with orders for the police and volunteers to mount up and join Dartnell beyond Mdutshana.

Lonsdale's Decision Point

At the top of the perilous ascent from the gorge, Lonsdale was confronted with a message from Dartnell asking for his support. It was already mid-afternoon; if the NNC battalions were to get back to Isandlwana by sunset, they had to turn for home now. Maori Browne implored Lonsdale not to get embroiled so late in the day. Sensing that Lonsdale was wavering the wrong way, he quickly called Duncombe over to give a second opinion. Duncombe also urged Lonsdale to turn for the camp, while there was still enough light to cross the plain in safety. The formal command and control relationship between Dartnell and Lonsdale is not clear. It seems unlikely that the general had directly subordinated Lonsdale to Dartnell. If he did, then Lonsdale had no choice but to move to Dartnell's support as ordered. If, as we might reasonably suppose, the arrangement was loose or unspecified, then Lonsdale could have played his trump card and declined the request. Ultimately, Lonsdale probably felt obligated to follow the lead of the older, more experienced man. Both were commandants of colonial troops, but their reputations as ex-regulars stood no comparison: Lonsdale was but a failed subaltern, Dartnell a successful field officer – a retired major, now the commandant of police and still a full-time professional. In any event, Lonsdale was a fiery young man and spurned the good advice offered by Browne and Duncombe. He told his two battalion commanders to rally their men on Hlazakazi as they ascended from the gorge, while he rode off to locate Dartnell and discuss the situation. It was a decisive moment. Had Lonsdale listened to his subordinates and sent a message politely declining to become embroiled so close to nightfall, then the first invasion may not have ended in disaster. It was not to be.

On the other side of Mdutshana, the mounted troops were engaged in a stand-off with the enemy. The Zulus had withdrawn to the high ground on the other side of the valley – the crest of Magogo Hill – a long, right-angled spur of the Phindo Hills. There was much broken and rocky ground along the line of the ridge and Dartnell knew that he would need the NNC infantry to clear such terrain. From where he had last seen them, scrambling in a long, snaking column up the side of the Mangeni Gorge, it seemed improbable that they could be brought up to attack the enemy before sunset. In discussion with Gosset and Buller, it was agreed that the ADCs should ride back to the camp to apprise the GOC of the situation, and seek his sanction for Dartnell's preferred course of action: to remain in the field overnight and make an attack on Magogo at first light. Although it is difficult to be certain, Lonsdale was probably also present at this discussion, and went back to Hlazakazi to bring up his battalions at about the same time that Gosset and Buller rode away.

In due course, the Zulus withdrew into dead ground on the reverse slope of Magogo. One of the essential tenets of reconnaissance is that once contact has been made, the enemy should be kept under observation until the main force has deployed to deal with them. Lose contact and they can slip away and will have to be found all over again. In order to prevent this happening, Dartnell sent a small patrol under Inspector Mansel to see where the Zulus had gone. By now Lonsdale had rejoined Browne and Cooper and was observing events from the cover of some rocks on the forward slope of Hlazakazi. Their main bodies were still concealed in dead ground behind them. As they watched, something in the region of 1,500 Zulus charged over the crest of Magogo, threw out left and right horns, and chased Mansel and his men back downhill. The patrol rode hell-for-leather back to Dartnell's position in the valley floor, whereupon the Zulus broke off the chase and fell back over the crest. There was a world of difference between 300 and 1,500 Zulus, not least because the all-up strength of the 'two Matyanas' had been estimated as a few hundred warriors. Most people leapt to what they thought was the obvious conclusion – this could only be the vanguard of the main *impi*. Dartnell withdrew from the valley floor immediately and made his way uphill to rendezvous with the NNC.

After Gamdana had gone on his way, Chelmsford and the staff went ahead with their plan to ride the length of the Nyoni escarpment and inspect the ground to the north of the camp. At the vedette on Itusi Hill, the two troopers posted there reported that they had spotted fourteen mounted Zulus in the undulating ground in the direction of Siphezi Hill only a few moments before. One of the staff remarked that this was the same area in which Lieutenant Browne's patrol had exchanged fire with a party of about forty Zulus earlier on in the day. Just then Lieutenant Berkeley Milne drew everybody's attention to a fresh but fleeting sighting of the mounted Zulus. Chelmsford remarked that they must make a point of properly scouting the ground to the north-east the next day. With that, he led off in the direction of the camp.

On the way in, Gosset and Buller cantered up to make their report. Chelmsford later declared himself to be irritated by Dartnell's decision to stay in the field overnight, but if a general officer considers a subordinate's actions ill-advised, then he should do something about it at the time; there is no justification for crying over spilt milk at some later point. In fact, when the staff returned to camp, a message approving Dartnell's intent was despatched in the care of Lieutenant Henry Walsh of the IMI. When the news migrated from the army staff to the column staff, Clery approached Glyn to express his personal reservations, and his fear that there was now every danger of the Mangeni expedition implicating the rest of the column in what he later described in correspondence as some 'compromising enterprise' up-country. This was probably a viewpoint that Glyn empathised with but, so far as is known, he kept his own counsel and raised no objection with the GOC. What good would it do anyway.

A Night in the Hills

On top of Hlazakazi a somewhat heated council of war quickly followed Dartnell's arrival. Again Maori Browne spoke out to urge immediate withdrawal to the camp. Dartnell over-ruled all protest and declared that the force would bivouac in two mutually supporting squares, NNC in one, mounted troops in the other. As the news spread, there was an outbreak of grumbling dissent amongst the NNC Europeans. They were tired and hungry; they had no rations or blankets; they were twenty kilometres from the nearest help; there was a strong enemy force on the other side of the valley; and the darker it got, the more nervous the levies were becoming. In a display of ill-disciplined petulance, Lieutenants Avery and Holcroft rode off in disgust. They were never heard of again and are presumed to have been killed at the camp the following day. Perhaps they died well; at least they were spared the indignity of a court-martial.

Some of the NNC officers had left camp armed only with pistols. Maori Browne quickly disarmed enough of his black riflemen to give each of the officers a Martini and a pocketful of cartridges. Convinced that the levies would bolt at the first sign of trouble, the whites clustered together in an inner ring in the centre of the square. When the sun went down, a large number of campfires were seen to spring up on the hillside opposite; the Zulus too it seemed, were settling down for the night. Most of the levies quickly convinced themselves that this was just a subterfuge and stared into the dark for the onset of the enemy. Thankfully, when Lieutenant Walsh and his twenty-man IMI escort arrived from Isandlwana with the GOC's reply, their horses made enough noise to convince the levies that they could not possibly be stalking Zulus. Walsh's men had brought four packhorses with a limited supply of tea, hardtack, bully beef and blankets. There was nothing like enough food to go round; no doubt it was the levies who went without. Dartnell drew Walsh to one side and explained how the situation had changed since the despatch of his first message. As Walsh had come across the plain in the half-dark, he stood a better chance than most of making it back again, now that it was pitch-black. Dartnell asked him to report that he now estimated the enemy strength to be in excess of 1,500 men, and that he would need to be reinforced with two or three companies of the 24th if he was to mount an attack in the morning as planned. Realising that numbers would provide no real defence on such a dark night, the fearless Walsh set off on the return journey with only three of his men.

Trained soldiers, accustomed to night-time sentry duty, know that if you stare long enough at a suspicious shape in the dark, sooner or later it will start to move – boulders and bushes alike. The more the NNC sentries stared into the gloom, the more they convinced themselves that they were looking at crouched or crawling warriors. In fact not a single Zulu crossed the valley all night. Suddenly a shot was fired, triggering an immediate panic. Men ran everywhere. The Europeans leapt to their feet and backed together to meet the enemy rush. Things were a lot calmer in Dartnell's square, where the police and volunteers rose to one knee, levelled their carbines and waited for orders. Mercifully, they all kept their nerve and there was no reckless firing into the night. In Lonsdale's square, Maori Browne and others were raging about, trying desperately to restore some semblance of order. Two isiGqoza companies were deployed along the rear face of the square and stood their ground, calling out that they would stab the next man who ran through their line. Nonetheless, a good many levies disappeared into the night, to hide amongst outlying clusters of boulders or thickets. Henry Harford had been brought up in Natal and spoke fluent Zulu. He spent the rest of the night trying to coax in the deserters. Eventually the square was re-formed and, after issuing a stream of dire threats against their men, the officers and NCOs lay down again. Somewhat disloyally, given that he had invited himself to become a member of 3rd NNC's officers' mess, 'Noggs' Norris-Newman decided to move across to the cavalry square. This time Maori Browne and others dozed with one eye open, a knobkerrie in one hand, and the reins of their horses in the other. When, in the early hours of the morning, a second panic occurred, it was much more quickly suppressed.

There was a huge sense of relief when at last the dawn began to break. Tired, hungry, and despondent, everybody was in a filthy mood. It had been a miserable twenty-four hours. At least, they consoled themselves, whatever hardships the new day would bring, they would be sleeping that night in the relative comfort of the camp at Isandlwana.

Part Two

In the Shadow of the Sphinx

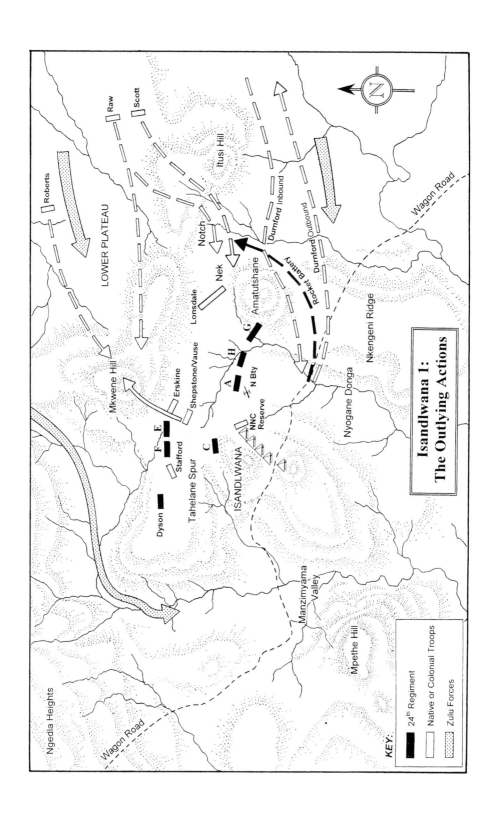

Isandlwana 1:
The Outlying Actions

Ngedla Heights

Wagon Road

Mpethe Hill

Manzimyama Valley

ISANDLWANA

Dyson

Tahelane Spur

F E

Stafford

C

Mkwene Hill

Erskine

Shepstone/Vause

Lonsdale

LOWER PLATEAU

Roberts

Raw

Scott

Itusi Hill

Nek

Notch

Amatutshane

G

H

A

N Bty

NNC Reserve

Durnford Inbound

Durnford Outbound

Rocket Battery

Nyogane Donga

Nkengeni Ridge

Wagon Road

N

KEY:

24th Regiment

Native or Colonial Troops

Zulu Forces

Chapter 4

Sunrise

The British Give Battle, a.m. 22 January

Not long after 1.00 a.m. on the morning of Wednesday 22 January, Lieutenant Henry Walsh reined in his horse to make the customary cautious silent hours approach to a picket-line. The night was 'intensely dark'. At the point at which the old wagon road crossed the Mpofane Donga, he was challenged from the gloom by an alert knot of men from Lieutenant Charlie Pope's G Company, 2nd/24th. Having duly identified themselves as friend not foe, Walsh and his companions were permitted to pass. Safely inside the perimeter, they spurred forward towards the saddle and the nearby headquarters tents. With the aid of the sentries, Walsh quickly located the tent of Colonel Glyn's chief of staff. After being shaken awake, Clery attempted with some difficulty to decipher Dartnell's hand by lamplight. He was quick to appreciate the import of the despatch and made his way to the column commander's tent to brief him. After hearing Clery out, and by now only too keenly aware that the movements and dispositions of No. 3 Column were no longer in his hands, Glyn immediately instructed him to refer the report to the GOC.

Lord Chelmsford's Decision and Plan

Chelmsford listened intently from the edge of his camp-bed as Clery ran through the text of the message once more. It seemed to lend collateral to all the general's notions regarding the principal direction of the enemy threat, but it was the revised estimate of enemy strength which seemed to Chelmsford to be the most significant element of the report. He drew the conclusion that Dartnell must be in contact with the van of the main *impi*. If this were so, then the whole force at Mangeni was in grave danger. Ultimately, there could be no question of leaving Dartnell in the lurch.

A few moments of thoughtful contemplation revealed to the general that his courses of action were limited. Peremptory recall of the troops was one option but, given the calibre of the NNC, it was unlikely that Dartnell and Lonsdale would be able to extricate themselves without some disaster befalling the native battalions. On the other hand, the plan of campaign required commanders to make every possible effort to fix the enemy, so that opportunities to bring them to battle could be grasped. There could be no doubting Dartnell's bravado in the current scenario. Maybe the situation could be turned to advantage. The Zulu army might well attempt to close with Dartnell's isolated detachment in the morning, the general reasoned. Perhaps by marching quickly, as the darkness receded into dawn, he might be able to engineer a meeting engagement and bring on a meaningful general action.

Chelmsford had already earned a reputation amongst the staff for snap decision-making and, sat on the edge of his camp-bed, he made just such a decision now. A flying column would march to Dartnell's succour with the dawn. It was to consist of the 2nd/24th under Henry Degacher, four of N Battery's six guns under Harness, the mounted infantry and the native pioneer company. All preparations were to be made in silence, without drums, bugles, bellowing or lamps. It was now 1.30 a.m. and it would be light in a little over three hours time. Optimum mobility would be essential, so no wagons could be taken along. A guard force centred on Pulleine's 1st/24th would have to be left behind at Isandlwana to protect the camp, the stores, the oxen and the wagons. The plan was hastily made in true Chelmsford style, entirely without consultation with his staff or subordinate commanders. In making it, Chelmsford took upon his shoulders alone, the responsibility for the further sub-division of No. 3 Column in the near but as yet unfixed presence of the enemy. Once divided across a distance of twenty kilometres, there could be no possibility of rapid reunification. A mere two and a half years earlier, George Armstrong Custer had committed this most cardinal of military sins and had been posthumously castigated for it.

Before dismissing Clery to get the enterprise underway, Chelmsford added a second peremptory instruction: Durnford's No. 2 Column was to come up immediately from Rorke's Drift to Isandlwana. By now, Crealock, in an adjacent tent to that of the general, had also been woken and was listening outside. He had listened in silence to the orders affecting No. 3 Column but ever jealous of his own standing, felt aggrieved at the idea of

Clery issuing orders to another column. He interjected through the wall of the tent, no doubt with a suitably hurt tone, 'Is Major Clery to issue orders to Colonel Durnford?' Anxious not to offend military protocol, or the sensitivities of his own somewhat precious chief of staff, Chelmsford replied, 'No, let you do it.'

Clery disappeared into the night to brief each of the principal commanders in turn. He can be presumed to have completed a circuit of the tents of Glyn, Henry Degacher, Harness, and Russell, a process which would inevitably have taken some time. In the meantime, Crealock busied himself with writing an order to Durnford. It was to contain nothing deeper than an executive instruction to move No. 2 Column to Isandlwana, some direction for Bengough's battalion, and some background information on the forthcoming operation. Importantly, nothing in the order suggested that Durnford should do anything other than move to Isandlwana and await further instructions.

Although it is often stated that Durnford was ordered up to supplement the guard force at the camp, it is apparent that, as far as Chelmsford was concerned, any tactical grouping which contained a few companies of regulars armed with the Martini-Henry could safely be regarded as invulnerable. A much greater worry to him than the strength of the force at Isandlwana, was the painful immobility of No. 3 Column and the difficulty he had so far experienced in scouting this part of Zululand to his satisfaction. Strung out on the move, over several miles, as it had been two days earlier, the lumbering column was extremely vulnerable at such times. That Monday was the first time that Chelmsford had attempted a general advance, the first time that it dawned on him just how ponderous the column truly was. He now knew too that the old wagon road was a road in name only. Any steep-sided watercourse, of which there were many, had the potential to delay the ox-drawn transport for days. Getting to Ulundi was going to take much longer than expected. The wagons had even failed to make the relatively simple move from the Buffalo to Isandlwana in a single day, necessitating their separation between two locations on the night of 20/21 January. Brimming with complacency as he undoubtedly was, even Chelmsford recognised that this was highly undesirable. In order to make safe and timely progress towards the king's kraals, he had to be confident that the immediate area of the column was not concealing any lurking *amabutho*, and that the transport was safely cocooned within a vast area of cleared ground. This was doubly important in the light of the intelligence that the main *impi* had taken the field. With matters seemingly coming to a head, he was keen to make Durnford's native cavalry more readily available; five additional troops of horsemen would prove invaluable in scouring such vexatious ground. In effect, Chelmsford was implementing a merger of No. 2 and No. 3 Columns. In such a scenario Durnford would be relegated to the role of regimental commander of the NNMC. This would have the added advantage, following his recent rush of blood, of bringing the excitable colonel under the general's immediate supervision. This was a private thought which Chelmsford rightly kept to himself. Nor was he ever able to make it public, for to do so would be to admit that he had placed a man in whom he had little confidence, at what would prove to be the decisive point. Crealock drafted the order as follows:

> You are to march to this camp with all the force you have with you of No. 2 Column. Major Bengough's Battalion is to move to Rorke's Drift as ordered yesterday. 2nd/24th, Artillery, and mounted men with Colonel Glyn move off at once to attack a Zulu force about 10 miles distant. J.N.C.

> PS. If Bengough's Battalion has crossed the river at Eland's kraal it is to move up here (Nangwane Valley) [*sic* – Mangeni Valley].

There was one glaring omission in the order: direction on command and control relationships. It does not seem to have dawned on anybody, and it really ought to have dawned on Chelmsford, Glyn, Crealock and Clery all, that Durnford as a substantive lieutenant-colonel was senior to Pulleine, who held his rank by brevet only. This would create an issue around the overall command of the combined force at Isandlwana. There was plenty of potential for such a command and control nuance to generate friction in the face of the enemy, but then again the enemy were not at Isandlwana, nor were they expected to be. In the absence of orders to the contrary, the formal principles of seniority would apply, and these meant that Durnford could not be subordinated to his junior in the Army List. Ordinarily the fighting arms would only happily defer in the matter of field command to Royal Engineers of the highest rank or standing, men of the ilk of 'Chinese' Gordon. Like it or not, though, sappers were now regarded as a fourth fighting arm and the rules of seniority applied just as much to them as they did to officers of the more 'fashionable' arms. Regulations notwithstanding, there is no doubt that Durnford's arm of the service, his shaky reputation, and Pulleine's technical parity in rank, combined to make the whole issue somewhat delicate. Essentially through absent-minded oversight, Chelmsford and the staff had provided for an incoherent command structure at Isandlwana. Nine times out of ten it would not have mattered, but for the sake of the one time when it might, this was precisely the sort of important detail which an efficient military staff ought to have attended to. Having departed the headquarters to rouse the senior commanders, Clery had no idea what Crealock wrote to Durnford, and Crealock had no idea what Clery wrote and said to Pulleine. It was inexcusably shoddy staff-work.

After the battle, and perhaps unable to believe that he had made such a fundamental error, Crealock insisted for a time that his written order contained a clause instructing Durnford to take command of the camp. With Lieutenant-Colonel Edward Durnford up in arms over Chelmsford's attempts to cast his late brother in the role of scapegoat, this was an important point. Eventually, no doubt to Crealock's considerable discomfort, the order was recovered from the battlefield and found to contain no such clause. The Durnfords at the time, and plenty of historians since, were quick to attribute sinister motives to Crealock. However, there is no evidence to substantiate a conspiracy theory, or anything to suggest that the affair amounted to much more than a lapse in Crealock's powers of recall. Which of us after all can remember the verbatim text of a memo or letter we wrote a week ago? Given the lack of clear-cut evidence, we are obliged to give Crealock the benefit of the doubt.

Pulleine's Orders

As the 1st/24th would be staying put and their camp was furthest away from the headquarters, Clery seems to have left briefing Pulleine to last. The GOC was and up and about very quickly. Glyn would not have been far behind him. Clery, too, had to get himself sorted out – properly dressed, mounted, armed and readied to go. Without having been given direct instructions on the matter, Clery eventually and rightly turned his thoughts to Pulleine's task: that of guarding of the camp. Pulleine's tent was several hundred metres away through a black night and so to save himself some time, Clery quickly scribbled out a written order on behalf of Glyn and despatched it in the hands of his orderly. He did so without consulting either Chelmsford or Glyn as to its contents. The instructions he gave were simple and apposite. It is difficult to know at what time Pulleine received this note, but it was probably not before 3.00 a.m. Later, when Clery found himself with a few minutes on his hands, he made his way to Pulleine's tent to confirm that he had received the written order, which he then discussed with both Pulleine and Melvill. Clery later recalled the content of the written order as:

> You will be in command of the camp in the absence of Colonel Glyn. Draw in your line of defence while the force with the General is out of camp. Draw in your infantry outpost line in conformity. Keep your cavalry vedettes still well to the front. Act strictly on the defensive. Keep a wagon loaded with ammunition ready to start at once should the General's force be in need of it. Colonel Durnford's force has been ordered up from Rorke's Drift to reinforce the camp.

It is important to note that this order did not survive the coming battle and Clery kept no copy of it. The text above is Clery's recollection of what it contained and cannot be guaranteed as a verbatim rendition. Recently it has been suggested that Clery gave no orders to Pulleine and that the words above are a work of fiction on his part. There is no evidence whatsoever to substantiate this and the allegation is deeply unfair to Clery; indeed there is source evidence to suggest otherwise. Although he had his faults, Francis Clery was still an archetypal 'officer and gentleman' of the high Victorian army. Not invariably the most professional of soldiers, as a caste of men they were at least well educated, extremely polite and highly courageous; above all else they held their personal honour dear. Clery could no more have told barefaced lies on such an important issue, than he could have robbed a bank. The ultimate responsibility for giving orders to Pulleine rested with the tactical commander and since Chelmsford had wrested command of No. 3 Column from Glyn, this meant the general himself. The truth is plain. Glyn no longer regarded himself as anything other than Chelmsford's second-in-command, whilst Chelmsford himself was pre-occupied with the advance of the flying column and gave the matter no thought. Clery spotted the omission and took steps to correct it. A chief of staff has every right to anticipate the commander's intent and issue orders in his name, and this is exactly what Clery did. He issued brief and simple instructions for a straightforward task, perceived at the time to be well within the competence of the man entrusted with it. There is a reference in *Historical Records of the 24th Regiment* to written orders being physically produced in the presence of an Isandlwana survivor, undoubtedly Cochrane. There is no issue here. The real issue in respect of these orders is how they subsequently came to be disregarded.

March of the Flying Column

The 2nd/24th would provide the major component of the flying column. With Lieutenant Gonville Bromhead's B Company back at Rorke's Drift, and Charlie Pope's G Company inextricably committed to night-time picket duty in front of the camp, Henry Degacher had A, C, D, E, F and H Companies available to him. The task of guarding the camp would fall to the five companies of the 1st Battalion. Since Pope was also being left behind, this would split the twelve companies of regular infantry equally between the flying column and the guard force. N Battery would also be divided. Lieutenant Henry Curling's two-gun division would stay in camp to support the 1st/24th, whilst the remaining four guns, the divisions of Lieutenants Fowler and Parsons, would go forward with Colonel Harness. Around a hundred mounted police, colonial volunteers and IMI would be left at the camp, either because they were next for vedette duty, or because their horses were already in poor condition. No. 9 Company, 1st/3rd NNC, and No. 4 Company, 2nd/3rd NNC, were, like Pope, committed to overnight picket duty and would also stay behind. Their respective daytime reliefs, No. 6 Company, 1st/3rd NNC, and No. 5 Company, 2nd/3rd NNC, would also be part of Pulleine's command. Captain Murray's No. 1 Company, 2nd/3rd NNC, had come in the previous evening with the captured cattle and would likewise remain at Isandlwana.

Lieutenant Horace Smith-Dorrien of the 95th Regiment was a special service subaltern assigned to Rorke's Drift as the representative of the transport staff. He had come up to Isandlwana on Tuesday afternoon to supervise the rearward move of a convoy of forty-five ox-wagons. These were due to set out for Rorke's Drift at first light on Wednesday, in order to replenish their loads from the commissariat store. Since there would now be insufficient troops left at Isandlwana to provide an escort, the move had just been cancelled by Captain Edward Essex, No. 3 Column's

Sub-Director of Transport. Relieved of his appointed task for the day, Smith-Dorrien found himself spare and was assigned instead to carry the orders to Durnford at Rorke's Drift. As soon it was light enough to see the ruts in the wagon road, he was on his way.

In the N Battery lines, four teams of limber horses were harnessed in readiness for the move – no easy proposition in the dark. In the adjacent 2nd/24th encampment, Henry Degacher's officers and colour-sergeants were ushering their men down to the parade ground in front of the tents. The troops were carrying only light fighting order, with the customary fifty rounds of ammunition in their pouches and a further twenty tucked away in their haversacks. In case of significant expenditure during the course of the day, Quartermaster Edward Bloomfield was ordered to keep the 2nd Battalion's first line reserve ammunition wagon, laden with an additional thirty rounds a man, at instant readiness to join the battalion main body should Colonel Degacher call for it. The fact that the infantry were not ordered to parade in full marching order indicates that, at this early juncture, their officers expected to be back at Isandlwana by last light. In addition to the ninety men of G Company, almost another eighty members of the 2nd Battalion would be left behind at Isandlwana on various administrative tasks, or on guards and duties. Not least, since the battalion was leaving all its tents and equipment behind, there was an issue around security against petty theft. It is probable that each of the colour-sergeants detailed two or three of their men to stay behind and keep an eye on the company's tents and kit.

A number of last minute quirks of fate determined who would live and who would die. Tailor-Sergeant Charles Twiggs had intended to stay behind to make a pair of trousers for one of the officers, but was detailed at the last minute to join the flying column. A discreet order passed around the 2nd Battalion officers to the effect that that the CO did not expect to see men fallen out from their companies to act as horse-holders, resulted in many of the subalterns leaving their animals in the camp. Since they would need feeding and watering during the course of the day, most of the soldier-servants stayed behind too. For some unknown reason, Lieutenant Pope's senior non-commissioned man, Colour-Sergeant Ross, and three privates of G Company* did go out with Degacher. No doubt they considered

---

* Privates Jones, Baker and Etbridge.

themselves lucky to be going where the action was likely to be; only later in the day would they come to realise the full extent of their good fortune. Initially, Degacher decided to leave his bandsmen behind, but then changed his mind when he got wind of the general's order that no wagons were to go out. In the apparent absence of any ambulances, the musicians were to fall in with the companies as stretcher-bearers. Bandmaster Harry Bullard secured permission to stay behind, and kept with him three teenaged boy-bandsmen who were probably too young to heave wounded men around on stretchers. As it turned out, the staff left Surgeon-Major Shepherd in the dark and, unaware of any orders to the contrary, he detailed Doctor Thrupp and two mule-drawn ambulance wagons to accompany the troops. Ordinarily a civilian surgeon in Natal, Thrupp had been attached to the 1st/24th when the regular army doctors were assigned to wider duties – Shepherd as the principal medical officer, and Surgeon Reynolds to the recently established hospital at Rorke's Drift.

Clery sanctioned one formal exception to the prohibition on wheeled transport. Mindful of the now protracted duration of the Dartnell–Lonsdale reconnaissance, he told Quartermaster Bloomfield to have a wagon loaded with rations for 2,000 men. This was a significant load and Bloomfield quickly identified that he had no wagon in his charge which could manage it. He made his way to the headquarters to report the problem, which was quickly solved when Coghill requisitioned a heavy wagon from the IMI squadron.

By the time the troops were formed and ready to march, dawn was just beginning to break, and a heavy morning mist hung over the hills to the south of the camp. The men staying behind were also up and about in accordance with normal morning routine. Not long after 4.00 a.m. Chelmsford gave the word and trotted off into the gloom at the head of the staff and the mounted infantry. He was keen to join Dartnell as quickly as possible, in order to ascertain the latest situation and be able to direct the deployment of the troops as they came up. The infantry and artillery were left in the wake of the mounted men, to make best speed under Degacher and Harness. Notwithstanding the early hour, there was much light-hearted banter as the 2nd Battalion companies marched past the 1st Battalion tents. Fond farewells were exchanged. Nobody second-guessed their finality, for the mood of the troops was one of confidence and excitement at the prospect of an engagement.

Picketing the Camp

Lieutenant Durrant Scott of the Natal Carbineers was responsible for the daytime cavalry vedettes that Wednesday. He took over the plan originally made on Monday afternoon by Inspector Mansel. Scott's task was to keep a weather eye on two principal arcs of observation: first, he needed to be able to look into the dead ground to the north and north-east of the Nyoni Ridge, and, second, he needed to watch the great expanse of plain to the east and south-east. He had around fifteen carbineers with him as he rode out of camp at first light. His own particular vantage point and the site of his command post, was to be at the top of the conical koppie, Amatutshane. Scott had briefed his men that they would be posted in pairs at various points, and that if they sighted the enemy they were to signal the alarm by cantering their horses in a circle.

Four pairs of troopers peeled off to take post along the rim of the Nyoni escarpment: one pair was sited on the Tahelane Spur directly north of the camp; a second on Mkwene Hill; a third just above the notch; and a fourth on Itusi Hill. Finally, two more pairs were flung out even further afield. Itusi Hill was the easternmost limit of the view along the escarpment from the camp. Beyond Itusi the escarpment turns away to the north-east; in effect it is 'around the corner' to an observer at the foot of Isandlwana. Qwabe Hill is a low koppie on the plain which runs parallel to this stretch of the escarpment to create a shallow valley, the mouth of which is obscured from Isandlwana by Amatutshane. Although Scott could see at least a part of the way up the valley, Itusi precluded a longer-range view, even from the summit of Amatutshane. Troopers Barker and Hawkins were therefore posted on Qwabe Hill, which placed them opposite the Itusi corner, with the eastern face of the escarpment in plain view. Crucially, they could be seen from Scott's lookout on Amatutshane, and could if necessary make the alarm signal to him. The sixth and most distant picket was on a high point over three and a half kilometres north of Qwabe Hill. This was Nyezi Hill, some ten kilometres from Isandlwana. It was a post so far from succour that it would require men with nerves of steel to man it. The unfortunate carbineers assigned to this post of danger were Trooper Whitelaw and a man whose identity has been lost to history. By the time all of Scott's men were in position, the sun had risen clear of the horizon and the chill of the dawn was no more.

By 6.00 a.m. it was fully light, the camp was busy, and Pulleine's force had been dismissed from morning parades to daily routine. It was almost time for breakfast. The appointed hour had come for relief of the previous day's pickets, by those assigned to duty for the next twenty-four hours. Exempt by virtue of their arm of the service from such tedious tasks as picket duty, the gunners busied themselves instead with their particular priority, the feeding and grooming of their battery horses. As usual the men saw to their animals first, before falling out to their own breakfasts.

The picketing arrangements have generally been poorly reported by historians, who often cite Pope's as the only picket company that day. In fact, the men of G Company had been relieved at six and had been dismissed to have breakfast and catch up on lost sleep. The daytime picket line described a great semi-circular arc across the plain, and each of the four battalions in No. 3 Column was expected to find a company to man its assigned sector. The two regular battalions held the right half of the line, for this was judged the most probable direction of enemy threat; the less esteemed NNC battalions were assigned to the left. The 1st/24th sector protected the right flank of the camp and ran out from the stony koppie, Mahlabamkhosi, to the Nyogane Donga. The 2nd/24th sector covered the centre-right and ran from the donga to the southern slopes of Amatutshane. The centre-left, from Amatutshane to the escarpment, was the task of 1st/3rd NNC. Finally, 2nd/3rd NNC was responsible for the extreme left, the high ground to the north. This was the camp's blind spot. To guard against a threat in this direction, the 2nd/3rd NNC's picket company had taken post on Mkwene Hill.

Historical Records of the 24th Regiment indicates that C Company, 1st/24th, had been on overnight picket duty alongside Pope. G Company should have been relieved at 6.00 a.m. by the 2nd Battalion's H Company, but it had marched with Degacher two hours earlier. Pope's diary, later recovered from the battlefield, records that he was relieved instead by the 1st Battalion, but does not specify by which company. This means that two 1st Battalion companies were now assigned to daytime picket duty, but there is no evidence with which they can be positively identified. In the event, neither would be left on the picket line for long.

On Mkwene Hill, Captain E. A. Erskine's No. 4 Company, 2nd/3rd NNC, was relieved by Captain A. J. Barry's No. 5 Company and made its way thankfully downhill to the camp. It had been a jittery night atop Mkwene for Erskine's amaChunu levies; periodically voices had called out to them from the darkness. Mkwene is not far as the crow flies from kwaSokhexe, and it is possible that these were threats of revenge from some of Sihayo's men, now scattered and living as refugees in the smaller kraals in the hills.

For some unknown reason, timings had gone astray in 1st/3rd NNC's arrangements, so that the appointed hour of relief came and went with No. 9 Company under Captain James Lonsdale, (a cousin of Rupert Lonsdale), still strung out between the escarpment and Amatutshane. This was one of Browne's isiGqoza Zulu companies, the most resolute of the clans in the NNC order of battle. Back in the camp, No. 6 Company was at last forming up under Captain Robert Krohn, but their lateness meant that the isiGqoza would be guaranteed a front row seat in the coming battle.

Early Morning at Rorke's Drift

Twelve kilometres back down the wagon road, in their encampment on the Zulu bank of the Buffalo at Rorke's Drift, Durnford's men had stood to under arms in the hour before the dawn. Durnford expected positive orders from Chelmsford to arrive before too long, so to keep his horses as fresh as possible, he directed that morning drills be carried out on foot.* If nothing else, it was a good way to warm his people up after the coldness of the dawn, a time of day which African soldiers have always detested. In the continuing absence of orders, Durnford himself would make an early morning start and head back into Natal on a foraging expedition. He was short of transport wagons and hoped to be able to requisition a few more from the Boer farms on the Biggarsberg.† He took the Edendale Troop with him as an escort, not necessarily to protect him from Zulus, along what was after all a safe stretch of the lines of communication, but more for the company of his favourite troopers and to cow any recalcitrant settlers who might to wish to dispute the loss of their wagons. Lieutenant William Cochrane, another special service regular, was Durnford's transport officer and rode with him. The troop splashed across the drift and cantered on into Natal, passing the mission station on the higher ground to the left.

---

* Lieutenant Vause.

† Lieutenant Cochrane.

Recruit training at Brecon Barracks. The barracks remains virtually unchanged to this day. The building on the extreme left is now the regimental museum. The building on the right has always been the officers' mess. *(RRW Museum)*

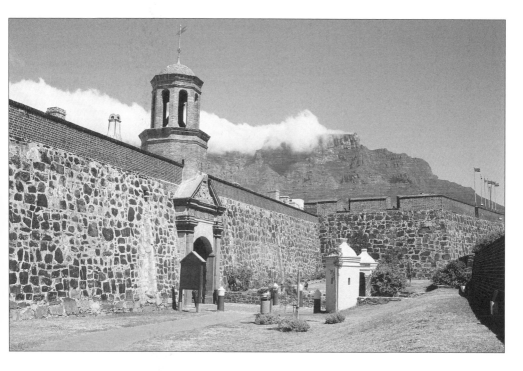

Cape Castle and Table Mountain. This was the old Dutch headquarters at the Cape and was home to the 24th on its arrival in South Africa. King Cestshwayo was detained here after the war. *(Author's Collection)*

Officers of the 2nd Battalion, 24th Regiment, Secunderabad, India, 1871.
Front row: A newly joined Charlie Pope is on the left in civilian clothes. Penn Symons, sporting an impressive beard, is third from the left. H. B. Church who like Symons was a captain commanding a company in the 2nd/24th on 22 January 1879 is seated on the chair at right with his head on his hand.
Second row: Captain Henry Pulleine is second from the left. Thomas Rainforth, who commanded a 1st/24th company at Centane, and was at Helpmekaar on 22 January, is two down from Pulleine.
Third row: Lieutenant H. M. Williams, who commanded C Company at Mangeni, is second from the left.
Fourth row: Fifth from the left is Younghusband. The presence of Pulleine and Younghusband indicates that officers moved freely between the 1st and 2nd Battalions on posting. *(RRW Museum)*

Sir Bartle Frere, ministers of the Cape government, officers of the staff,
and regimental officers of the 1st/24th photographed at King William's Town in 1878,
during the 9th Cape Frontier War.
On the ground: Lieutenant Nevill Coghill (24th – KIA, 3rd Column Staff),
The Honourable W. Littleton (Frere's private secretary).
Seated left to right: Lieutenant Pat Daly (24th – KIA with F Company), The Honourable C. P. Brownlee
(Cape Cabinet and member of Frere's War Council), Sir Bartle Frere,
Lieutenant-General Sir Arthur Cunynghame (GOC South Africa), Colonel Richard Glyn
(CO 1st/24th and Commander Transkei), The Hon J. X. Merriman
(Cape Cabinet – and *de facto* Minister for War within the War Council).
Standing left to right: Captain W. T. Much (24th, invalided home before the Zulu War),
Captain Rainforth (24th, at Helpmekaar 22 January 1879), Major & Paymaster Francis White (24th, KIA)
Captain Hillier (staff), Captain Henry Hallam-Parr (staff), QM James Pullen (24th, KIA),
Lieutenant Francis Porteous (24th – KIA with A Company), Major Henry Pulleine (24th – KIA as CO 1st/24th),
Lieutenant George Hodson (24th – KIA with C Company), Lieutenant-Colonel F. W. E. Walker (staff),
Mr J. Silverwright (manager of the Telegraph Company), Lieutenant Charles Atkinson (24th – KIA with H Company),
Capt George Wardell (24th – KIA as OC H Company). *(RRW Museum)*

Colonel Richard Glyn, CB. Military commander of the Transkei in the 9th Cape Frontier War and commander of No. 3 Column for the Zulu War, Glyn was destined to be pushed into the background by the GOC. *(RRW Museum)*

Lieutenant-Colonel Henry Degacher, CB. As a major he had been in the Cape with the 1st/24th but, having taken command of the 2nd Battalion in England, he soon received orders to embark for South Africa. *(Royal Collection)*

Lieutenant Pat Daly, 24th Regiment. Born in March 1855, Daly was commissioned into the 24th in February 1874. He served in the 9th Cape Frontier War and would fall at Isandlwana as a member of F Company. *(Royal Collection)*

Lieutenant George Hodson. Born in Dublin in November 1854, Hodson served as Sir Bartle Frere's ADC and as Colonel Glyn's orderly officer in the war with the Xhosa. Hodson was in C Company at Isandlwana. *(Royal Collection)*

The 1st Battalion, 24th Regiment at a halt. By 1879 the battalion was widely
regarded as the best unit in the colony. *(Illustrated London News)*

Lieutenant Teignmouth Melvill, the able and highly regarded
adjutant of the 1st/24th. *(Ron Sheeley Collection)*

Soldiers of the 1st/24th in the field in the Transkei during the
fighting against the Xhosa. Bush conditions took a heavy toll
of the men's uniforms. *(Lloyd/RRW Museum)*

Paddy Brennan, A company defending his pot.

A sketch by Lieutenant William Lloyd of the 1st/24th, showing a skirmish in Zululand later in the war. *(Lloyd/RRW Museum)*

Left: Company photograph of Captain Henry Harrison's B Company, 1st/24th, which remained at Port St John's throughout the Zulu War. Harrison is on the extreme left in tweeds. Here the men wear their Glengarry headdress; when deployed in the field the lightweight cork foreign service helmet was worn for protection from the sun. *(RRW Museum)*

Below: Picket Duty. Another Lloyd sketch, showing a company commander and his two subalterns bedding down for the night on picket duty. *(Lloyd/RRW Museum)*

Officers of the 1st/24th. *(L to R)* Porteous, Cavaye and Degacher, all killed in action at Isandlwana. *(RRW Museum)*

Colour-Sergeant Edward Wilson, killed in action at Isandlwana. *(RRW Museum)*

The Corps of Drums of the 2nd/24th. These men were at Mangeni on 22 January. Note the regimental mascot on the right. *(RRW Museum)*

High Commissioner for Southern Africa and Governor of the Cape, Sir Bartle Frere *(RRW Museum)*

The GOC South Africa, Lieutenant-General Lord Chelmsford. *(Ron Sheeley Collection)*

No. 4 Column commander, Colonel Evelyn Wood, vc. *(Ron Sheeley Collection)*

No. 2 Column commander, Lieutenant-Colonel Anthony Durnford, RE. *(Ron Sheeley Collection)*

Brevet Lieutenant-Colonel Henry Pulleine and his wife Frances, an archetypal husband and wife portrait of the era, taken in Malta in 1871. *(RRW Museum)*

Ntshingwayo kaMahole. He co-commanded the *impi* with Mavumengwana but is traditionally thought of as the principal architect of the Isandlwana victory. *(RRW Museum)*

The Buffalo River at Rorke's Drift with Isandlwana in the distance. The river is in spate here, exactly as it was in January 1879. This is the view of Isandlwana that caused men of the 24th Regiment to remark on its resemblance to the Sphinx, which many considered to be a bad omen. *(Author's Collection)*

View upstream from the mission buildings at Rorke's Drift. The photograph was taken later in the war, at some point between April and August 1879. *(RRW Museum)*

The Batshe Stream. The high ground on the right is the Ngedla Heights. In the centre is the v-shaped cleft into which Black and Hamilton-Browne made their attack on 12 January. This is the point at which Lieutenant McDowell had to build a causeway for the wagons. *(Author's Collection)*

Lieutenant-Colonel John Crealock, 95th Regimant. Although officially designated Lord Chelmsford's 'military secretary' Crealock was to all intents and purposes his chief of staff. *(Royal Collection)*

Major William Dunbar, 24th Regiment. Dunbar commanded the advanced camp in the Batshe Valley until he was insulted by Lieutenant-Colonel Crealock. *(RRW Museum)*

Nqutu Plateau

Ngwebeni stream

Raw's position on Mabaso Ridge

Above: Where Lieutenant Charlie Raw encountered the Zulu army. An outstanding piece of natural cover, which nonetheless left the army commander, Ntshingwayo, with a 'real estate' problem. *(Author)*

Below: View from the notch into the Isandlwana 'Bowl'. From here many of the warriors of the chest gained their first view of the enemy. As they emerged from the dead ground above the camp, in this general area, the two RA 7-pounders opened fire from the rocky ridge at a range of 3,000 yards. Zulu skirmishers operating in advance of the regimental main bodies destroyed Major Russell's rocket battery in the low ground between the escarpment and the conical koppie, Amatsutshane. *(Author)*

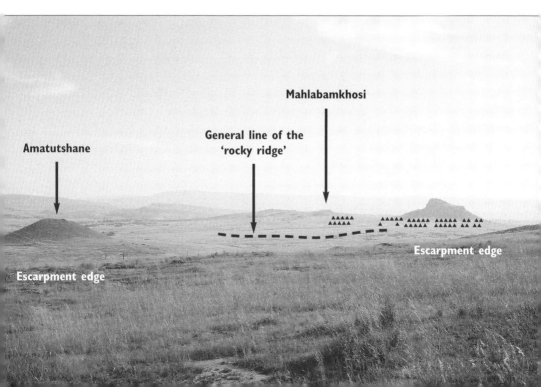

Mahlabamkhosi

Amatutshane

General line of the 'rocky ridge'

Escarpment edge

Escarpment edge

Above: Cavaye and Mostyn on the Tahelane Spur. This photo is taken from Mkwene Hill, the high point on the escarpment. A regiment of the right horn put in an early appearance on the spur, before veering away to the right to take up a hidden position in the approaches to the Manzimyama Valley: this caused Pulleine to deploy E Company to the spur, where it was joined in due course by F Company. Shepstone brought up Vause's troop to support the infantry, counter-attacked from the spur towards the camera, and drove back the uNokhenke skirmishers before, in turn, having to fall back in the face of the regimental main body. Dyson's position was further along the spur to the right. *(Author)*

Below: Advance of the right horn. View of the action on Mkwene Hill and the Tahelane Spur from a Zulu perspective. The route taken by the right horn is indicated. The ring shows the killing area into which the 24th companies directed their fire. On sighting the advance of the uNokhenke from his right, Captain Erskine fell back from Mkwene to join the regulars on the spur. Pulleine's orders to retire on the camp pre-empted the arrival of the uNokhenke from Cavaye's right. In due course the uNokhenke would wheel in to mount an attack down the spur. *(Author)*

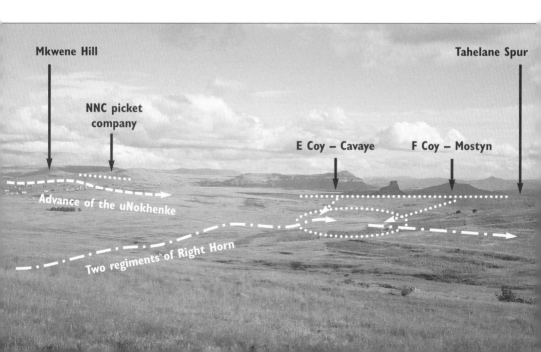

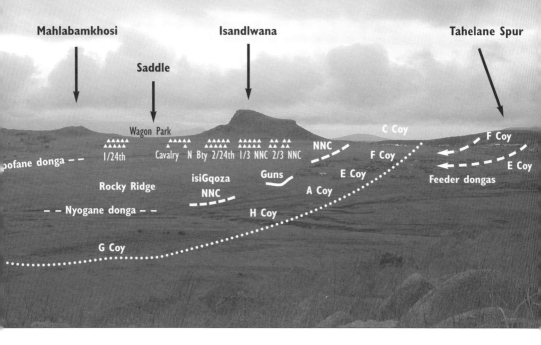

Above: The firing line: initial positions. F and E Companies fell back to the firing line from Tahelane. The right flank companies, G and H, were extended down the forward slope of the rocky ridge at this stage, in the direction of Amatutshane, which is just off the left edge of the photograph. *(Author)*

Below: The firing line: right flank refused. The increasing threat to the right of the firing line caused G and H Companies to wheel back to the top of the rocky ridge as seen here. The Zulu chest took cover in the dongas in front of the firing line. *(Author)*

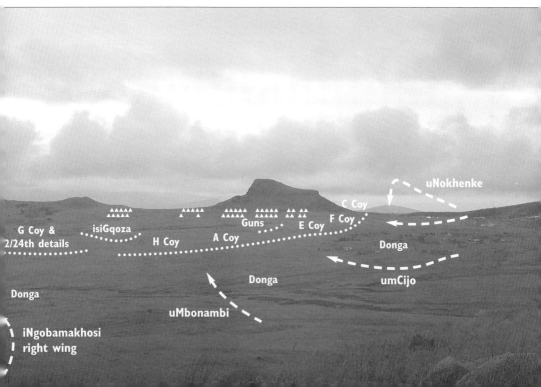

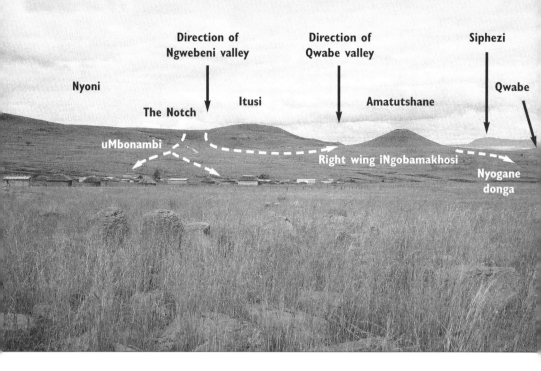

Above: The view from the rocky ridge to the notch. This typifies the field of fire that Captain George Wardell's H Company riflemen had after they had fallen back to the top of the rocky ridge. It was around here that Colour-Sergeant Wolfe and his rearguard section were over-run. *(Author)*

Below: The centre right of the firing line from the camp. How the Zulu attack looked to the men amongst the tents. Although the firing line is shown at the top of the rocky ridge, most riflemen would have been a few yards down the forward slope and thus out of sight – their position would have been indicated by drifting clouds of white smoke. Note that, once the uMbonambi and umCijo were down in the Nyogane Donga, they could not be seen from the camp. The right half of G Company's first position is also indicated. *(Author)*

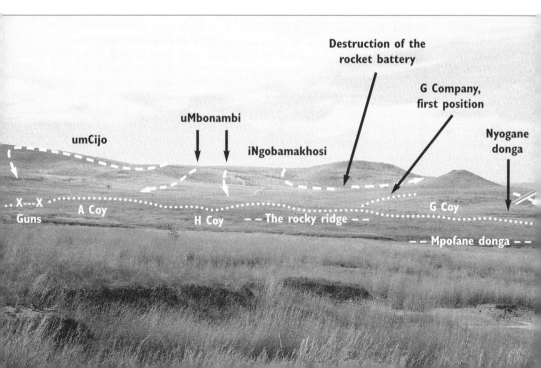

Labels on upper image: Hlazakazi, Malakatha, Durnford's retreat, uVe, Durnford's stand in the Nyogane Donga, Nkengeni Ridge, Firing line – G Coy & 2nd/24th rear details

Above: View along the right of the firing line. This shows how the uVe, the left horn regiment, moved along the Nkengeni Ridge to outflank Durnford's position in the Nyogane Donga, and then moved on to drive in Charlie Pope from the British right. The 2nd/24th fell back up the slope in the direction of the camera, not off camera to the right, the direction of the saddle – which was not an option due to the uVe's rate of advance. *(Author)*

Below: The destruction of G Company. A view from the direction of the saddle. Pope's firing line on the rocky ridge was enveloped by the uVe from the British right, once Durnford's men had abandoned the Nyogane Donga and fallen back up the slope towards the camera. Pope's cairns, which are difficult to see because of the long grass, denote G Company falling back along an impromptu line of retreat from right to left. None of the 2nd Battalion contingent made it back to the saddle. *(Author)*

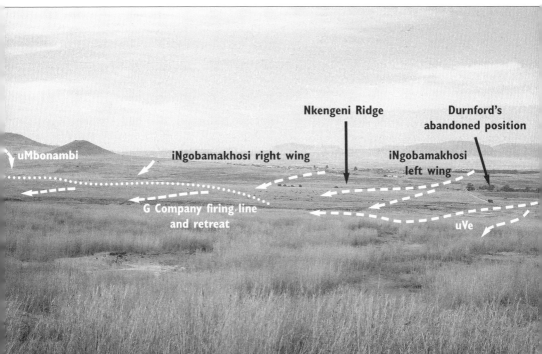

Labels on lower image: uMbonambi, iNgobamakhosi right wing, Nkengeni Ridge, Durnford's abandoned position, iNgobamakhosi left wing, G Company firing line and retreat, uVe

Site of QM Pullen's delaying action

Flight of mounted natives and NNC

Wagon park

Mpofane donga

24th 'withdrawing slowly'

Above: Escape of the guns. A view from the rocky ridge to the saddle. Smith and Curling had to traverse this ground with the 7-pounders. The line of the Mpofane Donga can just be made out; the guns had to go around the head of the donga, by keeping to the right. The uVe and Ngobamakhosi were attacking uphill from the left. Colonel Pulleine was unhorsed about here, as he was riding to the left of the line to organize a rallying point. Wardell's H Company was withdrawing to the saddle in square, just off the left of the shot. Tents are shown purely symbolically. *(Author)*

Below: Withdrawal to the saddle. Melvill brought the Queen's Colour from the Guard Tent in the saddle to Pulleine, on the right of the photo, and was almost immediately ordered to take it to safety. Shortly afterwards Pulleine was shot dead. Degacher's A Company was caught in front of the tents by the charge of the uMbonambi from the Mpofane Donga. The fight raged back into the 2nd Battalion camp, where about fifty A Company men made a stand in square. This enabled C, E, F and H Companies to continue their withdrawal to the saddle. *(Author)*

Death of Pulleine

A Company's last stand

C, E & F Companies

H Company

Labels on image: Pullen/Durnford stand · Mahlabamkhosi · H Company last stand · 1st/24th camp · Cavalry lines · Left Horn

Above: Where H Company crossed the Mpofane Donga. *(Author)*

Below: Last stands on the British right. QM Pullen organized a rally at the foot of Mahlabamkhosi, with the idea of holding back the iNgobamakhosi on the glacis slope. He was joined by Scott and the Carbineers and then Durnford. After falling back in square, H Company under Wardell effected a junction with the Durnford group in front of the 1st/24th tents where about 100 men formed a square. Under relentless pressure the square was broken up into its constituent groups which fell back through the tents and wagons to the positions where they were eventually cut down. *(Author)*

Labels on image: Pullen/Durnford stand · Mahlabamkhosi · H Company last stand · gobamakhosi · 1st/24th wagons · uMbonambi · 1st/24th tents

Right Horn

Anstey

C Company last
stand & charge

E/F Company
square

Chest

Above: The end in the saddle. C, E and F Companies fell back into the saddle in the face of the Zulu chest. On the left side of the photo, they formed square and for a time held back the attack from the Manzimyama Valley. When the square was broken up, Anstey broke out to the left with about sixty men. Younghusband fell back to the terrace with two-thirds of C Company. The remnants of E and F Companies, about seventy men, formed square where the 24th Monument is. Here they were cut down. At the end Younghusband led a supremely defiant bayonet charge into the turmoil below. The slaughter on this ground was bloody in the extreme. *(Author)*

Below: Attack of the right horn and pursuit of the fugitives. The photo is taken from the side of Mpethe Hill and show how the onset of the right horn drove successive groups of fugitives along an increasingly pronounced left oblique – or further and further from the Rorke's Drift road. The vegetation in this area was much less dense in 1879. The early fugitives included Henderson's Basutos, Zikhali's Horse and most of the NNC. The last few mounted fugitives to get out of the camp included Melvill, Coghill, Smith, Curling and Brickhill. Some time later Lieutenant Anstey attempted to break out with a party of 24th men. The last of Anstey's men were killed just short of the stream. *(Author)*

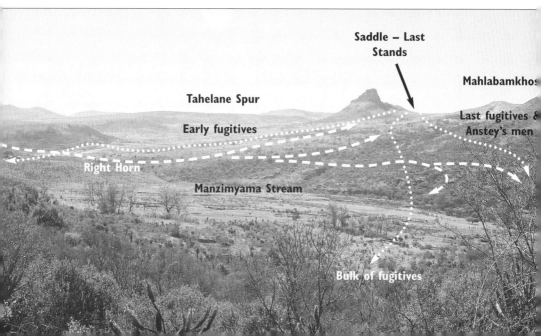

Saddle – Last
Stands

Mahlabamkhos

Tahelane Spur

Early fugitives

Last fugitives &
Anstey's men

Right Horn

Manzimyama Stream

Bulk of fugitives

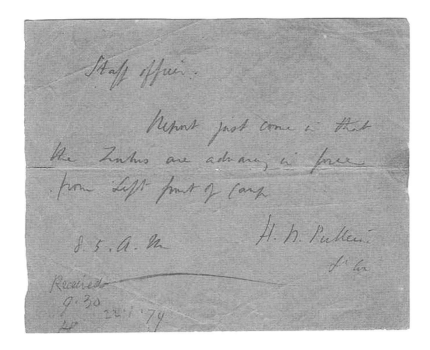

Pulleine's 8.05 a.m. despatch. The note is preserved at the regimental museum in Brecon.
Its receipt by the staff at 9.30 a.m. is acknowledged at the bottom left hand corner
by 'HP' – Captain Henry Hallam-Parr. *(RRW Museum)*

Levies of 1st Regiment, Natal Native Contingent. These men are believed to be members of Major Harcourt Bengough's
2nd Battalion, which crossed the river into Zululand at Eland's Kraal on the day of the battle but which somehow avoided
being destroyed by the main *impi*. *(RRW Museum)*

Brevet Lieutenant-Colonel Henry Pulleine

Lieutenant & Adjutant Teignmouth Melvill

Lieutenant Nevill Coghill

Quartermaster James Pullen

Honorary Major Francis White (Paymaster)

Captain William Degacher

Lieutenant Francis Porteous

Right: Company officers, C Company, 1st/24th. Younghusband was killed on the mountain leading a last defiant bayonet charge; Hodson probably fell in Younghusband's charge.

Captain Reginald Younghusband

Lieutenant George Hodson

Right: Company officers, E Company, 1st/24th. Cavaye and Dyson both died during the battle but the circumstances of their deaths are not known.

Bottom row: Company officers, F Company, 1st/24th. Anstey was killed leading an attempted breakout from the saddle; the circumstances of Mostyn's and Daly's deaths are not known.

Lieutenant Charles Cavaye

2nd Lieutenant Edwards Dyson

Captain William Mostyn

Lieutenant Edgar Anstey

Lieutenant Patrick Daly

Left: Company officers, H Company, 1st/24th. Wardell ws killed in the H Company square and Atkinson probably died there also.

Middle row: Battalion staff officers, 2nd/24th. Dyer was stabbed in the heart during H Company's last stand; Bloomfield was shot dead on his ammunition wagon; Griffith died in action but the circumstances are unknown.

Captain George Wardell

Lieutenant Charles Atkinson

Lieutenant & Adjutant Henry Dyer

Quartermaster Edward Bloomfield

Sub-Lieutenant Thomas Griffith

Left: Company officers, G Company, 2nd/24th. Godwin-Austen and Pope fell fighting alongside each other behind the Mpofane Donga.

Lieutenant Charlie Pope

Lieutenant Fred Godwin-Austen

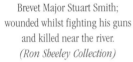

Officers of the Royal Artillery

Brevet Major Stuart Smith;
wounded whilst fighting his guns
and killed near the river.
(Ron Sheeley Collection)

Brevet Major Francis Russell; shot dead
at the foot of the notch.

Lieutenant Francis McDowel,
Royal Engineers; killed in action,
circumstances unknown.

Officers of the Natal Mounted
Volunteers

Lieutenant Durrant Scott (Natal
Carbineers); killed alongside Durnford
at the foot of Mahlabamkhosi.

Captain Robert Bradstreet (Newcastle
Mounted Rifles); killed fighting alongside
Durnford and Scott.

At Bay. Although this illustration from *The Graphic* might be regarded at first glance as a typically melodramatic and over-romanticised Victorian representation of the scene, it actually conveys the horrific and terrifying nature of the final phase of the fighting rather well. This is how the last moments of the H Company square must have been. Note the Zulus using the bodies of their own dead to drag down the bayonet points. *(RRW Museum)*

Wardell's last stand. This is where the H Company square was surrounded and cut down. The 24th Regiment Monument on the horizon serves as a good marker for the general position of C, E and F Companies at this time. *(Author's Collection)*

Isandlwana by Jason Askew. *(By kind permission of the Artist)*

Saving the Colours by Alphonse de Neuville. Melvill and Coghill attempt to cut their way out with the Queen's Colour. *(1 RRW)*

Captain Edward Essex, 75th Regiment, of the transport staff. Essex would be one of only five regular officers to survive Isandlwana. *(MOD Library)*

Surgeon-Major Peter Shepherd. Shepherd was killed on the fugitives' trail after stopping to aid a wounded man in the Manzimyama Valley. *(Royal Collection)*

Private Samuel Wassall, vc. A member of the 80th Regiment's mounted infantry section, he was awarded the Victoria Cross for his selfless rescue under fire of a drowning comrade. *(Royal Collection)*

The 24th Regiment Monument. About seventy men of the 24th formed square here and made their stand. Another sixty men fell back onto the rocky shelf on the right hand side of the mountain, and were then driven back against the sheer rock face behind them. Then came the dramatic denouement – Younghusband's charge. *(Author's Collection)*

The Fugitives' Trail. The saddle is to the left. The Zulu right horn attacked from the right foreground. The cairns mark the line of retreat – the left oblique in the direction of the Manzimyama Stream. *(Author's Collection)*

Sothondose's Drift from Mpethe Hill. This is the deadly downhill approach to the river; Natal is on the far bank. The water was low when this photo was taken but on the day of the battle the river was up to the high water mark and was extremely fast flowing. *(Author's Collection)*

Where Melvill and Coghill died. This is a contemporary photograph taken from the Natal bank of the river, with Mpethe Hill in the background. The white cross in the centre stands above the grave of the two officers. Importantly this shows that the hillsides were much more sparsely vegetated in 1879 than is the case today; the fugitives moved much quicker across the ground than is commonly imagined. *(RRW Museum)*

Mr L. P. Dubois 'The enemy has scattered us this day.'
Dubois was killed in flight on the fugitives' trail.
(Ron Sheeley Collection)

'Maori' Browne, the colourful commandant of 1st Battalion,
3rd Regiment NNC. He trusted only his three companies of
isiGqoza Zulus. *(Ian Knight Collection)*

Sunset. From atop the 24th Regiment Monument the author describes Lord Chelmsford's return to Isandlwana
to a visiting group of soldiers from the Royal Regiment of Wales. *(1 RRW)*

A poignant image of the burial cairns where Captain George Wardell's H Company square was finally cut down. It conveys something of the famously 'brooding' atmosphere at Isandlwana. *(Author's Collection)*

A newly arrived sapper officer, Lieutenant John Chard RE was camped beside the ponts. Chard was an officer of No. 5 Company, Royal Engineers, which was even now marching up from the coast to join in the war. Chard had been sent ahead with a small advance party to supervise the ponts and oversee the construction of a redoubt to cover the crossing. Captain Rainforth's G Company, 1st/24th, had been at Helpmekaar for a week, and was due to come up to Rorke's Drift to build and garrison the new redoubt. It should have arrived on 20 January, but due to a misunderstanding Rainforth believed he could not move forward until he was relieved at Helpmekaar by Major Russell Upcher's D Company, 1st/24th. Upcher and his men left Durban on 7 January and had been marching hard ever since. They had in fact arrived at Helpmekaar at 6.00 p.m. the previous evening, to find that fresh orders required both companies to move to Rorke's Drift, one to build the redoubt and the other to move up to Isandlwana to join the rest of the battalion. In the event, it was to be mid-afternoon before either of them set off.

Chard expected to be able to make a start on the redoubt by Thursday at the latest. In the meantime, he had only a corporal and four enlisted men of his corps with him. Late the previous day, he had received orders from the column staff instructing that the RE detachment should move up to Isandlwana; no doubt the sappers' expertise would prove useful in supervising the unskilled labour of the native pioneers. Chard was unsure whether he was personally required up-country, as Francis McDowel was already up with the column providing its engineering advice. Chard had resolved to cover both eventualities; he would accompany the detachment with his batman, his Cape Coloured wagon driver, his black *voorlooper*, his kit and his wagon, just in case it proved necessary to stay at Isandlwana. He planned to ride on ahead to clarify the situation, and return post-haste to turn back his wagon and servants if he was not required. For a mere eight men to march twelve kilometres through enemy territory was reckless in the extreme, but this was indeed Chard's rather casual plan. He set off with his intrepid band as soon as he had breakfasted and his kit had been loaded.

It took Chelmsford and his escort only a couple of hours to get to the foot of Dartnell's overnight bivouac. Henry Harford was doing his morning rounds at the time and was amongst the first to spot the column of horsemen on the plain. Having ridden down to greet them, he soon found

himself being bombarded with questions. Harford gave the best account
he could of recent events, before leading Chelmsford and Glyn to where
Dartnell and Lonsdale were to be found. In making his report, Dartnell was
obliged to break the unwelcome news that not a single Zulu had been
seen since daylight. The deserted slopes of Magogo Hill were indicated to
Chelmsford as the place where the Zulu campfires had been. His lordship's
disappointment at the apparent disappearance of the enemy was palpable.

Whilst Dartnell and Lonsdale conversed in a huddle with the GOC,
Maori Browne came across to chat with Richard Glyn, with whom he was
on cordial terms, the colonel having served under Browne's father as a
young man. The hills permitted only limited fields of view and, having
now seen for himself the ground on which Dartnell and Lonsdale had
spent the night, Glyn must have been appalled at the risk they had run.
He greeted Browne's approach with, 'In God's name Maori, what are you
doing *here?*' Browne recalled: 'I answered him with a question. "In God's
name sir, what are you doing here?" He shook his head and replied, "I am
not in command." And fine old soldier as he was, I could see he was much
disturbed.' Whereas previously some historians have been inclined to
dismiss many of Browne's recollections as retrospective poetic licence,
now, given our earlier consideration of the significance of Glyn's exclusion
from the decision to launch the 21 January operation, this suddenly begins
to sound like a vivid recollection of a very real conversation.

There was much to unsettle an experienced campaigner. Not only had
No. 3 Column been fragmented into three widely separated components,
Pulleine's camp-guard, the Dartnell–Lonsdale combination, and the flying
column, but during the course of the morning the dongas astride the route
had necessitated the man-handling of the guns and limbers; as a result the
2nd/24th and the artillery were now strung out in a long and vulnerable
snake, trailing back across the plain. Nowhere was there a concentration
of reliable troops sufficiently strong to make a stand against a large-scale
Zulu attack. Indeed this parlous state of affairs was to persist throughout
the morning. No doubt Glyn hoped for a long pause, so that he could
gather in the regular infantry and the guns, but Chelmsford had not done
with the exercise of tactical command; already he was hatching plans to
despatch the troops even further afield as they came up. Such casual
manoeuvres bespoke an attitude of utter contempt for the enemy. Little
wonder Glyn was worried.

Not long after 7.00 a.m., Smith-Dorrien rode into the No. 2 Column encampment in search of Durnford. Captain George Shepstone took delivery of the message in his absence. Designated initially as Durnford's 'Political Assistant', presumably to deal with the 'native affairs' arising from the levy of the NNC, Shepstone seems by now to have assumed a role as his military chief of staff. Correctly judging his commander's mood and his acute anxiety to become more actively involved in the campaign, Shepstone gave orders to strike the camp, saddle the horses, and come to immediate readiness to move. Lieutenant Alfred Henderson, the troop leader of Hlubi's Basutos, was sent to bring Durnford back. His duty done, Smith-Dorrien crossed the river and rode up to the mission station. Over breakfast he told Gonville Bromhead that he intended going back to Isandlwana and asked him if he had any spare revolver cartridges. Bromhead gave him eleven rounds. Neither man imagined for a moment that, within a few short hours, the gift would save Smith-Dorrien's life.

Henderson caught up with his colonel quickly. On reading the despatch, Durnford remarked to Cochrane, 'Just what I thought – we are to proceed at once to Isandlwana. There is an *impi* about eight miles from the camp, which the general moved out to attack at daybreak.' With this, the colonel wheeled his riders in the road, and set a brisk pace back to the drift.

Chelmsford had the Malakatha/Hlazakazi high ground on his right along the entire length of his early morning ride. Now, two kilometres beyond the point at which he met Dartnell, the Phindo range ran directly across his path. Ahead and to the half-right, Hlazakazi and the Phindos were separated by the upper Mangeni Valley, which dropped away near Mdutshana into the precipitous Mangeni Gorge. To the left, two long spurs, Magogo and Silutshane, ran down off the Phindo Hills at right angles to define a pair of parallel valleys. The upper Mangeni Valley, on the right, was by far the more significant. Five kilometres beyond Silutshane was Siphezi Hill. Chelmsford's immediate area of concern, though, was Magogo, the location of the Zulus' overnight bivouac. The spur made its descent to the plain over a number of steep scree-terraces, but further up the valley, in the area of Mdutshana, it was gentler in gradient and much more accessible to troops.

Chelmsford decided to probe both valleys simultaneously, in the hope of locating the enemy and precipitating an action. Dartnell was told to proceed directly along the upper Mangeni Valley with the mounted police and the volunteers. He was to cross the stream above the waterfall and then swing north behind Mdutshana. Here he was to probe the junction of Magogo with the Phindo range. Maori Browne and 1st/3rd NNC would support him. In the meantime, Russell and the IMI would swing to the rear of Magogo, and clear up the Silutshane Valley. Cooper's 2nd/3rd NNC would support this second probe. When the valleys were declared free of the enemy, the two NNC battalions were to reunite on top of Magogo and clear along the spur towards Phindo Hill. When the 24th and the guns were up, they were to proceed up the Silutshane Valley behind the IMI.

Back at Isandlwana, the morning had started quietly enough for Colonel Pulleine. Overnight the staff had paid only cursory attention to the arrangements for the camp, and Pulleine himself had not been at all involved in the planning. His first task therefore, was to get to grips with the true state of affairs at Isandlwana. He was assisted in this, as in all things, by his adjutant, Lieutenant Teignmouth Melvill. The two men knew each other well. Notwithstanding the wide gulf in their ranks, a mere four years separated them in age. Pulleine also had to continue with the business of settling in as commanding officer, a post he had held for less than a week. On hand to advise and assist with this second task, was the former acting CO, Captain (Acting Major?) William Degacher. It is not altogether clear whether Degacher had been retained as second-in-command, or whether he had returned to duty with A Company. As the sources are silent on his role in the coming battle, it is to military logic that we must turn for an answer. Degacher does not appear in any of the sources as being in the company of Durnford, Pulleine and Melvill, during any of the discussions that took place at the 1st Battalion headquarters later in the morning, discussions in which it is certain a second-in-command figure would have participated. The post of battalion second-in-command was in any case a later innovation; as we have seen, at this juncture a battalion at full strength had two majors, each commanding a wing of four companies. With only five companies in the field, the 1st/24th was unable to operate by wings in any bona fide fashion. Degacher may well have reverted to his substantive rank on 17 January, when he handed the battalion over to Pulleine. Such formalities would be normal in the British military, where acting rank is granted only for a specific purpose and period.

Historians have repeated *ad nauseam* that as Pulleine was now in command of the camp and its wider garrison, he would have handed command of the 1st Battalion back to Degacher. Not only is there no evidence to support this contention, but there is no element of military probability on which to base it. Such a step would be taken only if the overall span of command had become unmanageable. The mere addition of some mounted troops and a few companies of native infantry would not qualify. It is improbable that, a week after attaining a new pinnacle in his career, Pulleine would pass the mantle of commanding officer back to his immediate predecessor. The strongest likelihood, therefore, is that Degacher had resumed his role as officer commanding A Company and reverted to his substantive rank. However, it is necessary to caveat this by saying that if this were not the case then A Company was commanded in the battle by the 31-year-old Lieutenant Francis Porteous. For the remainder of this reconstruction, however, the role of A Company commander is assigned to Degacher.

Composition of the Force at the Camp

With the departure of the flying column, around sixty officers and 1,300 men had been left in the camp at Isandlwana. Around 800 of the other ranks were Europeans and 500 were black levies. In addition, there were anything up to 300 civilian non-combatants, mostly black wagon drivers, *voorloopers*, grooms and servants, with a couple of dozen white drivers and foremen. The major fighting component was the 1st/24th. This could field its small headquarters element, its band, and five companies: A Company under Captain William Degacher, C Company under Captain Reginald Younghusband, E Company under Lieutenant Charles Cavaye, F Company under Captain William Mostyn, and H Company under Captain George Wardell. Each of the companies was between seventy and eighty strong. This included the company commander, one or two subalterns, a colour-sergeant, three or four sergeants, a similar number of corporals, a couple of drummers and sixty to seventy privates. In all there were thirty-five senior NCOs on parade that morning. The most senior man amongst them was Sergeant-Major Frederick Gapp, the man who today would be referred to as the Regimental Sergeant-Major or RSM. In 1879 there was only one sergeant-major in a battalion, who was known accordingly as *the* Sergeant-Major. The five company colour-sergeants were James Ballard,

Thomas Brown, William Edwards, William Whitfield, and Frederick Wolfe. The second senior non-commissioned man after Gapp was Quartermaster-Sergeant Thomas Leitch, right hand man to Quartermaster James Pullen. Other prominent figures included Drum-Major Robert Taylor, Armourer-Sergeant Henry Hayward, Pay-Sergeant George Mead, the orderly room clerk Sergeant Gerald Fitzgerald, and the Sergeant Instructor of Musketry, George Chambers. Accompanying the battalion in a civilian capacity was the now retired Mr William Seaton, who had been Gapp's predecessor as sergeant-major, and had since found gainful employment as the battalion's canteen steward. In all the 1st Battalion fielded fifteen officers,[*] including the paymaster and the quartermaster, thirty-five senior NCOs, seventeen corporals, 332 privates, twelve adult drummers and two boy-drummers. In addition there were also six privates of the 90th Foot[†] who had been found a temporary home with the 1st/24th. All-up this amounted to fifteen officers and 404 other ranks.

As Charlie Pope's G Company was the only 2nd Battalion sub-unit left at Isandlwana, he would have been expected to regard himself as being temporarily under Pulleine's command. In addition to the ninety or so men

---

[*] Coghill, serving as Glyn's 'orderly officer' or aide, was the sixteenth 1st/24th officer in camp. There were other 1st/24th enlisted men in the camp that morning, such as the men serving with No. 1 Squadron IMI, and the eight other ranks serving with Russell's rocket battery. These two groups are not included in the 1st Battalion's parade state quoted here. There are discrepancies in most unit muster rolls for the Battle of Isandlwana. This was a function, in the case of the 1st/24th, of the wholesale annihilation of its battalion headquarters, and the loss in the looting of the camp of the battalion's nominal rolls and order books. In a truly herculean effort, the late Norman Holme spent many a long year researching the 24th's parade state. His work, originally published as *The Silver Wreath* and later updated and re-released as *The Noble 24th*, is strongly commended as the authoritative source on the subject. Recently Major Martin Everett, curator of the Brecon Museum of the Royal Regiment of Wales was tasked with compiling a nominal roll of the 24th men who fell at Isandlwana, in the hope that the regiment could record their names on the battlefield. In quoting these strengths, I have followed Major Everett's list, which he will freely acknowledge owes a large debt of gratitude to Holme's work and to more recent follow-up work by Julian Whybra. Where muster rolls and parade states are concerned, in both this work and its companion volume *Like Wolves on the Fold*, I have drawn heavily on Norman Holme and on Julian Whybra's *England's Sons*. A nominal roll for the 24th Regiment at Isandlwana appears as an appendix to *Like Wolves on the Fold*.

[†] The 90th was with Wood's column. These men may have been sick or employed on miscellaneous duties when their battalion moved to join Wood. They were Privates Broadhurst, Edwards, Healey, Puttock, Walsh and Wickham.

of G Company, the 2nd/24th contingent also included the battalion guard of two sergeants, two corporals and eighteen men from A Company, a handful of C Company men, the quartermaster and his helpers, and around twenty of the officers' soldier-servants. The all-up 2nd Battalion strength that morning was three officers, nine senior NCOs, seven corporals, 148 privates, two adult drummers, two boy-drummers and three boy-bandsmen. The two senior non-commissioned men were Quartermaster-Sergeant George Davis and Bandmaster Harry Bullard. Later in the day, two more 2nd Battalion officers, Dyer and Griffith, would return to camp and fight in the battle, to give a final total of five officers and 171 men.

Seventy-one members of N Battery were still in camp under the command of Lieutenant Henry Curling. Only twenty of these men were the gunners and drivers of Curling's own division; the remainder were the administrative staff of the battery. A miscellany of mounted men had also been left behind, some of whom were at their ease amongst the tents, and some of whom were posted at far-flung points as vedettes. The senior officer amongst them was Captain Robert Bradstreet of the NMR. In all there were five officers and around 101 mounted troopers at Pulleine's disposal. There were twenty-one men of the IMI, made up of a handful of soldiers from each of the 2nd/3rd, 1st/13th, 1st/24th, and 80th Regiments;* thirty-four men of the NMP; two officers and twenty-seven men of the Natal Carbineers; two officers and twelve men of the NMR; and one officer and seven men of the BBG.

There were still five companies of the NNC in camp. Maori Browne's 1st/3rd NNC was represented by Nos. 6 and 9 Companies under Captains Krohn and Lonsdale respectively. In all, the battalion fielded eleven officers, thirty-one European NCOs and around 200 levies. The officers included Quartermaster McCormack, Doctor Buée, the interpreter Mr Grant, and, it is presumed, the disillusioned Lieutenants Avery and Holcroft. The three 2nd/3rd NNC companies were No. 1 under Captain Murray, No. 4 under Captain Erskine and No. 5 under Captain Barry. These amounted to nine officers, including Quartermaster Chambers, twenty-eight European NCOs and about 300 levies. Minor contingents included a lieutenant and ten men of the Army Hospital Corps; eleven assorted regular soldiers acting as servants to the staff; ten black pioneers; and three men of the Army Service Corps.

---

* Ten more mounted infantrymen would arrive back at the camp with Gardner.

The First Alarm

At around 7.30 a.m., as the men of the 1st Battalion were either eating breakfast or queuing for it, a galloper was seen dashing in from the direction of Amatutshane – clearly one of Durrant Scott's men. He was seen by Private John Williams, Glyn's groom, to rein in at the headquarters tents and make a report to Lieutenant Coghill. It has been generally assumed that Pulleine had by now based himself on the column headquarters, but with the staff all deployed in the field there was no particular reason for him to do so, and the fact that the report was made to Coghill would suggest that the colonel was not immediately at hand. In fact, it seems certain from references in the sources that he remained in the familiar surrounds of his own 1st Battalion camp. Private James Bickley of the 1st Battalion Band saw the same rider make his report to Pulleine and Melvill. Since we know that moments later Bickley was posted to guard the 1st Battalion officers' mess tent, this places the CO and adjutant squarely in the 1st Battalion camp at the time the report was made. It seems certain, therefore, that the galloper stopped at the column headquarters first, and was then sent on by Coghill to the 1st Battalion camp.

Pulleine and his adjutant conferred briefly inside the colonel's tent. Melvill then emerged to order the 1st Battalion duty bugler to sound 'Assemble'. A galloper dashed out to recall the two 24th picket companies. Lieutenant Anstey of F Company was out with a work party improving the wagon road but was not called in immediately. Traditionally historians have placed Anstey in front of the camp, where the road crossed the Nyogane Donga, but this is militarily illogical. He would not have been left in so exposed a position, while the rest of the force stood to arms behind him. Rather, it is clear that Anstey and his men were at the rear of Isandlwana, improving the troublesome crossing point over the Manzimyama Stream. The red-coated men scattered by fours across the right half of the picket line, quickly coalesced into larger groups around their officers and NCOs, and marched back to the camp. The two NNC picket companies, Barry's amaChunu on Mkwene Hill, and Lonsdale's isiGqoza to the left front of the camp, were not recalled. For five minutes or so, there was a brisk sense of urgency as the colour-sergeants formed their companies. Having given their NCOs the requisite head start, the company officers then strolled down from the tents to take over.

Whilst the 1st Battalion fell in on the right of the camp, Pope's company would have fallen in on the 2nd Battalion parade ground, on a flat open area in front of their tents. In the artillery lines, there was a rush to get the two limber-teams into harness. This took around ten minutes. It took the police and volunteers about the same length of time to saddle their horses and form up under Captain Bradstreet. Pulleine gave orders for the 1st/24th companies to march down to join Pope on the 2nd Battalion parade ground, as it was in a much more central position than their own. He also ordered Quartermaster James Pullen to do something about the stray transport oxen grazing in front of the camp. The majority of the herd was in the Manzimyama Valley, where there was water and grass, and they would not interfere with the troops. Pullen sought out the column interpreter, Mr James Brickhill, with whom he shared a tent, and sent him to tell the conductors and *voorloopers* to tether the stray animals to the wagons in the saddle. Brickhill probably shouted the order to the nearest cluster of loafing *voorloopers* and allowed the message to be relayed from group to group. Like all relayed messages, it was subject to misinterpretation, and some of them would in-span their oxen as if for a move. They may have been anticipating an order to laager the wagons, but no such order would be given.

Down on the 2nd/24th parade ground, the 1st Battalion formed up in column of companies. This meant that the companies were formed one behind the other in lettered sequence, A Company at the front, H Company at the rear. Within each company the men were formed two ranks deep with a frontage of about thirty-five files. No firing line was formed as it would take only minutes for the companies to double forward and extend themselves alternately left and right of A Company. After a few minutes, Curling trotted up with his two guns and took post beside the infantry. The men waited patiently in the ranks for half an hour, but no orders came. There was a brief moment of excitement when small parties of Zulus were sighted on the edge of the escarpment. They put in only a momentary appearance, before vanishing just as suddenly.

After a while, the colour-sergeants allowed the men to stand easy and converse quietly in the ranks. The sunshine became uncomfortable. Still nothing happened. Pulleine was obeying his written orders to the letter; he was acting 'strictly on the defensive'. The officers became bored and coalesced into chatting groups. There was some humorous banter at the prospect of an attack developing whilst the general was out chasing shadows.

Pulleine's response to the 7.30 a.m. alarm is significant. Left to his own devices, he remained very close in on the camp, deployed nobody to far-flung positions, and kept his infantry balanced and tightly concentrated. Let the enemy come to him. It was calm, it was measured, and it was tactically sound. Clearly Pulleine at least, could be trusted to obey his orders. But what had triggered the alert?

The galloper who had ridden in to Pulleine was in fact Trooper Whitelaw. At about 06.30 a.m. Barker and Hawkins on Qwabe Hill, and Whitelaw and his partner on Nyezi Hill, had sighted parties of the enemy and had been compelled to abandon their outposts. The particular object of attention from Qwabe had been some mounted men whom Barker and Hawkins at first failed to appreciate were a Zulu patrol. When the truth dawned on them, they signalled the alarm to Lieutenant Scott, and then cantered back to Amatutshane to make a full report. Despite the generally commanding view, there were no enemy in sight, so Scott decided to accompany the pair back to Qwabe to see for himself. As they were crossing the intervening low ground, Scott caught sight of the vedette pair from Nyezi galloping down the valley towards him. Across on Qwabe a small number of Zulus were now in plain view. There also appeared to be a few Zulus in the direction of Nyezi. Reining in hard, Whitelaw blurted out some truly significant news. From Nyezi he and his mate had observed a body of several thousand Zulus moving above the escarpment. As an eyewitness Whitelaw was the ideal choice to ride the news into camp: Scott despatched him with orders to make his report to Colonel Pulleine in person.

With his defensive arrangements in hand, Pulleine decided to send a brief report to his superiors. Just after 8.00 a.m. he pulled a piece of blue writing paper from his bureau and scrawled a few lines in black ink. The note survives to this day in the collection at the regimental museum at Brecon.

> Staff Officer. Report just come in that the Zulus are advancing in force from left front of camp. 8.5 am. H.B. Pulleine, Lieut Col.

The blandness of the despatch is remarkable. It is inconceivable that Pulleine failed to ask Whitelaw to put a figure on the strength of the enemy.

Whatever the estimate was, and it was certainly in the thousands, Pulleine chose to use the militarily vague expression 'in force' instead. 'In force' means different things to different people; ultimately it can mean any number higher than a few hundred. Even if Pulleine distrusted Whitelaw's estimate, it must nonetheless have been clear to him that a significant enemy force had been located. Its presence can only have served to suggest the possibility that the main *impi* had slipped past Chelmsford to the north. If Pulleine had quoted the enemy as 'several thousand' strong, rather than merely 'in force', it is certain that Chelmsford would not have been as disinterested in the 8.05 despatch as he was to prove. Instead, he may well have deduced that he had been out-manoeuvred, and turned his whole force back for Isandlwana. There would have been just enough time for the infantry and artillery to threaten the rear of an attacking *impi*. There was certainly ample time for the mounted troops to play a full part, and 200 carbine-armed troopers could have made all the difference to the defence of the camp. Had Chelmsford ridden back himself, or sent back Glyn, then the irresponsible Durnford might have been dislodged just in time. Essentially through over-caution, Pulleine had now missed his only chance to recall the flying column to his assistance. A trooper of the NMP was summoned and given instructions to deliver the colonel's note to the first staff officer he came across. As the man galloped into the plain, there was still no sign from the camp of the Zulu force that had triggered the alert.

Around 8.00 a.m. Durnford and the Edendale Troop arrived back at the Rorke's Drift encampment in a clatter of dust and hooves. It was an encampment no more. Everything had been packed into the ten wagons available, though they were not yet inspanned. Durnford told Cochrane to stay with the civilian conductor, Mr McCarthy, until the wagons were on the move, and then gallop on at best speed to catch up with the troops. With this, Durnford led off his command along the old wagon road. Outwardly, he cut a dashing figure. Here was a man who had firmly cast himself in the role of heroic frontier fighter. In his broad-brimmed slouch hat, jauntily hooked up on one side, in the manner which would come to characterise Australian military headgear, and with his great drooping moustaches, a passing American might have been forgiven for thinking he had seen the ghost of George Custer. Like Custer, Durnford pushed his horses hard. By now the morning had grown hot and cloudless. The two amaNgwane infantry companies, D and E Companies, 1st/1st NNC, and the mule-borne rocket battery under Major Russell, struggled along well behind the mounted men. It must have been at least half an hour later that the ox-wagons set off. Mr McCarthy must have been well imbued with the spirit of the frontier: as he and his *voorloopers* urged their straining teams into the heart of enemy territory, they found themselves utterly defenceless.

Skirmish at Mangeni

Out at Mangeni, the NNC and the mounted troops had positioned themselves for the twin-pronged probe into the hills. Although the vanguard companies of the 2nd/24th were just about up, the guns were still straggling far to the rear. Dartnell and his men trotted out beyond Mdutshana as planned and, not long after splashing over the Mangeni Stream, made contact with the enemy. This was just after 8.00 a.m., precisely as Pulleine was penning his first despatch, and around the same time that Durnford moved off from the river. Detecting a party of about eighty Zulus, which scattered immediately, Dartnell rode at the forefront of a dashing hot pursuit. The warriors fled for the most part in the direction of the Phindo high ground. The police and volunteers cantered after them, firing from the saddle. Some Zulus returned fire from the rocks, some hid as best they could and some sought refuge in caves. A number of stragglers were captured and questioned about the location of the main Zulu army, but no significant intelligence could be gleaned. The men in the caves were well protected and could not easily be flushed out. In the hour that Dartnell and his men were skirmishing in the valley between Mdutshana and the Phindo Hills, the IMI drew a blank in the Silutshane Valley, and Cooper and Browne cleared Magogo without incident.

At about 9.00 a.m. Lonsdale swung his battalions to the right and continued his advance in the direction of Phindo Hill. Heavy firing broke out almost immediately. Chelmsford and the staff had been watching the IMI clear through the Silutshane Valley, and were thus unable to see what the cause of the firing was. Behind them, the leading elements of the 2nd/24th had just arrived. Degacher had paired off his companies and had them marching in lettered sequence, so that it was A and C Companies who arrived first. They were commanded by Captain J. M. G. Tongue and Lieutenant H. M. Williams respectively, with Major Dunbar in overall charge. Dunbar was told to climb out of the Silutshane Valley to the top of

Magogo, and then advance to the support of the NNC. Not long after Dunbar started uphill, Degacher himself came up with D and E Companies. Chelmsford decided to go to the top of Magogo to see what was going on for himself, and sent instructions for Degacher to follow on behind. Chelmsford paused occasionally to scan the wider situation with his field glasses and identified that there were more Zulus across on Siphezi Hill. Thus far, though, he had seen nothing to indicate that the main *impi* was to be found in this direction. The arrival of the infantry meant that Chelmsford could now afford to cut the IMI loose, and Russell was sent to scout the situation around Siphezi. Meanwhile, F and H Companies under Major Black were still a considerable distance to the rear, acting as N Battery's escort.

Cooper's battalion quickly became heavily embroiled around Phindo, with parties of Zulus which may have totalled 500 men in all. Recovered from their overnight fit of the jitters, the men of 2nd/3rd NNC pressed their attack well, driving the enemy before them. The Zulus were well provided with firearms, so that there was heavy firing on all sides. The noise of the firefight rebounded loudly from hill to hill; indeed, as we shall see, the sound was carrying for miles. At one point, Browne and Lonsdale galloped off in pursuit of a mounted induna. Lonsdale seems to have lost himself in the hills during the chase, because thereafter he was absent for a protracted period. Harford's memoirs give a good feel for the severity of the fighting on Phindo:

> Here we met with rather a warm reception; bullets began to rain down upon us from all directions, and a few men were hit. It became quite clear that a systematic attack would have to be made on the position, so the two battalions were closed in and formed up in as sheltered a position as we could find, for the companies to be told off for specific work on the front and flank . . . In Lonsdale's absence I sent the companies off on their different ways, and continued to conduct the operations myself. Being day instead of night, our men showed nothing of the fear they had exhibited at the bivouac and under the leadership of their officers did uncommonly well, tackling several very nasty situations. At one spot alone thirteen men were shot down one after another, and others were quite game to make further attempts had I not gone up

myself and put a stop to an impossible undertaking. Nothing but some high explosive like dynamite could have effected an entrance to the cave . . . At another place where several of us were being held up by snipers, I spotted a man at the entrance hole of a mass of large rock some twenty or thirty yards off taking a deliberate aim at me, and I quickly shot at him. I then went after him, and, crawling on all fours, found him badly wounded, with a dead Zulu lying close to him.

Watching the fighting from a safe distance, 'Noggs' took particular note of young Harford's gallantry. Observers remarked that he seemed to have a charmed life.

It was 9.30 a.m. when Pulleine's police galloper approached the cluster of staff officers intently watching the skirmishing to their front. Captain Henry Hallam-Parr, of Glyn's staff, spotted the messenger first, and relieved him of the 8.05 despatch. He then signed it and noted the time of receipt in the bottom left hand corner. Next he took it to Clery, who in turn rode it across to Chelmsford. The general quickly scanned the note and handed it back without comment. 'What is to be done on this report?' asked Clery. 'There is nothing to be done on that,' Chelmsford replied. Lieutenant Berkeley Milne, the naval ADC, had a powerful seafarer's telescope and a few minutes after the arrival of the message was sent by Chelmsford to observe Isandlwana from the top of Silutshane. Captain W. P. Symons,* commanding D Company, 2nd/24th, tagged along with him. A little while later, when the two of them made their report, it was to the effect that the only thing of note was that the transport oxen seemed to have been moved into the camp; or to interpret their words more closely, they could see cattle in the saddle. Having delivered the 8.05 despatch, the police galloper went across to where D and E Companies were sat down in the grass awaiting developments. He managed to cause a stir amongst the men, with his stories of imminent attack at Isandlwana. Having presumably been told the contents of the note by Clery, Degacher went across to reassure his soldiers that there was nothing in it to give cause for alarm.

---

* Later Major-General Sir William Penn Symons. Symons was killed in the first battle of the Second Boer War; the Battle of Talana Hill, fought on the outskirts of Dundee. He was killed leading from the front as he attempted to restore the momentum of a stalled attack.

Chelmsford's Change of Plan

By now, Chelmsford had concluded that his hope of bringing on a major engagement was not about to be realised by the current phase of operations. He would make the most of things by advancing Pulleine and the transport to join him at a new campsite near his present location. He had liked the look of the Mangeni Falls area, where he had met Dartnell and Lonsdale first thing that morning: this is another pointer to Chelmsford's poor eye for ground, for it would undoubtedly have made an indifferent defensive position. Captain Alan Gardner, one of Glyn's staff officers, was summoned to take an order to Pulleine instructing him to pack up the camp and come on to Mangeni. It was a tall order in the daylight hours remaining, and certainly meant that Pulleine would have to make an immediate start. Yet the enemy was 'advancing in force from the left front of the camp'. More poor generalship; the time and space simply did not add up.

No doubt Glyn and other experienced African campaigners were bemused by the decision. With well over half the force out of camp, there was huge potential for administrative chaos. As the word went round, a number of officers gathered to accompany Gardner back to the camp, in order to oversee their unit arrangements. Degacher decided to send back Sub-Lieutenant Thomas Griffith, who had drawn a short straw the day before the invasion and found himself detached from his company to be employed on the transport staff. *Historical Records of the 24th Regiment*, authored by 2nd Battalion officers who were there that morning, described the administrative problem and how it came about that the 2nd Battalion would also lose its adjutant:

> It must be remembered that the men had been called up at 1.30 a.m. on an intensely dark night, and as no lights were allowed to be struck all their small belongings, of such comfort to a soldier campaigning, were of necessity scattered about the tents. They had brought with them only their ball bags, haversacks and water-bottles; and to collect and pack all the articles left behind in the camp – the equipment of a battalion – there were only the company left on picquet and a few stray men. Whilst discussing how the order was to be carried out with as little confusion and loss to the men as possible, Lieutenant and Adjutant Dyer, 2nd Battalion 24th,

remarked that he had perhaps better ride back with Lieutenant Griffith and help the quarter-master. So the two young officers rode away and rode to their death.

Chelmsford decided that Maori Browne's battalion should go back to oversee the NNC interest and provide Pulleine with a labour force. A mounted orderly was sent to recall him and guide him to the GOC. Browne was engaged in a skirmish when he was located and had his blood up; he seethed when told to break off the engagement. Galloping across to Cooper, he arranged for 2nd/3rd NNC to pick up the skirmish and then extricated his own men. Not long afterwards the fighting began to peter out anyway.

After their long morning ride, and with little happening to command the attention of an army staff, Chelmsford and his aides had turned their thoughts to breakfast. Before long a pleasant picnic was underway. They were still thus preoccupied, when Browne put in his appearance. Chelmsford greeted him and asked him if he had breakfasted. To his credit, Browne replied that he had not, nor had his men. As he remarked in his memoirs, he might have added that they had had no lunch or dinner the previous day either. Pointedly, he asked Chelmsford if he had been aware that his battalion had been engaged at the time of his recall. No doubt sensing Browne's irritation, Crealock took him to one side to give him his orders. They inferred a march of twenty kilometres, some rushed manual labour, and another twenty-kilometre march back again, all before sunset. With the European NCOs close to exhaustion, it was an impossibly tall order. Browne also doubted his battalion's ability to survive a significant contact. As he wrote in his memoirs:

> I nearly fell off my horse. Could these men know of the close proximity of the enemy? Were we all mad or what? However I was only a poor Devil of a Colonial Commandant and as a simple irregular not supposed to criticise full blown staff officers, so I saluted and said, 'If I come across the enemy?' 'Oh,' he said, 'just brush them aside and go on,' and went on with his breakfast.

It is astonishing to reflect that Crealock's glib complacency was a mere reflection of Chelmsford's own attitude. That Maori Browne and his battalion did not come to grief that afternoon was no thanks to either of them.

Gardner, Dyer and Griffith readied themselves to depart in the company of a dozen mounted infantrymen who had been acting as Chelmsford's personal escort up to that point. Lieutenant McDowel, who had no men of his own to worry about, decided to ride back as well, probably for personal reasons. So, too, did Lieutenant Andrews of the Pioneers. A sixth officer was picked up as Gardner and his companions descended from the high ground and passed the guns. Hearing of the new plan for the first time, Colonel Harness decided that his battery second-in-command, Major Stuart Smith, should also go back to Isandlwana, where there would now be much important administrative work for N Battery's rear details to attend to.

It is noteworthy that the written order to Pulleine seems to have differed from the widely held understanding of the officers at Mangeni. Whereas the word had gone around that the whole camp was to be moved forward, two key witnesses who saw Pulleine read the orders aloud described their gist in quite different terms. These were Gardner and the interpreter Brickhill, both of whom were to record that the order was to send forward tents and rations for the men at Mangeni, leaving the 1st/24th and heavy transport in place at Isandlwana. It is possible that in between his declaration of intent to call Pulleine forward, and Gardner's departure, somebody prevailed on Chelmsford to modify his plan, given the relative lateness of the day. More than likely this would have been Glyn, the only officer senior enough to venture crossing swords with the GOC, who is known to have had a tendency to irritability when suggestions were volunteered by the staff,* a not uncommon element of military arrogance. Even given the change in the orders, the move of tents and rations would involve at least a small convoy of ox-wagons which would need escorting back across the plain. It is highly improbable that such a move could have been completed before nightfall. At least Glyn, if he was indeed the one who took the general to one side, had prevented an unnecessary and large-scale administrative disaster. In the event, No. 3 Column would be engulfed by a disaster of infinitely greater magnitude.

First Sight of the Enemy from the Camp

John Chard cantered on ahead of his wagon as planned and arrived at Isandlwana at around 9.00 a.m. to find the troops still under arms. He

---

* Clery refers to this trait.

would remain for perhaps forty-five minutes. At the column headquarters he was told that he should continue to regard Rorke's Drift as his place of duty. Just then the enemy came into sight above the escarpment:

> A NCO of the 24th lent me a field glass which was a very good one and I also looked with my own, and could see the enemy moving on the distant hills, and apparently in great force. Large numbers of them moving to my left, until the lion hill of Isandlwana, on my left as I looked at them, hid them from my view. The idea struck me that they might be moving in the direction between the camp and Rorke's Drift and prevent my getting back, and also that they might be going to make a dash at the ponts.

The passage above comes from Chard's personal report to Queen Victoria, written at her request early in 1880. It is of crucial importance, in that it reveals that a substantial body of Zulus swept along the escarpment in plain view of the camp, at some point between 9.20 and 9.45 a.m. Self-evidently, whatever it was that Chard saw, everybody else in the camp would have seen too. If Chard's description is accurate, and there is no reason to suspect otherwise, then a large body of Zulus came into sight to the west of Mkwene Hill, moved further west along the Tahelane Spur, and then disappeared from sight behind Isandlwana. This must have entailed a narrow scrape for Barry's company, which must by chance have been on the blind side of Mkwene, or was intentionally hidden by Barry at the enemy's approach. Wherever his main body was concealed, Barry had positioned himself to get a good view of the proceedings. Within a few minutes, he sent in a report to Pulleine, which described the enemy as moving in three columns. Two of these had retired again to 'the north-east', but a third had been moving north-west when it disappeared from view. It was this third column that had been visible from the camp.

In previous accounts of the battle, no numerical estimate has been appended to these movements, but in fact, it is clear that what Chard saw, what Barry reported, and what Charlie Pope logged in his diary, are one and the same movement. The diary, recovered from the battlefield some time later, makes it clear that the Zulu force on the escarpment was estimated by somebody, most probably Barry, at 7,000 men, of whom 4,000 continued to push west for the rear of Isandlwana. This has a fundamental bearing on our understanding of the battle, for although the numerical estimates were not precisely accurate, such large bodies of warriors can only have been the Zulu right horn manoeuvring above the escarpment.

Historians have repeatedly remarked upon how quickly the right horn came forward from the Ngwebeni Valley, but after twenty years of pondering the time and space equations of the battle, it is clear to the present writer that it cannot have been in the Ngwebeni Valley to begin with. The distance from the Ngwebeni Valley to the point where Cavaye first brought the right horn under fire is ten and a half kilometres, whilst the distance to the point at which Durnford made contact with the left horn is a mere four and a half kilometres, with no significant difference in the going. Yet Cavaye and Durnford would come into action at broadly the same time. The conclusion that the right horn could not have had the same start point as the left is inescapable.

Barry's report of Zulus retiring to the north-east has traditionally been interpreted as a long-range sighting across the length of the plateau, in the direction of Mabaso Ridge. If the Zulu columns went in that direction, then they must have gone all the way back to the Ngwebeni Valley, as there is nowhere on the plateau for such large bodies of warriors to conceal themselves. Change the compass bearing only marginally from north-east to north-north-east, a fine distinction seldom made by professional soldiers, let alone by a volunteer officer who probably did not have a compass, and the sighting was not along the length of the plateau in the direction of Mabaso Ridge, but across the width of the plateau in the direction of the Ngedla Heights. Follow a bearing of north-north-east on the map, to the nearest points at which large bodies of warriors could have concealed themselves behind the Ngedla Heights, and the distance from the Zulu start point to Cavaye's killing area is reduced to a downhill stretch of between four and a half and six kilometres. Thus, it is contended that the movement observed by Barry took place much closer to Mkwene Hill than has hitherto been suspected and that two of the Zulu columns retired over the heights a mere three kilometres or so NNE of Barry. After sweeping along the Tahelane Spur, the third column moved off to the north-west, and can only have moved down into the valley of the Manzimyama Stream. Importantly then, the British rear was under threat before the battle had even begun. It was this movement which would cause the subsequent consternation about Durnford's wagons. Finally, with three distinct moving parts clearly identified by the British, it surely cannot be coincidental that the right horn is known to have consisted of three regiments.

Zulu Intent

Some modern writers advance the theory that the Zulu attack was always intended for 22 January, regardless of the traditionally inauspicious 'day of the dead moon', or the start of the lunar cycle. Indeed some contend that the attack was already underway, when Raw's and Roberts's troops made contact. Conversely, other writers will point to the volume of Zulu sources which say that they did not intend to attack on the 22nd, but on the morning of the 23rd. Certainly ritual doctoring was not yet complete and the principal induna's pre-battle harangue had not yet taken place. Sihayo's son Mehlokazulu, a junior induna in the iNgobamakhosi regiment, was quite emphatic on the point:

> We slept the night before the battle in a valley rising from the Nqutu range and running eastwards towards the King's kraal. It [Ngwebeni] abounds with scrubby bush and small stones. We did not see Lord Chelmsford's army leave the camp on the day of the battle, but heard the report of firearms and [after the battle] saw him returning. No orders were given as to the attack; it was not our day. Our day was the following day; it being the new moon we did not intend to fight. Our intention was to attack the camp the next day at dawn, but the English forces came to attack us first.

The early morning attack described by Mehlokazulu would fit neatly with Zulu doctrinal norms, and a number of the Zulus interviewed after the war by Bertram Mitford corroborate his statement. Compellingly, a letter from Cetshwayo to Sir Hercules Robinson, the then Governor of the Cape, written from captivity on 5 April 1881, described exactly what happened to bring on the battle a day early. The king's version of events coincides with other relevant sources. But the question remains: if the attack was to be on Thursday 23rd, why were there significant Zulu movements mid-morning on the 22nd?

The main *impi* had arrived in the Ngwebeni Valley late on Tuesday 21 January, with insufficient time in hand to complete the reconnaissance and other preparations necessary to mount the dawn attack called for by Zulu tactical doctrine. Thus, regardless of native superstitions, still to this day an extremely strong phenomenon in Zulu society, there were sound military reasons why the attack could not be made on Wednesday morning. The army rested in the valley overnight, with the intention of utilising the following day for reconnaissance and preliminary moves.

Regardless of the purely military factors in play, Ntshingwayo, the army commander, was also subject to an important political imperative. The king had instructed him to send some indunas forward, to attempt to open last-minute negotiations with the British, before any recourse to open hostilities. Accordingly, Ntshingwayo and his regimental commanders met on Tuesday evening, to decide who should go down to the camp the next day. The meeting broke up inconclusively, but the indunas agreed to continue their discussions the next morning. Probably there was no real expectation of a positive British response to the king's overtures. On the assumption that their delegates would be rebuffed during the course of the day, the attack could be planned to go in at dawn on Thursday morning.

At the heart of Ntshingwayo's military preparations on Wednesday was real estate management, one of the principal elements in the art of higher command. In today's British Army, where large scale armoured exercises are much less frequent than they once were, young officers have to be reminded on courses just how much real estate an armoured unit or formation will require. Often they are surprised at the great tracts of land indicated to them. Ntshingwayo was an old hand, and knew exactly how much ground was required for an attack by an army of almost 25,000 men. He had found an outstanding place of concealment in the Ngwebeni Valley: it had water; it was close to the enemy, but not too close; it was on the enemy's flank; it had good exit points; and it was concealed from view in all compass directions. Its weakness was that the orientation of the valley to the direction of the coming assault was wrong: it was lengthwise on to the plateau; consequently the *impi* was at rest in great depth but insufficient width. The army needed a huge frontage to throw out its flanking horns rapidly – the most essential tenet of Zulu military doctrine at the army level. If all 25,000 warriors had to squeeze up over the Mabaso Ridge, then the horns would be doing nothing quickly. Whilst the left horn would have all the room in the world to extend into the Qwabe Valley and the plain beyond, the right horn would be constrained on the plateau by the line of the Ngedla Heights. The approach across the plateau, which was on average some three kilometres wide, was vital real estate for the four regiments of the chest. Between them, the uNokhenke, the umCijo, the uMbonambi, and the iNgobamakhosi totalled around 12,000 men, or four warriors for every metre of frontage, even without allowing for intervals between companies and regiments. The right horn must therefore find its own place of concealment behind the Ngedla Heights. Since its destination in the coming assault was the rear of Isandlwana, best approached from the plateau by following the line of the Manzimyama Stream, then the further west its start point was the better: otherwise the route from Ngwebeni would be over fourteen kilometres in length.

The three regiments concerned then, the uDududu, the iMbube and the iSangqu, known collectively as the uNodwengu Corps, were sent forward in regimental columns early on Wednesday morning to find concealment along the Ngedla Heights – the most significant of Ntshingwayo's preparatory moves for the coming attack. In such a scenario, Ntshingwayo would certainly have exposed his battle plan to the indunas of these regiments before detaching them, though as ever, it was based on the simple and standardised manoeuvre of double envelopment, and thus did not require a great deal of amplification. The sighting of thousands of warriors on the move, made by Trooper Whitelaw and his comrade from the summit of Nyezi Hill, enables us to fix the move of the right horn out of the Ngwebeni Valley as occurring at around 7.00 a.m. on the morning of the battle.

The False Start

Zulu sources indicate that, during the course of the morning, firing in the direction of Mangeni triggered a false alarm, which resulted in a precipitate forward move by the umCijo regiment. Its warriors were only recalled with difficulty. In the words of one of them:

> We were sitting resting when firing was heard on our left, which we at first imagined was the iNgobamakhosi engaged, and we armed and ran forward in the direction of the sound. We were soon told however that it was the white troops fighting with Matshana's people some ten miles away to our left front [more accurately their left rear], and returned to our original position.

Many writers have mistakenly asserted that it was this movement which Trooper Whitelaw saw and reported to the camp – but the first firing of the day was by Dartnell, and did not occur until just after 8.00 a.m., by which time the troops at Isandlwana had already been under arms for half an hour in response to Whitelaw's alert. Furthermore, Dartnell's firing at that time was sporadic, and took place in the upper Mangeni Valley, on the far side of the high ground from Ngwebeni; it is highly unlikely to have carried as far as the heavy firing which took place on top of the high ground at or around 9.00 a.m., when Lonsdale's two battalions brought the best part of 250 rifles to bear on the Zulus defending Phindo. Probably a hundred or more Zulu weapons returned this fire. This was the most significant outbreak of firing from the direction of Mangeni during the course of the morning – and logically it must have been the loudest noise which precipitated the only false alarm known to have occurred. Clearly then, the excitement in the umCijo was the result of the action around Phindo Hill and cannot account for Whitelaw's sighting of over two hours earlier. What Whitelaw saw was the preliminary move of the right horn regiments in the direction of the Ngedla Heights.

Yet if the attack was not to be made until the morning of the 23rd, how could it be that the uNodwengu Corps went on to betray the presence of the main *impi*, by manoeuvring in the open, to the north of the camp, on the morning of the 22nd? The key to this question is the time at which the compromise occurred. Since Chard was present at Isandlwana from 9.00 a.m., and had completed his business at the column headquarters when one of the three regiments swept along the top of the escarpment, we can fix the movement as occurring at some time between 9.20 and 9.30 a.m. This means that they left their place of concealment, roughly four kilometres away over the Ngedla range, at around 9.00 a.m.; precisely the same time as Lonsdale's NNC became engaged in the heavy skirmish in the Phindo Hills.

In such close proximity to the enemy, all the Zulu regiments were on edge and bristling with eagerness for the fray. We know that the sound of gunfire played all sorts of acoustic tricks around the hills that day. The leaders of these three regiments heard the firing to the south-east and were deluded into thinking that the main body was in contact at Ngwebeni. Accordingly, they advanced from cover to execute the plan of attack. As the indunas led their men down the forward slopes of the Ngedla Heights in regimental columns, they looked to their left and saw exactly what they expected to see – phalanxes of warriors coming up onto the plateau from the Ngwebeni Valley – the umCijo's false start. The right horn was well into the open and had been spotted from Mkwene Hill by Captain Barry, when the indunas of the two left hand regiments realised their mistake. To their left, the umCijo had been recalled, and there was now no sign of a major attack across the plateau by the regiments of the chest. In response, they wheeled their regimental columns back the way they had come.

By now the third regiment was screened from the other two by the northwards-projecting spur of Mkwene Hill, which is over a thousand metres long. Oblivious to the wheel of their comrades, this third regiment kept advancing until it reached the Tahelane Spur. On looking down into the Isandlwana bowl, the indunas realised that the regiment was on its own. They quickly wheeled the column to the right and trotted along the length of the spur in plain view of the camp. The right wheel continued until the regiment reached the upper reaches of the Manzimyama Valley. So, the movement seen by Chard had in fact been an unsupported regimental attack which was averted only at the last minute. Quite how the day would have developed if this attack had been pressed is an intriguing but ultimately irrelevant issue.

All three of the uNodwengu regiments were 1,200–1,500 strong. Therefore the true figures connected with the British morning sightings can be calculated in broad order terms as follows: Whitelaw saw all 4,000 warriors moving towards the Ngedla Heights; Barry saw 4,000 warriors split between three regimental columns but estimated them at 7,000; Chard and everybody else in the camp saw about 1,500 warriors sweeping along Tahelane, a group which Pope, at least, estimated at 4,000.

The British Response

The spur was only a few hundred metres to the north of the camp. Concerned at this highly significant threat to his left, Pulleine ordered that Lieutenant Charles Cavaye's E Company, 1st/24th, be despatched from the camp to take up a position on Tahelane.* The purpose of the deployment

---

* Historians have been divided on precisely when this deployment took place and who ordered it. There is no hard evidence to say one way or the other that Pulleine ordered it, or that it was done at Durnford's insistence before he left the camp. As with many aspects of this battle, however, one can make a reasonable inference from an absence of evidence. Cochrane

was to protect the north end of the camp from any attempt by the third Zulu column, last reported as having moved off to the north-west, to double back and mount an incursion down the spur. Cavaye was to advance up to the high ground in skirmishing order,* and establish a firing line which would deny Tahelane as an unopposed avenue of approach. The deployment also offered some succour to Barry's by now rather nervous company. If he was again pressed by the enemy, Barry could fall back across the downhill kilometre separating Mkwene Hill from the spur, and shelter his men behind Cavaye's firing line.

Chard decided that he had better get back to Rorke's Drift to apprise Major Spalding, the senior officer at the post, of the potential threat to the ponts. Turning back through the saddle, he began his return journey to the river. A short distance down the wagon road, he encountered Durnford at the head of his mounted troops. Chard briefed the colonel on the situation at the camp, and expressed his concerns about the Zulu column seen moving to the north-west. He must have spoken with conviction as Durnford immediately inferred a threat to the rear of his own column, by now well strung out along the road behind him. Durnford told Chard that somewhere behind his five troops of horsemen, he would find two companies of native infantry and the rocket battery. He was to tell Major Russell to drop off a company with the wagons, and hurry on with the other. Entirely in keeping with his contrived buccaneering image, Durnford himself would press on at best speed with the mounted troops. Riding on, Chard soon met his little party of sappers. His batman, driver and *voorlooper* were told to turn about with the wagon, whilst the other four unfortunates were instructed to march on to the camp. Chard then cantered on, to pass on Durnford's instructions to his slower-moving subordinates. He found them as he approached the Batshe Valley. Russell quickly called in the two NNC company commanders to discuss the orders. It was agreed that Captain Walter Stafford would hang back with E Company to escort the wagons, and that Captain Cracroft Nourse's

---

seems to have stayed at Durnford's side throughout all the interchanges with Pulleine and makes no mention in his accounts of such a deployment being discussed or agreed, as it must have been, had it taken place after Durnford's arrival in the camp. The most rational explanation, therefore, is that Pulleine ordered the deployment at approximately 9.30 a.m. as a response to the significant Zulu movement along the Nyoni Ridge.

* Statement of Private John Williams.

D Company would dash on with Russell and the rocket battery. Dropping off E Company was little more than a token gesture to the protection of the transport – there would be little chance of Stafford's lightly armed amaNgwane successfully resisting a strong enemy force. After a few minutes, Stafford detailed Lieutenant Wallie Erskine to remain with the wagons with a squad of sixteen men, and then hurried on with the remainder. Perhaps, like his colonel, he too was anxious not to miss any excitement up-country.

Within twelve to fifteen minutes of first receiving the order, Cavaye and E Company were at the top of the Tahelane Spur. They could see no sign of the enemy in the valley beyond. The crest was rocky underfoot, with plenty of clusters of larger boulders where riflemen could take up well-protected positions. There was an excellent field of fire to the north. A gentle slope fell away to a stream just under a kilometre away. Another kilometre beyond the stream were the relatively gentle south-eastern slopes of the Ngedla Heights.

The stream ran along a shallow gully immediately in front of Cavaye's position, but to the half-left it disappeared behind a convex westward projection of the spur. From there the stream meandered back to the north-west in dead ground, where it then fed into the Manzimyama. This then flowed south for a further four kilometres, until it emerged from the hills directly behind Isandlwana. Concealed somewhere in these upper reaches of the Manzimyama, of course, was a regiment of the Zulu right horn. The line of the stream offered a good cross-country avenue of approach to the rear of Isandlwana, but anybody moving along it from the north-east would now be in plain view from Cavaye's position, over an exposed stretch of open ground, some 600–700 metres in width. Captain Edward Essex would later judge the range to this gap as about 800 yards, but judging distance downhill is frequently deceptive and it was closer to a thousand.

Cavaye looked to his flanks only to find that neither was particularly satisfactory. To his right, the gradient sloped uphill to the Mkwene highpoint, where Barry's amaChunu infantry were huddled. Although this was his limit of visibility to the right, the position was at least picketed by friendly troops who could warn him of any developing threat from the east. To the left, however, there was nobody. Because of the spur's western projection, Cavaye could see less than a kilometre and had no view of the

Manzimyama Valley. To counter the problem, he instructed 2nd Lieutenant Dyson to take a section further along the spur, to a position where he could obtain a view to the west. This would separate the two parts of the company by a substantial distance. Cavaye instructed the three remaining section commanders to deploy along the crest. Having been posted by their sergeants, the men made themselves comfortable amongst the boulders and settled down to await developments.

In the camp the atmosphere had become tense. Krohn's No. 6 Company was in reserve in front of the tents, where its officers had no particular task. Krohn was told to send an officer to obtain an update from Barry. First, Lieutenant Gert Adendorff was despatched. When he returned, his report was garbled and threw but little light on matters; it cannot have helped that English was not his first language. Lieutenant Walter Higginson was sent out to see if he could do better. Higginson took a white NNC sergeant-major called Williams along for the ride.

Durnford Arrives at the Camp

At around 10.00 a.m. Durnford and his horsemen cantered over the saddle. As the column reined in behind the camps of the volunteers and the artillery, Durnford's mind was racing with dreams of military glory; perhaps today would be his day. Leaving his troop officers to dismount their men near the hospital tents, Durnford rode across the saddle to meet with Pulleine. Cochrane accompanied him and was a key witness to what then ensued. When the two colonels met, Pulleine's welcome was civil but less than whole-hearted, as he knew that the rules of seniority demanded that he hand over command. His brief moment of glory, an independent command in the near presence of the enemy, seemed, disappointingly, to have been terminated.

The conversation that followed, as far as it is known, has been endlessly debated but, if Cochrane reported it reasonably accurately, then, at its simplest, Pulleine offered up overall command and Durnford, at least at first, declined to take it. Pulleine said, 'I am sorry you have come, as you are senior to me and will of course take command.' These words of themselves sound cold and even hostile, but delivered with an ironic smile they would have quite a different tone. Durnford is said to have replied, 'I'm not going to interfere with you: I'm not going to remain in camp.' The last thing a buccaneering frontier fighter needed was to be responsible for a static position, for a great lumbering wagon train, for rows of tents, for guards, duties, and pickets, for logistics. Like it or not, though, he was the senior officer present, and until such time as he received orders to move on from Isandlwana, he was the overall commander there. Pulleine knew and understood the importance of this most basic of military precepts and continued to defer to Durnford, notwithstanding the latter's apparent reluctance to accept responsibility for anything other than his own immediate command.

Regardless of Durnford's disinterest, Pulleine went on to brief the composition of the force in the camp, the movements of the Zulus so far as he understood them, and the orders he had received from Clery that morning. Perhaps he sensed Durnford's restlessness, for Cochrane tells us that during the course of the conversation, Pulleine repeated 'two or three times' that the orders were to defend the camp. There were four sightings of the enemy for Pulleine to itemise. First, there was Whitelaw's report describing several thousand warriors moving in the hills to the north-east at around 7.00 a.m. Second, there was the fleeting sighting of small groups of Zulus standing on the escarpment and apparently observing the camp. Third, there was Barry's very recent report of the enemy manoeuvring just behind the escarpment in three columns. Fourth, there was the element of this last movement that had been seen from the camp.

In the traditional rendering of the Isandlwana story, Pulleine and Durnford have little idea of the strength of the Zulu force in the hills above the camp, and no idea whatsoever that they are facing the main *impi*. This is a myth. Pope's diary entry for 22 January proves that a very definite estimate of the enemy's strength was widely known in the camp. As we have seen, the figure at issue is 7,000 men. If Pope knew this figure, then it was known to Pulleine, and if it was known to Pulleine then it would certainly have been cited in his handover to Durnford. To lend collateral to this contention, William Cochrane's evidence tells us that when Durnford and his men arrived at Isandlwana, it was to find that, 'A number of Zulus had been seen since an early hour on top of the adjacent hills and that an attack had been expected.' If there were indeed several thousand Zulus on the high ground, and Pulleine must himself have seen the body of '4,000' (actually 1,500) moving along the escarpment, then the two colonels should have operated on a worst-case basis and assumed that a very large *impi* lay not to the south-east, but to the north-east. All this must have a fundamental bearing on how the performance of the British commanders is judged in history.

The exchange on command of the camp clearly took place immediately after No. 2 Column's appearance and demonstrates that Durnford arrived determined to retain his independence by not associating too closely with No. 3 Column. It has been argued, not unreasonably, that he conflated the GOC's guidance of 14 January with the order of that morning – that he arrived expecting to be called forward to join Chelmsford in operations against the 'two Matyanas'. However, during the course of his conversation with Pulleine, it would have become clear that no such order had yet been given. In these circumstances he would have had to await further developments. Desperate to redeem himself after the sorry affair at Bushman's River Pass, he yearned for the fame and glory that would flow from a general action against the Zulu. Given the chance he could humble his critics, salvage his professional reputation, end his career on a high note and attain a state of personal fulfilment. These were dark psychological demons, lurking in the deepest recesses of his mind, but ultimately nothing could or would dispel them. If nothing else, Pulleine's briefing had indicated that that the camp itself might well be the immediate focus of enemy activity. It seems clear from the subsequent passage of time that any initial misapprehension was corrected and that Durnford accepted that, for the time being at least, he would be staying put.

The initial conversation between the colonels probably lasted less than 10 minutes, at which point Durnford went to brief his officers. The mounted troops were to ride over to the NNC lines, where they could dismount and rest, but not off-saddle in order that they remain at the same high state of readiness as the imperial troops. About ten to fifteen minutes after the NNMC had trotted off, Cracroft Nourse's D Company and the rocket battery appeared over the saddle, and were directed to join the mounted troops. Then, to Durnford's surprise, Stafford and E Company marched in too. Where were the wagons? The information which Pulleine had provided on the enemy manoeuvre to the north-west, reinforced the potential threat to movement between Rorke's Drift and Isandlwana. Durnford summoned Lieutenant Wyatt Vause and instructed him to take No. 3 Troop back along the road to see the wagons safely in. With fifty carbine-armed riders, Vause's troop was a much more credible escort than Stafford's company could ever have been. Stafford, however, was also sent back over the saddle to bring the wagons in as originally instructed. He probably went with a flea in his ear. The uphill climb from the Manzimyama Stream is hard work on a hot day and, having completed it once, the men of Stafford's company could hardly have been delighted at the prospect of doing it all over again.

By the time No. 2 Column had come up in its entirety, the camp would contain seventy-one officers, 870 enlisted Europeans and just over a thousand levies. Allowing for black non-combatants there may have been 2,200 souls in all. It was an impressive military force and it was in the field against a 'primitive' enemy, yet few of its members would live to see the sunset.

The troops in camp had been under arms in a hot sun for well over 2½ hours; having been disturbed at breakfast, many of them were hungry. Since there had been no major developments since the sighting on the Tahelane Spur some fifty minutes earlier, and there appeared to be no imminent threat to the camp, Durnford suggested that the men be dismissed under orders to keep their equipment on and their weapons close at hand. Pulleine raised no objection and directed his adjutant to give the necessary instructions, whilst he and Durnford adjourned to the mess tent for something to eat. A few minutes later, the 1st/24th companies marched back to their own camp and were fallen out. The company officers had soon filed into the mess to join the two colonels and their immediate staff officers. Curling trotted his guns back to the RA camp, where he left his teams harnessed, and then joined his 1st/24th friends in their mess. Whilst, no doubt, Durnford joined in the social pleasantries with everybody else, inwardly he was burning with impatience; he ate standing. The enemy was just beyond the Nyoni escarpment, within easy striking distance for mounted troops such as his own. He could not be sure exactly where, for Barry's reports were imprecise, but yes, somewhere out there was the enemy. His mind was racing, as Custer's had raced at Little Big Horn, as Ney's had raced at Waterloo.

It is unclear where the next series of developments took place, but after their belated breakfasts, Pulleine, Durnford and their respective aides probably strolled back to the 1st/24th headquarters tent. Higginson was back. He approached Pulleine to make his report, but Pulleine told him to deliver it to Durnford instead. From Barry's position, Higginson had watched some '600 Zulus' manoeuvring on the plateau, about a thousand metres to the north-east. This may have been a rearguard covering the withdrawal of the right horn to the heights, though Higginson probably did not interpret it that way. It is likely that Durnford would have asked some supplementary questions, and it is possible that Higginson's answers were in some way vague or unsatisfactory. Perhaps irritated by the lack of clarity in the various reports of the outposts, Durnford decided to send out some of his own men to reconnoitre. He gave orders for Captain William Barton to scout the ground behind the escarpment with Nos. 1 and 2 Troops of Zikhali's Horse, under Lieutenants Charlie Raw and Joseph Roberts respectively. Captain George Shepstone would accompany Barton. The two troops would ride up onto the high ground via the Tahelane Spur,* and then push north-east across the plateau, paralleling the escarpment. The NNC company at Mkwene Hill could be picked up en route, to operate in support of the mounted troops. Next, Durnford sent Higginson to post a party of NNC men on top of Isandlwana itself. He had been taken in by the geography, for whilst the summit of Isandlwana can appear commanding, it actually offers no great view over the escarpment. Shepstone, Barton and the two troops cantered away not long after 11.00 a.m.

At some point in the next twenty minutes, a report was received from Higginson which was phrased in such a way as to indicate that the enemy was 'retiring everywhere'. It is not possible, in the time available, that the men sent to the top of the Sphinx made this report. Whilst its source is uncertain, it served to push Durnford over a judgemental edge; if there were to be no fight at the camp, he would seek one in the plain. Turning to Pulleine he expressed a vague concern about a threat to the GOC's rear and announced his plan. Raw and Roberts would be ordered to press their scout east across the plateau. He himself would ride into the plain with the Edendale troop and Hlubi's Basutos, where he would skirt the foot of the high ground and attack any enemy force driven in his direction. He would take Russell's rocket battery in support, with Nourse's company as its escort.

---

* In his somewhat confused *Survivor's Account*, in which compass directions are frequently used, but cannot be relied upon, Brickhill says that the two troops went back the way they came, that is to say back into the Manzimyama Valley. This makes no particular sense given the existence of a native path running up the Tahelane Spur just to the left of the NNC camps. It seems likely that what Brickhill saw was in fact Vause's Troop going back over the saddle to escort Durnford's wagons. Private Bickley reported, 'A part of Colonel Durnford's Basutos was sent up a hill to our left.'

As he heard the plan described, Pulleine was no doubt silently perplexed by such flagrant disregard for orders, but then Durnford completely overstepped the mark. He asked for two companies of the 24th to accompany him. Quite what role he had in mind for them is unclear, as they would certainly have been much slower-moving than the mounted natives. Pulleine quickly expressed his disapproval and produced the written orders he had been given that morning.* Durnford did not immediately back down. Under pressure, and with Melvill having apparently stepped outside the tent on other business, Pulleine conceded that if Durnford insisted and directly ordered it, then the companies would have to go. For a few moments Durnford seemed to have got his way. Then came a crucial intervention. Pulleine went to brief his adjutant, but Melvill was having none of it. He knew that his CO was too polite a man to have a stand-up row with a nominal superior, but he was quite certain in his own mind that Durnford had taken leave of his senses. Melvill was a good soldier and knew the mettle of the Zulu; for the past thirty-six hours he had despaired at the all-pervading air of complacency displayed by the general and the staff. He had discussed his reservations with old hands such as Major Dunbar. Now Durnford proposed sallying forth with 400 native troops against an enemy force which had been estimated at 7,000 strong. The speed with which Durnford backed down suggests that Melvill's approach was fiery, though in what he said he did not step outside the limits of military decorum. Experienced officers cultivate a way of telling a senior officer that he is being a fool with their eyes, demeanour and tone. Melvill must have employed all these techniques. 'Colonel, I really do not think Colonel Pulleine would be doing right to send any men out of camp, when his orders are to defend the camp.' Sensing that he was not going to get his way without an unseemly argument, Durnford replied, 'Very well, it does not much matter; we will not take them. I will go with my own men.' Then, turning back to Pulleine, he said something to the effect of, 'My idea is that wherever Zulus appear we ought to attack. I will go alone, but remember if I get into difficulties, I shall rely on you to support me.' Higginson was sent to ride after Barton and Shepstone to advise them of the new plan. With this Durnford turned on his heel and was gone. It was now approximately 11.30 a.m.

* *Historical Records of the 24th Regiment.* Though the witness to the production of the written order is not named, it is clearly a reference to Cochrane.

Within minutes of Durnford's departure, Charlie Pope made a final rushed entry in his diary, recollecting the events of the morning. In doing so, he inadvertently consigned the truth about Colonel A. W. Durnford to history.

Four am, A, C, D, E, F, H 1 and 2/3 NNC, mounted troops, and four guns off. Great firing. Relieved by 1st/24th. Alarm. Three columns of Zulus and mounted men on hill E. Turn out. Seven thousand more E.N.E., four thousand of whom went around Lion's Kop. Durnford's Basutos arrive and pursue with rocket battery. Zulus retire everywhere. Men fall out for dinners.

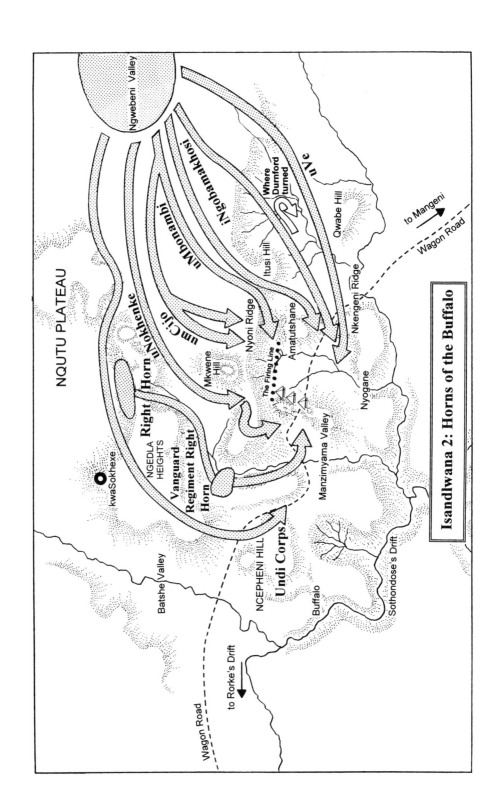

NQUTU PLATEAU

Ngwebeni Valley

iNgobamakhosi

uMbonambi

uVe

Where Dumford turned

Qwabe Hill

to Mangeni

Itusi Hill

Wagon Road

umCijo

Nyoni Ridge

Nkengeni Ridge

Mkwene Hill

Amatutshane

The Firing Line

Nyogane

Right Horn

Nokhenke

NGEDLA HEIGHTS

Manzimyama Valley

Vanguard Regiment Right Horn

kwaSokhexe

NCEPHENI HILL

Undi Corps

Batshe Valley

Buffalo

Sothondose's Drift

Wagon Road

to Rorke's Drift

Isandlwana 2: Horns of the Buffalo

Chapter 5

Horns of the Buffalo

The Onslaught

As Pulleine and Melvill scanned the plain with their field glasses, they could see nothing to suggest the coming onslaught. Commanding officers and their adjutants often have confidential conversations, and it is likely that they had one now about the extraordinary bravado of Colonel Anthony Durnford. What passed between them is unlikely to have been charitable. The two troops of amaNgwane riders under Raw and Roberts had long since ridden out of sight, somewhere beyond the escarpment. Near Amatutshane, a cloud of dust indicated the swift progress of the Basuto and Edendale Troops under Durnford himself. Still in plain view was a much slower moving procession, consisting of the rocket battery and its NNC escort. Between Amatutshane and the escarpment, James Lonsdale's isiGqoza remained deployed in a series of huddles that passed for a picket line. On the high ground Barry's amaChunu had now departed Mkwene Hill, having been ordered forward in Durnford's name by Shepstone. Here and there men of Cavaye's company could be seen nestled between the boulders on the top of the Tahelane Spur.

Amongst the rows of bell tents, the men of the 24th stood in huddles scanning the horizon. Faithful to their orders, they were still fully equipped to fight at a moment's notice. Left and right on their waist-belts were their ammunition pouches, each containing two sealed paper packets of ten Boxer cartridges. The bayonet frog suspending the lunger's formidable twenty-two inches of cold steel hung from the waist-belt above the left buttock. Below the right ammunition pouch was the black leather expense pouch with ten loose cartridges ready for immediate use. Over the left shoulder was slung the Oliver pattern water-bottle, and, over the right, a white canvas haversack with a few biscuits, perhaps some personal belongings, and a further two packets of ammunition. In all then the NCOs and privates each had seventy cartridges on their person. There was now an air of suspense. Surely, people reasoned, something must come of such a determined reconnaissance of the high ground to the left of the camp. The atmosphere may have been tense, but there was no unease as such. Filled with the sense of inherent national superiority which has always characterised the British professional soldier, the men of the 24th were confident in their supremacy over any African foe.

Now that Pulleine was in sole charge again, he turned his attention once more to the protection of the vulnerable northern flank. From his position on the Tahelane Spur, Cavaye had a good view of the ground to the north-west, but now that Barry's company had been dragged forward with Zikhali's Horse, the camp was blind to the north-east. As it was essential that the commander in the camp had his own eyes and ears on Mkwene Hill, it would be necessary to backfill the NNC outpost there. Accordingly, Captain Edward Erskine's No. 4 Company, 2nd/3rd NNC, was ordered to return to its position of the previous evening.

Scouting the Plateau

Behind the escarpment, the men of Zikhali's Horse fanned out across a two-kilometre frontage and began to scour the plateau. Their progress to the north-east was funnelled between the Ngedla Heights on their left and the Nyoni escarpment to their right. A stream ran along the axis of advance, dividing the horsemen either side of it – Raw and No. 1 Troop to the right, Roberts and No. 2 Troop to the left. The ground was undulating but fields of view were generally good. Barry's amaChunu infantry had only reluctantly come out of cover onto the open plateau, and were moving slowly along at the rear. To their great relief the ground ahead appeared to be clear of the enemy. It was a hot day and the men on the plateau were moving at a steady rate of advance, aimed at not over-exerting themselves or their ponies. Durnford, meanwhile, was moving at a sharp trot on the plain, where the going was somewhat better for mounted troops: notwithstanding the head start that Zikhali's Horse had been given, it was not long before he had closed the gap and come up roughly parallel with Raw and Roberts. With the escarpment intervening between the two halves of the command, however, neither group was aware of the position of the other.

After riding five to six kilometres across the plateau, the troopers with Raw and Roberts identified a number of small parties of Zulus in the distance, some of them herding a few head of cattle. No significant enemy force was apparent, however. The men quickly kicked their horses into a canter to close the gap. When at length they were within striking distance, some of them opened fire from the saddle, whilst others dropped to the ground to take a better-aimed shot. Charlie Raw and others rode in hot pursuit of the cattle-herders. The sound of the firing carried to the camp as a distant crackle of shots to the north-east. Not everybody heard it, and not everybody who did paid it much attention. As Raw and his troopers galloped forward, the ground started to rise towards a scree-covered ridge which entirely obscured the terrain beyond. The particular group of Zulus on which Raw had set his sights, quickly slipped over the ridge and out of sight. There were a great number of boulders strewn along the higher ground, obliging the amaNgwane to slow their ponies and pick their way carefully through the obstruction.

From Mabaso Ridge, as this crest is now known, the ground falls away steeply into a hidden valley, at the bottom of which is the Ngwebeni Stream. Raw and his men now experienced one of the most dramatic surprises in the history of warfare. At one moment they were chasing a handful of warriors, droving a few cows. Now, from the top of Mabaso, they were looking downhill at a great military host of around 20,000 men. Unbeknown to Raw, a further 4,000 warriors, the men of the right horn, were concealed behind him on the Ngedla Heights and in the upper reaches of the Manzimyama Valley. Where, a few minutes before, there had been stillness and silence on the floor of the valley, there was now uproar and movement. Alarmed by the sudden outbreak of firing from beyond Mabaso, the nine Zulu regiments concealed below it were now rousing themselves to battle. The following passage from Cetshwayo's letter to Sir Hercules Robinson should dispel any lingering doubts inspired by modern writers as to whether the battle was brought on early by the British, or initiated as planned by the Zulus:

> I told Tyingwayo [sic] who was at the head of these troops, not to go to the English troops at once, but to have a conference and then send some chiefs to ask the English why they were laying the country waste and killing Zulus, when they had plainly said they had not entered the country to fight but to talk about the settlement. Well the troops (the Zulu troops) travelled two days and on the third

day they reached the hill called Ingudu [*sic* – Nqutu]. Here they encamped, and the officers of the different regiments assembled in order to come to an agreement as to which chiefs they should send to confer with the English about their proceedings [i.e. laying waste to Sihayo's region] . . . During this time the several regiments had sent out foragers to bring in food. When day dawned my chiefs were again consulting about sending to the English before fighting; but suddenly they heard the roar of guns and saw the dust and smoke rising up to Heaven, and our foragers rushing back to the encampment and saying 'that the cavalry was near'. Then the chiefs, knowing that the work of death was being executed, broke up the meeting and went to their several regiments. The troops then moved up a little hill [Mabaso Ridge], and on coming to the top met the English troops . . .

Captain George Shepstone had been riding along behind No. 1 Troop in the company of Durnford's civilian commissary, Mr James Hamer. The pair now galloped up alongside Nyanda, the black sergeant-major of Zikhali's Horse, to see what the fuss was about. One can imagine their jaws dropping as they did so. They may have had time to marvel briefly at what a brilliant place of concealment the Ngwebeni Valley was. There were even quick-exit routes left and right of the valley floor, where two wide re-entrants ran uphill to the plateau. After the earlier false alarm, parts of the umCijo* had settled down just behind Mabaso, much closer to the crest than the *amabutho* below. Loosing a fusillade at the encroaching riders on the ridge, the regiment quickly took the offensive; while in some places the amaNgwane were driven back almost immediately, in others handfuls of troopers were able to hold on a minute or two longer and fire a few pinprick volleys into the valley. Responding to instruction by their indunas, the warriors below raced into their regimental phalanxes and, with scarcely a pause, jogged instinctively to their assigned places in the great 'horns of the buffalo' formation.

As we have seen, there were four regiments assigned to the chest. The uNokhenke and umCijo regiments, on the right side of the chest, would have pushed uphill to the plateau via the northernmost re-entrant. To the left of these two regiments, the uMbonambi and the iNgobamakhosi

* Also known as the uKhandempemvu.

clambered up Mabaso Ridge itself which, although it was relatively steep, presented no serious obstacle to their rapid advance. On the extreme left, 3,500 men of the uVe regiment raced for the southernmost re-entrant. This was the youngest *ibutho* in the army and had been assigned to duty as the left horn. Further back down the valley to the east, the indunas of the four reserve regiments roared commands of restraint. It was essential to the Zulu battle drill that these regiments were held in check, until the three forward elements of the army had shaken out into battle formation. As is always the way when trained soldiers execute a familiar and well-rehearsed drill, it all happened surprisingly quickly.

Although the NNMC troops are traditionally credited with the discovery of the main Zulu *impi*, it was in fact sighted from its left flank just a little while earlier. At about the same time as the amaNgwane horse spotted the cattle herders, a small patrol of Natal Carbineers was operating above the escarpment, some way north-east of Itusi Hill, when they made contact with a party of the enemy estimated by Trooper Barker to be 200 strong. As the patrol loaded carbines and prepared to skirmish, the Zulus withdrew over a low ridge and disappeared from sight. Barker and a few others trotted up the slope to investigate and found that they now had a view into parts of a low-lying valley – Ngwebeni. Thankfully, in his later account of events, Barker resorted to completely unambiguous language, 'We saw a large army sitting down.' However, unlike the much better known NNMC contact only a few minutes later, the carbineers' sighting took place at a range of some 600 yards, with a couple of low ridges intervening, and, for the time being at least, the Zulu main body remained oblivious to its detection. The little group of horsemen slipped quietly away from their vantage point and rode back towards Lieutenant Scott's new position to report their dramatic news. (Scott was certainly above the escarpment by now, most probably at or near Itusi Hill, from where he would have observed the advance of Raw and Roberts across the plateau). Troopers Barker and Hawkins were ordered to continue on into camp via the notch and report the fresh sighting of the enemy at the headquarters tents. It would seem likely that Scott took the rest of his men and pushed forward in the direction of the Ngwebeni Valley – by now there was firing coming from the direction of Mabaso where the amaNgwane horse had made contact.

Out beyond the Ngedla Heights, the three right horn regiments, the uDududu, iMbube and iSangqu, stirred in their hidden positions at the sound of a fresh outbreak of heavy firing. Undoubtedly, their indunas would have dashed forward to commanding vantage points to see what was happening; this time they had no intention of going off at half-cock. It did not take them long to ascertain that this was the real thing: the main *impi* had been compromised; now there could be no question of waiting for the morrow. Within a few minutes, the two regiments concealed NNE of Mkwene Hill were on the move down the forward slope of the Ngedla Heights. They moved rapidly in the direction of their vanguard regiment, with which they had lost contact some two hours earlier, but which they knew was concealed north-west of Isandlwana in the valley of the Manzimyama.

Prudently, Raw and his men did not hang around to dispute Mabaso Ridge with the Zulu chest. Rather they cantered back downhill, re-formed their skirmish line at a safe distance from the crest, and waited for the warriors to break the skyline. To Raw's left flank, Barton and Roberts were executing a similar manoeuvre. The wait was a short one; first one man appeared, then a dozen, and then thousands. At Raw's bellowed command, a second volley was fired, tumbling a handful of Zulus into the scree. Return fire toppled one of the amaNgwane troopers from the saddle and killed a horse. On the left, Roberts's men volleyed, then Raw's again. Untrained as cavalry mounts, the African ponies reared and shied at the frightening and unaccustomed sound. The amaNgwane struggled to control their excited animals, at the same time as ejecting spent cartridges from their carbines, and fumbling in their bandoliers for fresh ones. None of this was calculated to aid the accuracy of their fire and there was no question of it arresting the Zulu advance.

In company with James Hamer, George Shepstone galloped across to speak to Captain Barton. Announcing his intention to ride back to the camp to warn Pulleine personally, Shepstone told Barton to withdraw in the face of the enemy, imposing as much delay and damage as possible. Beckoning to Hamer to join him, Shepstone yanked his horse around and was gone. The two men set a furious pace for the notch in the Nyoni Ridge. It was whilst the amaNgwane horsemen were in the low-lying ground at the foot of Mabaso, concentrating on the enemy to their front, that the two regimental columns of the right horn descended from the Ngedla Heights unseen. By the time Barton, Raw and Roberts had broken clean to the west, gaining a little height in the process, the two *amabutho* were themselves in low-lying ground to the north and north-east of Mkwene Hill, pushing hard for the Manzimyama Valley. Thus, due to the lie of the land, the NNMC officers were oblivious to the presence of a significant enemy force ahead of them. Fortunately for Zikhali's Horse both sides were moving in broadly the same direction and were destined not to come to blows by virtue of the intervening distance.

If the quality of the shooting amongst the amaNgwane was indifferent, the sound of synchronised volley firing drifting down from the hills, did at least serve to give early warning to the camp. It was an unmistakeable sound and could only indicate the onset of a general action. As yet, it was still some considerable distance away, and since the men were already fully armed and equipped, Pulleine did not immediately sound the alarm.

Mehlokazulu, who left the most valuable account of the battle from a Zulu perspective, stated that the horsemen on the plateau halted in the path of the chest four times. He also recalled that there were two troops of blacks and one of whites, falling back in front of the *amabutho*. Clearly then, Lieutenant Durrant Scott and his vedettes were also caught up in the action at this time. During the course of the morning, Scott seems to have been reinforced by an additional party of mounted volunteers; it is not known whether Captain Bradstreet sent them out at his own initiative, or whether it was at Pulleine's instigation. Including his original parties of vedettes, he probably now had around thirty carbineers and police under his command. Whatever task they had been engaged in when contact was made, they were now withdrawing in the face of the *impi*, along the top of the escarpment.

With the chest and horns safely launched, Ntshingwayo could now release the *amabutho* of the reserve. A Zulu source:

> The Undi Corps [consisting of the uThulwana, iNdluyengwe, and iNdlondlo] and the uDloko formed a circle and remained where they were. With the latter were the two commanders Mavumengwana and Ntshingwayo, and several of the king's brothers, who with these *amabutho* bore away to the north-west, after a short pause, and keeping on the northern side of Isandlwana performed a turning movement on the right without any opposition from the whites, who from the nature of the ground could not see

them.

Durnford Makes Contact with the Left Horn

Riding at the head of the Edendale and Basuto Troops, Durnford was over two kilometres beyond Itusi Hill when he heard the sound of firing. He had just crossed a big donga running down off the eastern face of the escarpment, and was on a flat, open part of the plain, with the high ground a few hundred metres to his left, and Qwabe Hill a similar distance to his right rear. About a kilometre ahead, the escarpment curved across his path. Importantly, he was about seven kilometres from Isandlwana, and invisible to Pulleine. Two hard-riding carbineers suddenly appeared over the edge of the escarpment from the left and raced for the head of the column. Reining in beside Durnford, the men said that they had a message from Lieutenant Scott: the colonel should turn about immediately, as the enemy was advancing in force and he was in danger of being surrounded. Lieutenant Harry Davies recalled that Durnford snapped back, 'The enemy can't surround us and if they do we will cut our way through them.' It was an unduly hard response to two enlisted men trying merely to do their duty; it was also wholly unrealistic.

Turning to his officers, Durnford asked where the rocket battery was. Davies replied that it had fallen behind and was no longer in sight. Next, Durnford expressed frustration that his scouts seemed to have disappeared. With the firing above the escarpment increasing in intensity, he must now have been having second thoughts about the viability of his plan. Turning back to the two carbineers, he instructed them to ride back to Scott and tell him to bring his men down to the Qwabe Valley, to marry up with his own command. The carbineers had seen the enemy array with their own eyes and this was clearly nonsensical rubbish. Given their rate of advance and great strength, there was every probability that Scott was no longer where they had last seen him. To save themselves being sent back into the path of the *impi*, one of the carbineers proffered a thinly disguised excuse, saying that Scott would not come, as he had been given strict orders by Pulleine not to leave his post 'on any pretext whatsoever'. Durnford replied, 'I am Colonel Pulleine's senior; you will please tell Lieutenant Scott to do as I tell him.' His irritability and insecurity are only too apparent in these words.

The carbineers were saved from a fruitless and dangerous journey by the timely re-appearance of the scouts, followed a little under a kilometre away, by the van of the left horn, already spilling in a wide black tide over the edge of the escarpment. For Durnford and his officers, there were a few moments of stunned contemplation, as the uVe and the left wing of the iNgobamakhosi fanned themselves out on the move. The Zulus had closed to 800 yards, when wisps of smoke indicated that they had opened fire. At such a range their fire was bound to be ineffective. Untroubled by incoming rounds, Durnford ordered his men to fall back to the donga, a few hundred metres to their rear.

The NNC Flee the Plateau

Originally well to the rear of Zikhali's Horse, Captain Barry's company was now squarely in the path of their retreat. The amaChunu had been reduced to a state of abject terror at the sight of the great dark shadows spilling over Mabaso Ridge ahead of them and the Ngedla Heights two kilometres to their left rear. There was nothing they could usefully do to dispute the advance of such strong forces; even to attempt resistance would be suicidal. Accordingly, Barry and his Europeans had no chance of preventing the spontaneous flight of their men. In twos and threes and sixes, the amaChunu fled back in the direction of Mkwene Hill, where they knew there was a footpath leading down to the sanctuary of the camp. Barry and his company second-in-command, Lieutenant the Honourable William Vereker, were without horses and may have struggled to get off the plateau, had it not been for the timely arrival of Lieutenant Higginson and Sergeant-Major Williams. Higginson felt the need to ride post-haste back to the camp, either simply to rejoin Captain Krohn and No. 6 Company, or to convey a warning to Pulleine. He instructed Williams to bring the other two officers to safety as best he could. Williams took one of them up behind him, and trotted off with the second officer jogging alongside, hanging on to a stirrup. When the man on foot was exhausted, they would quickly change places, and in this way Williams would get both men safely back to the camp.

Captain Edward Erskine had not been back on Mkwene Hill for very long. From his familiar vantage point, he had a good view of the developing situation and knew that his first problem would be keeping No. 4 Company in hand, when Barry's men ran past, babbling in their native tongue that all was lost. To the north he could see the two *amabutho* of the Zulu right horn descending the Ngedla Heights. To Erskine's intense relief, they made no move on Mkwene, but instead swung to the west, following the line of the stream. If the regiments continued on their current course, they would pass well to the north of his outpost and plunge into the valleys leading to the rear of Isandlwana. Their route was certain to expose them to the fire of the 24th company on the spur. Some way to the north-east, however, the uNokhenke and the umCijo were steering a direct collision course for Mkwene Hill. Erskine decided to pre-empt the arrival of Barry's men, and that of the enemy, by withdrawing immediately to the spur. The intervening downhill kilometre was covered quickly. At the foot of the slope, Erskine positioned his nervous levies on Cavaye's right.

Durnford's Withdrawal

As Durnford reined in at the big donga in the Qwabe Valley,* his men threw themselves from the saddle and dashed to line its eastern edge. The uVe were coming on at full tilt, but Durnford knew the limitations of the cavalry carbine well, and waited for them to close to 400 yards before unleashing a volley. A shudder ran through the regiment as the rounds struck home, spilling a number of warriors into the grass. A second volley followed, but the Zulus were already thrown out over a much wider frontage than two troops of irregular cavalry could ever hope to cope with, so that there could be no question of standing fast. Moments later, the troopers were hauling themselves back into the saddle, to gallop clear of the donga. Inevitably such a scrambled withdrawal caused a degree of confusion, but as they rode back down the valley, the men ejected the spent rounds from their weapons and steered their ponies back into an evenly spaced skirmish line. This was a drill they had practised repeatedly under Durnford's watchful eye, and they knew they would be ordered to dismount a little further down the valley. Sure enough, after a short gallop Durnford reined in again, and wheeled his horse round to face the enemy.

Taking their cue from the colonel, Henderson and Davies swung into line on either side of him, the Edendale Troop to his left and the Basutos to his right. Working in groups of four, three men sprang to the ground with their carbines, quickly passed the reins over the heads of their ponies, and placed their animals in the safekeeping of the fourth man. The horse-

---

* Visitors to the battlefield should note that this donga is now much deeper than in 1879.

holders then wheeled a few yards to the rear. Durnford kept his nerve and then some. First, he found time to shout orders to the two lieutenants: when he gave the word, they were to retire down the valley by alternate troops. When the Zulus had again closed up to 400 yards, all seventy-five carbines were discharged as one, causing the ponies to spin, rear and whinny. The horse-holders worked hard to calm the momentary panic and, above all else, keep a firm grip on the reins. Again the dismounted troopers raced for their animals and vaulted back into the saddle. Durnford led off at a canter. This was good flat ground, free of the scree-boulders that were such a hindrance to mounted troops elsewhere in the area, so that before very long the uVe and iNgobamakhosi had been safely outdistanced.

The Second Alarm

Captain Alan Gardner and his companions were even now trotting into the camp from the plain, with Chelmsford's orders. They found the place astir, with a great many men standing in huddles, looking intently in the direction of the distant firing. As Gardner headed for the 1st/24th lines in search of Pulleine, the rest of the party dispersed to their units: Major Smith to take over N Battery from Curling; Dyer and Griffith to join Pope at the 2nd Battalion camp; the ten men of the IMI escort to join their mates in the cavalry lines. Moments before Gardner arrived in the 1st Battalion camp, Shepstone and Hamer clattered in from the opposite direction and threw themselves from the saddle. The first person they met was James Brickhill, the interpreter. Shepstone gasped Pulleine's name and Brickhill quickly led him in the right direction. One of the 24th officers drew the colonel's attention to their arrival, and Pulleine emerged from his tent to meet them. Shepstone was completely winded by his frantic gallop and at first could only gasp and gesticulate incoherently.

At precisely that moment Alan Gardner trotted up, saluted, and handed over the GOC's orders. Brickhill tells us that Pulleine read the note aloud. Its verbatim contents are lost to history, but Brickhill recalled:

> It was an order to strike camp and come on at full speed, leaving a sufficient guard behind to protect such portion as could not be moved without delay.

At the subsequent board of inquiry, Gardner testified that it was an order to:

> . . . strike that part of the camp belonging to the troops with Lord
> Chelmsford and send it on with certain stores.

He specified that the stores at issue were seven days worth of rations and
forage. These are damning words, indicating as they do that Chelmsford
was prepared to divide his force for a sustained period.

The contents of the note would certainly have taken Pulleine by
surprise, and probably caused him considerable consternation. It was
already noon, and any order to pack a portion of the camp and move it
twenty kilometres before sunset, really needed to have come by mid-
morning at the very latest. It was going to be a problem. The firing beyond
the escarpment meant that he was in no position to comply immediately,
and seemed, whatever its cause, to bespeak even further delay. Pulleine
was probably quick to realise that he had been given an unachievable task.
Brickhill remarked in his account that Pulleine looked 'totally nonplussed
as to what he ought to do'. Indeed, as well he might.

By now Shepstone had regained his composure and made an urgent
interjection. 'I am not an alarmist sir, but the Zulus are in such black
masses over there, such long black lines, that you will have to give us all
the assistance you can. They are fast driving our men this way.' 'Under
the circumstances,' said Gardner, 'I should advise your disobeying the
general's orders, for the present at any rate. The general knows nothing
of this. He is only thinking of the cowardly way in which the Zulus are
running before our troops over yonder.'* Pulleine told Melvill to have the
alarm sounded. Shepstone and Hamer mounted up to ride back to Barton.
Just then, Vause's troop came cantering over the saddle, with Stafford's
company and Durnford's wagons strung out in their train. Vause had
heard the firing from the plateau and had come on at a trot in search of
his colonel. This was a timely reinforcement and Shepstone dashed back
along the column, to harry Stafford's men up over the saddle.† Hamer
would have done better at this juncture to remain with the wagons and
attend to the availability of No. 2 Column's reserve ammunition, but
crucially, he failed to do so.

The troops in camp had been anticipating an alarm for some minutes,

---

* Meaning the Zulus at Mangeni/Phindo.

† Cochrane was unaware of Shepstone's role on the plateau and mistakenly believed that
he had gone back for the wagons with Vause.

so that the notes of the bugle call came as no surprise. Their response was quick and slick. In only a couple of minutes, the four 1st Battalion companies still in camp were formed and marching towards G Company on the 2nd Battalion parade ground, exactly as before. As all the horses in camp had been kept harnessed and saddled since the 10.30 a.m. stand down, both Bradstreet's mounted troops and Curling's gunners were as quick to their muster points as the 24th. In the N Battery lines, Major Smith quickly took charge, pausing only long enough to exchange his weary charger, 'Black Eagle', for a fresh horse, before then trotting off with Curling's division to join the infantry. In the few minutes it took the troops to assemble, Pulleine and Gardner withdrew into the colonel's tent to draft a reply to Chelmsford. Pressed for time and aware that he must immediately turn his attention to the tactical situation, Pulleine again adopted the same peremptory style that had characterised his earlier note:

> Staff Officer. Heavy firing to left of camp. Cannot move camp at present. H B Pulleine, Lt Col.

It is usually assumed by historians that Pulleine fought his battle from a command post amongst the tents, but this is highly improbable. His style of command will be examined in some detail in the next chapter. For the time being, suffice it to say that it is far more likely that he and his adjutant mounted and rode down to join the troops on the parade ground, and that they remained mobile throughout the ensuing action. With no other particular function to perform, Coghill and Dyer probably joined Pulleine to act as additional aides. Aware that the colonel had been in a hurry, Gardner held the galloper for a moment longer and wrote his own note in further amplification of the situation. He, too, was forced to rush the job as he had been specifically instructed by Pulleine to remain with him as an aide, and would have to catch up with the colonel quickly:

> Heavy firing to the left of the camp. Shepstone has come in for reinforcements and reports that the Basutos are falling back. The whole force at camp turned out and fighting about one mile to left flank.

All of a sudden, the troops in the camp heard the unmistakeable crash of a regular infantry volley. Then came another. E Company had come into action on the spur, and if Cavaye was firing company volleys it could only mean that he was engaging a substantial Zulu force. It served to verify everything Shepstone had said. Glancing to the north, Pulleine and the other officers could now see Barry's amaChunu making their panicky flight down from the escarpment.

Cavaye Comes into Action Against the Right Horn

At the sound of firing to the north-east, Cavaye stood his men to. They were soon disposed on a firing line along the crest of the spur, where they knelt in the cover of the larger boulders. Sergeants Thomas Fay, John Edwards and George Bennett strode up and down behind their sections, ensuring that everything was in good order. One of these three would have been out on the extreme left with young Mister Dyson. The terrified crowd of amaChunu infantry, Barry's men, were soon streaming down the path on Cavaye's right, intent only on finding sanctuary somewhere to the rear. Probably many of their kinsmen also deserted Erskine at this juncture. Then, a thousand yards to Cavaye's front, one of the regiments of the Zulu right horn appeared, jogging along the line of the stream in the direction of the Manzimyama Valley. Although the warriors were squarely in E Company's sights, they were passing across the front of the firing line from right to left, making no attempt to close with it. A range setting was quickly bellowed out, and with the words of command 'Ready . . . Present!' Cavaye initiated the first of the many thunderous volleys fired by the 24th Regiment that day. The men quickly loaded, raised their rifles to the shoulder on the executive 'Present', took aim whilst counting in their heads the British infantry's regulation pause of 'two – three,' and then squeezed their triggers as one. The noise of the volley was deafening; E Company's position was instantly wreathed in a cloud of white smoke, but the men were well dispersed and there was only brief obscuration of the target. The rounds struck home in the massed target presented by the right horn, leaving a number of broken bodies sprawled beneath the jogging feet of their comrades. As the redcoats thumbed fresh cartridges into the breech, they were expecting the Zulus to begin wheeling towards them. To everybody's surprise, the enemy paid them no attention whatsoever. Cavaye's voice came again to those nearest him, the sergeants echoing his words of command up and down the line. Another thundering volley, and still the right horn raced on, with no change of direction towards the spur.

Pulleine Deploys the Guns and Infantry

On his way out of camp, Major Russell had quickly realised that Durnford had no intention of being slowed down by the plodding mules of the rocket battery. The colonel had set a pace that the battery had no hope of matching. Russell watched Durnford ride to the right or south side of Amatutshane, and then disappear on a left oblique towards the Qwabe Valley. It has been suggested that Russell realised he could cut a corner, if he went not to the right of Amatutshane as Durnford had done, but to the left. This would keep him close to the foot of the escarpment and take him on a more direct line for the Qwabe Valley. This was not the case, however. He went to the south of Amatutshane, exactly as Durnford had done. Not long afterwards, an outbreak of firing from the direction of the escarpment indicated that Zikhali's Horse was in contact.

With heavy firing going on along the length of the escarpment, Pulleine could no longer be in any doubt that a significant attack was underway, even if it had not yet manifested itself in plain view. He made three fresh deployments on this basis. Firstly, in order to help Durnford's command extricate itself, he ordered Major Smith to deploy the guns into a forward position on the rocky ridge. From here they would be able to cover the entire length of the escarpment, and could fire in support of Durnford's troops as they fell back on the camp. The guns could not be left unprotected, so Degacher's A Company would go out to the ridge to support them. The third deployment was made in support of Cavaye: Captain William Mostyn was told to take F Company, 1st/24th, to the top of the spur.

Pulleine has been repeatedly criticised for his decision to reinforce Cavaye. Typically, the deployment is portrayed as further foolish scattering of the troops by the British. In fact, it was a perfectly understandable reaction to the situation as Pulleine read it at the time, and most battalion commanders would have done the same thing. Armies are not generally in the business of abandoning their forward positions as soon as firing breaks out; least of all is the British Army prone to such faint-hearted practice. Rather, the inclination will always be to support the forward troops. Armies only generally start moving backwards when they are forced to do so by enemy action. This is at the very heart of the psychology of warfare. He who fights and runs away will indeed live to fight another day, but sooner or later he is going to lose the war. Pulleine's critics, not normally military men, have completely missed the relevance of the fact that everybody in the camp, the colonel included, could see and hear Cavaye in action, but could not see his target. As far as Pulleine was concerned, E Company was under direct frontal attack on the spur, not merely firing on a passing target at long range. It was absolutely the doctrinal norm in 1879 for the battalion commander to send forward 'supports' to thicken up the forward firing line. It was then up to the forward company commanders to decide whether to hold their ground, or fall back to the main position. By reinforcing Cavaye, Pulleine was merely broadening his subordinate's tactical options. With two companies on the high ground, an attempt could be made to hold the spur, and if, in the event, the position proved untenable, then far better that two companies were present to support each other in an orderly withdrawal, than that one company should be left to its own devices. With two companies leapfrogging back alternately, a bold front can be maintained at all times, and any enemy pursuit can be driven to ground with fire. Pulleine's decision must be seen in the context in which it was made and not with the benefit of hindsight. In the event, no harm would come of the deployment to the Tahelane Spur, as the companies would withdraw successfully to protect the north end of the camp, a crucial task which would have been a necessary part of any defence plan. The criticism of Pulleine on this particular point is one of the great red herrings of the Isandlwana debate.

Not long after Cavaye came into action, Scott and his *ad hoc* troop of police and carbineers came galloping down the notch at breakneck speed. They were accompanied by some of Raw's troop, who had also been driven in the same direction. At the foot of the escarpment, they rode through the No. 9 Company picket line. No doubt Scott reined in to advise Captain James Lonsdale to get the hell out of it. Nobody had seen fit to give Lonsdale any orders, so that his isiGqoza were still spread out between Amatutshane and the escarpment. Cavaye's volleying and the indecent haste with which the mounted troops had come through were more than enough to persuade Lonsdale that Scott's advice was sound. Since matters were clearly hotting up, he contracted his line and fell back in the direction of the rocky ridge, where he could now see some of the regular infantry and the artillery moving up to adopt battle positions. Scott quickly moved on to rally his scattered troopers. When they had gathered around him to listen to his instructions, some of them told him that they would soon need a replenishment of carbine cartridges. Scott detailed a number of men to gallop back to the camp and fetch more rounds from Quartermaster London. He then led the balance of his troop in the direction of the rocky ridge, to await the imminent arrival of the regulars.

It is Scott's withdrawal that allows us to deduce that Russell did not in fact take the rocket battery through the short cut to the north of Amatutshane. If he had done so, he would have met Scott and his men coming the other way, and the encounter would have been recorded in the sources.* Indeed, Scott would have prevented Russell from pushing on, as there was now nothing between him and the enemy. Scott cannot have descended any later than this, or he would have been behind the skirmishers of the Zulu chest, and under fire from the artillery. So at the exact moment Scott galloped down from the high ground, Russell was to the south of Amatutshane, screened from the notch by the koppie itself. Only once he had rounded it to the east, did Russell change direction for the escarpment. He did so in response to the firing he had first heard whilst blind-sided to the south. This is the only way in which the paths of Scott and Russell can be reconciled.

Events on the Tahelane Spur

Captain Edward Essex was writing in his tent when Cavaye opened fire. He must have been concentrating hard on his correspondence, as he does not seem to have heard the first few volleys. A passing sergeant popped his head into the tent and told him that the infantry had come into action on the escarpment. Essex decided at once to ride out to the scene of the action:

> I had my glasses on my shoulder and thought I might as well take my revolver; but did not trouble to put on my sword, as I thought nothing of the matter and expected to be back in half an hour to complete my letters.

Captain William Mostyn was afoot alongside his men, doubling them up the path to the spur, when Essex trotted up alongside him. Barry's amaChunu were long gone, but now significant numbers of Zikhali's Horse

---

* In particular Captain Nourse, and Privates Grant, Trainer and Johnson, who were survivors from the rocket battery.

were riding down in the opposite direction. Essex had no particular business to be out there with the forward troops, but like most officers of the Victorian army, he felt the need to be in the thick of things. Mostyn asked him to ride on ahead, to warn Cavaye that he intended to bring F Company up on his left. This would place Mostyn and his men between Cavaye's main body and the detached section under Dyson. It would also mean that 150 of the 24th's Martinis would be in action on the spur, a significant amount of firepower, which it would be difficult for the Zulu to dislodge. Essex spurred on to deliver the message. He recalled that a few moments later:

> Captain Mostyn moved his company into the space between the portions of that already on the hill, and his men then extended and entered into action. This line was then prolonged on our right along the crest of the hill by a body of native infantry [Erskine's company]. I observed that the enemy made little progress as regards his advance, but appeared to be moving at a rapid pace towards our left. The right extremity of the enemy's line was very thin, but increased in depth towards and beyond our right as far as I could see, a hill [Mkwene] interfering with extended view.

Concurrent with Mostyn's move to the spur and Scott's descent through the notch, Smith and Curling trotted out of camp for the left end of the rocky ridge, where there were many fewer boulders and the guns could pass without damage or mishap. The gun-position selected by Smith was on a flat piece of ground just above the upper reaches of the Nyogane Donga. Twelve hundred metres to the front, Amatutshane cut out the view in the direction of the Qwabe Valley, but otherwise the position offered an excellent field of fire. This was especially true in the direction of Itusi Hill and the notch just to the left of it – the best enemy avenue of approach to the low ground by far. Whilst Curling wheeled his guns into position and began to unlimber, Smith scanned for targets. He noted Lonsdale's isiGqoza jogging back across the bowl towards him, but of much greater interest were the parties of Zulu skirmishers appearing at the top of the notch. Smith ordered the gun crews to prepare to come into action at a range of 3,000 yards.

Cantering their ponies just ahead of the enormous Zulu host, and turning occasionally to fire from the saddle, Zikhali's Horse had been comprehensively scattered during their seven-kilometre withdrawal. In vindication of amaNgwane horsemanship, though, they had suffered barely any casualties. Most of Roberts's men, and some of Raw's, stuck to the advancing Zulu chest, falling back in the path of the uNokhenke and the umCijo, all the way to Mkwene Hill. As we have seen, the balance of No. 1 Troop had been driven back not to the vicinity of Mkwene but to the notch, where in company with Durrant Scott's men, they made a rapid descent to the plain. Perhaps two-thirds of the hundred or so troopers who had set off from Mkwene, made it back there. Some of these men now dismounted to fight from the crest, whilst others, more faint-hearted than their comrades, followed the example of Barry's amaChunu and fled to the foot of the escarpment, passing Essex and F Company on the way up. The men who tarried on the hill had a spectacular view out across the advance of the Zulu chest. Some 2,000 warriors of the uNokhenke were now only just over three kilometres away, heading straight for Mkwene and closing the distance fast. The regimental main body was preceded by bands of skirmishers, who were considerably closer. There was very little point in hanging around any longer, so these men now also fell back on Mostyn and Cavaye. It was probably just as well that the men down on the spur could not see what the amaNgwane had seen.

Shepstone, meanwhile, had arrived at the foot of the spur at the head of Vause's No. 3 Troop and Stafford's E Company. In as much as he had a plan at all, it was to support the redcoat infantry on the crest as best he could. He would do this by moving the native troops to the flanks of the regulars in the approved fashion. As Edward Erskine's No. 4 Company was now on the right of Cavaye, Stafford was sent to take post on Mostyn's left. Shepstone and Vause would take the amaNgwane horsemen of No. 3 Troop further to the right of Erskine. On their way up the slope, the officers rallied some of Raw's and Roberts's men and led them back uphill. As he neared the crest, Vause told off horse-holders to stay in the cover of the reverse slope, before leading the rest of his command forward to join the firing line. In all the British now had anything up to 500 men deployed on the spur. From left to right, the skirmish line consisted of: Dyson and twenty men of E Company, 1st/24th; Stafford and around 150 amaNgwane levies of E Company, 1st/1st NNC; Mostyn and seventy-five men of F Company, 1st/24th; Cavaye and the balance of around fifty men of E Company, 1st/24th; Erskine with seventy to a hundred amaChunu infantry; and finally, on the extreme right, Shepstone and Vause with about eighty men of Zikhali's Horse. A further score of amaNgwane troopers were holding horses behind the line.

Soon after Vause arrived on the extreme right, Mkwene Hill fell to the skirmishers of the uNokhenke. There was a sharp exchange of fire between the hill and the spur, so that for a short while at least, the troops on the spur found themselves involved in two simultaneous but ultimately indecisive skirmishes. As the two companies of the 24th continued to volley at long range into what were now the rearmost elements of the uNodwengu Corps, the native horse to their right were engaged over a much shorter distance with the skirmishers of the right flank regiment of the chest.

Essex attached himself to the 24th and soon found himself fulfilling the role of a company officer, directing the men's fire and shouting encouragement. He recalled later, that the native troops to the right of the line, 'blazed away at an absurd rate'. This can only have been a reference to the fire of Vause's command against Mkwene Hill. His remark offers us an interesting glimpse of the standard of musketry in the troops of native horse; their fire discipline was poor, but this is hardly surprising of newly raised troops operating without a leavening of experienced NCOs. When the last of the right horn warriors disappeared into dead ground to the half-left of the infantry, Mostyn and Cavaye gave the order to cease fire.

Although it was certainly an inadvisable thing to do, Shepstone and Vause had decided in the meantime to mount a counter-attack against Mkwene Hill. The dismounted amaNgwane troopers pressed the attack gamely, skirmishing forward in bounds, and maintaining a heavy covering fire. Sky-lined on the crest as they were, and with their regimental main body only a few minutes away, the Zulu riflemen saw little point in disputing possession of Mkwene at the cost of their lives. Thus it took Shepstone and Vause only a few minutes to regain the high ground. The uNokhenke skirmishers fell back ahead of them, knowing full well that the 2,000 men just to their rear would shortly put the issue beyond doubt. When Shepstone and Vause saw what lay beyond the hill, they ordered an immediate withdrawal back to the horses. The troopers of Zikhali's Horse came running back down the hill considerably faster than they had gone up it.

Destruction of the Rocket Battery

In the Qwabe Valley, Durnford's command had gone into the cavalry battle drill of withdrawal by alternate troops. As Henderson's Basutos leapt to the ground and handed over their animals to the horse-holders, Davies's Edendale Troop cantered past their flank and rode back a further 200 yards, where they, too, began to dismount. The Basutos had fired their volley and were remounting, as the feet of the Edendale men touched the ground. By the time the Edendale troopers had steadied themselves in the aim, the Basutos were galloping past the right of their line, heading for a new position a further 200 yards to the rear. So it continued, back down the length of the valley. The withdrawal was disciplined, controlled and calm. If Anthony Durnford had a moment of military glory, it was this fifteen minutes in the Qwabe Valley. Ultimately, though, as the senior officer in the field, he was failing in his duty; he would have been much better advised to break clean and ride back to the camp at best speed, in order to agree a co-ordinated defence plan with Pulleine.

On the eastern side of Amatutshane, out of sight of just about everything happening around him, Russell's powers of judgement were about to fail him badly. He had decided to move up through the notch to the high ground. In order to get the mules up, it would be necessary to lighten their loads; a number of Nourse's levies were called forward to act as porters. During this delay, two carbineers rode up to speak to Russell. Private Johnson thought that they were offering to show him a good route up to the high ground. In fact, the two carbineers were Troopers Barker and Hawkins, and in Barker's version of the encounter he claims that they advised Russell to turn back. However good the advice was, such a course of action was entirely at odds with the major's orders from Durnford. Russell decided that the best thing he could do was to check the situation above the escarpment for himself, so leaving the battery where it was, he spurred up his horse and rode on alone.

With A Company, 1st/24th, moving forward to the support of the guns, Pulleine was left with C and H Companies of the 1st Battalion and G Company of the 2nd Battalion still in reserve, in front of the camp. It took Degacher only a few minutes to catch up with the guns. He quickly fanned his men out left and right of them, in an extended-order skirmish line. As the 24th were taking post, the 7-pounders came into action against

* A remark which has been repeatedly misinterpreted to mean that a body of NNC was formed up in front of the guns as part of the firing line. Not so.

the notch. A warrior of the umCijo called Uguku, said that the first rounds landed amongst his *ibutho*. In fact, as is so often the case, the first ranging salvo dropped short. Brickhill saw the rounds, 'burst half way, nearly over our native foot contingent'* – a lucky escape for Lonsdale's men as they were doubling back to the rocky ridge. Just to the right of the notch, the lower slopes of Amatutshane denied Degacher and Smith any view of what was happening to Russell and Nourse. Over their left shoulders, the volume of fire from the spur suddenly doubled – this was Mostyn's company coming into action.

Russell was only halfway up the notch, when Smith's second salvo found the range and exploded a few hundred yards to his front. Clearly he could not continue in this direction any longer. Of more immediate concern was the target of the guns; dozens of Zulu skirmishers had appeared in the notch and were now pushing rapidly downhill, posing a very real threat to the rocket battery at its foot. Turning rapidly about, Russell galloped back to his men shouting, 'Action front!' Bombardier George Goff and the eight 24th men immediately sprang into action, racing to set up the rocket troughs where they stood. The Hale's 9-pounder rocket was about a foot long and three inches in diameter. It was fired from a V-shaped steel trough, supported by a pair of bipod legs; effectively it was a precursor of the modern mortar. To the rear of the battery, Nourse's company had been seized with panic: the majority of his levies took to their heels as soon as the Zulus were sighted. Nourse himself and a handful of his more resolute NCOs and amaNgwane riflemen, loosed off a ragged fusillade of shots. In the meantime, one of the rocket troughs had been readied to fire. At Russell's order, one of the men tugged hard at the lanyard, and sent the round screeching away to explode against the face of the escarpment.

Under fire from Nourse, and perhaps startled by the noise and sparks of the rocket, the Zulu skirmishers took cover amongst the rocks. They were probably within a hundred yards of the rocket troughs when they opened fire. It was a devastatingly effective volley: Russell was badly wounded and reeled from the saddle; five of the 24th men were hit and the frightened mules were scattered in all directions. In that brief moment, the rocket battery ceased to exist. Bombardier Goff and Privates Hector Grant, William Johnson and James Trainer were the only men to survive

* Curling.

unscathed. Private Johnson ran to Russell's aid and began to help him away, but before they had gone more than a few paces, the major was hit again and killed. Johnson then ran in the direction of the few remaining members of Nourse's company, only to find that a number of the riflemen were struggling to eject the spent cartridges from their rifles, a damning indictment on the state of the NNC's training. In fairness this was probably the first time they had fired them. Johnson offered to assist, but none of the levies would hand over their weapons. More of them turned and fled, until only Nourse himself and five others remained, blazing away with their Martinis as rapidly as they could load and fire. Under the cover of their desperate fusillade, Johnson ran off in the direction of Amatutshane. Trainer, too, got away on foot, whilst Grant, who had been holding a number of mules as the battery came into action, was able to escape on one of them, in company with Bombardier Goff.

Pulleine's Battle Plan

Pulleine could now see much larger bodies of Zulus appearing above the notch. The 7-pounders had found the range, and were playing on them effectively enough as they came up, but they were still well outside the range of Degacher's infantry. Strangely, they then appeared to come to a halt.* Occasional glimpses of a significant movement along the top of the escarpment to the west, indicated a developing danger of the troops on the spur being attacked in force from their right. Any large-scale Zulu descent through the notch to the plain also had the potential to cut the men on the spur off from the camp. The time had come to establish a coherent defensive perimeter with which to shield the tents and wagons at the foot of Isandlwana. Pulleine knew that he had only moments left in which to finalise his battle plan. His snap decision was to establish a battalion firing line just to the north of the camp, and at a right angle to it. The left flank would be anchored on Isandlwana and the right on Amatutshane. Any enemy descent from the escarpment would be defeated with volley fire in the open killing area at the foot of the high ground. It was time to get the companies moving.

Pulleine decided to commit H and G Companies to the right flank. They were to occupy the sector beyond Degacher and the guns, and would have a key part to play in blocking the seemingly imminent attack down through the notch. Captain George Wardell was ordered to double H Company forward, to take post immediately to Degacher's right. This would leave him extended down the forward slope of the rocky ridge, between the guns and the Nyogane Donga. Next, Pulleine was alongside Charlie Pope. He was to follow H Company down to the rocky ridge and, once Wardell had wheeled left into line, he was to extend G Company out as far as the lower slopes of Amatutshane. Turning next to Melvill, Pulleine instructed him to ride hard for the spur, to recall the troops there to the close defence of the camp. Finally, Pulleine sent Captain Reginald Young-husband to the left with C Company. His orders were to anchor the left flank on Isandlwana, and be prepared to cover the withdrawal of Cavaye and Mostyn with fire. When E and F Companies fell back, they would slot into the gap between Younghusband and Degacher. These four companies would cover the left and centre. With all the companies in motion towards their battle positions, the parade ground in front of the tents was suddenly deserted. One of the officers with Pulleine rode down to Stuart Smith, to tell him to bring one of the guns about and cover the withdrawal from Tahelane. For the next few minutes, on opposite sides of the battlefield, the Zulu indunas and the British company commanders were engaged in the same activity; all were urging their men to make haste to their designated battle positions for the imminent clash of arms.

The Zulu Formation

The *amabutho* of the Zulu chest were made up of young men in the prime of life, and were closing fast on Isandlwana across the plateau. On the outside right of the great arc, the 2,000 30-year-olds of the uNokhenke had been launched into battle knowing that they had farthest to go. Advancing rapidly, they covered the extra distance to Mkwene Hill and the spur a few minutes before the other three regiments reached the escarpment. To the left of the uNokhenke, the 2,500 28-year-olds of the umCijo were now wheeling by their left flank in order to hit the escarpment between Mkwene Hill and the notch. Heading for the notch itself, was the 32-year-old uMbonambi regiment, fielding some 1,500 men. On the left side of the chest was the iNgobamakhosi, a huge body of around 6,000 24-year-olds. Its indunas had been forced by the real estate problem to split their men between the plateau and the Qwabe Valley. The right wing of the regiment was heading for the notch behind the uMbonambi, whilst the left had descended into the low ground to chase after Durnford on the right of the uVe. With well over 3,000 23-year-olds jogging along in the left horn, the uVe was the second largest regiment in the field.

Withdrawal from the Spur

When Melvill arrived at the top of the spur, it was to find that Edward Essex was the only other mounted regular officer present. Reining in beside him, Melvill asked him to ride to the left, passing the word to withdraw as he went: Melvill himself would go to the right. It was about now that one of the 7-pounders started firing in this direction: the target at this stage can only have been Mkwene Hill and the approach to it from the east. Mostyn's F Company had been on the ridge for as little as ten minutes when the order to withdraw came; Shepstone, Stafford and Vause for about the same length of time. Whilst Mostyn had been in action for only about half this period, the native horse had been firing throughout. As short a time as this was, it had been more than long enough for the native troopers seriously to deplete the ammunition in their bandoliers. Essex kept riding until he reached young Dyson. By the time he turned back for the centre, everybody else had slipped away down the reverse slope. Looking over the lip, Essex could see the E and F Company redcoats scrambling down through the rocks, with Stafford's and Erskine's native infantry scattered ahead of them. The amaNgwane had retrieved their ponies from the horse-holders, and were similarly making for the low ground, mixed up amongst the 24th. Finding himself alone, and with the uNokhenke regiment now pushing in strength from behind and over Mkwene Hill, Essex nudged his horse gingerly down through the boulders. There is some suspicion that, at about this time, Lieutenant Joseph Roberts of No. 2 Troop was killed by friendly fire from the artillery.

At the foot of the spur, there was momentary confusion and plenty of shouting, as the officers and NCOs of E and F Companies re-formed their men along a new firing line, facing back uphill. These were a dangerous few moments. Order was restored quickly, however, and the withdrawal continued safely towards the camp. Shepstone, Vause and Raw dismounted their men near the head of the Nyogane Donga, a little over 200 metres from the foot of Mkwene Hill. It may be safely assumed that Dyson took the opportunity to double his section through Mostyn's men, to rejoin his own company. Echeloned about 300 metres to the left rear of E and F Companies was Younghusband's C Company, ready, as Pulleine had instructed, to fire in support of the other companies as they withdrew. Though parties of the uNokhenke pressed forward to occupy the spur almost as soon as it was abandoned, from where they opened a heavy fire, there was no immediate large-scale pursuit. When E and F Companies came level with Younghusband's right, Mostyn and Cavaye halted their men and shuffled them left and right, until they had the gap between Younghusband and Degacher covered.

Few of the NNC rallied at the foot of Tahelane. Rather, they fled back to the northern edge of the NNC encampments where Krohn's and Murray's companies were still formed up in reserve. Probably the officers and NCOs of these companies were instrumental in arresting the further flight of Erskine's and Stafford's men. They may have waved pistols about to stop the rot, but would not have been universally successful. Looking back over their shoulders, and seeing that there was no pursuit, most of the levies hesitated long enough for their leaders to get amongst them and rally them. As ever the principal means of doing so was physical violence or the threat of it.

It is important in comprehending the course of the Battle of Isandlwana, to understand that, notwithstanding all the excitement on the Tahelane Spur, the action here amounted to no more than a minor skirmish. True, the 24th companies had fired at long range on two regiments of the right horn, a significant body of not less than 3,000 warriors, but this force did not swing at the spur, and the British were not driven from their position there. They withdrew out of concern for their flanks, a threat which did not ultimately unfold in any meaningful way due to the timeliness of the withdrawal. Barely any British casualties had yet been sustained in the action, but neither had very much damage been done to the right horn.

The Firing Line

All six companies of the 24th were now disposed along a battalion firing line, stretching from Isandlwana on the left, to Amatutshane on the right. It was facing northwards, directly towards the line of the escarpment. It will be beneficial to recap the British dispositions briefly at this stage. On the left flank, closest to Isandlwana, was C Company under Captain Reginald Younghusband and Lieutenant George Hodson. Next came the companies which had withdrawn from the Tahelane Spur. F Company under Captain William Mostyn and Lieutenants Pat Daly and Edgar Anstey, was immediately to Younghusband's right. Then came E Company, under

Lieutenant Charles Cavaye and 2nd Lieutenant Edwards Dyson. In the centre of the line, disposed on either side of the guns, was A Company under Captain William Degacher and Lieutenant Francis Porteous. Running down the forward slope of the rocky ridge as far as the Nyogane Donga, was H Company under Captain George Wardell and Lieutenant Charles Atkinson. Further down the slope to Wardell's right was G Company, led by Lieutenants Charlie Pope and Fred Godwin-Austen. Pope and his 2nd Battalion men held the extreme right flank, from the donga to Amatutshane. All the companies were in single-rank extended order and, in the inveterate way of the infantry, the company commanders had reached out with their flanks, to secure them on their immediate regimental neighbours.

There were no significant gaps between companies, as is often stated, and no formed bodies of colonial troops were allowed to disrupt the integrity of the battalion firing line. Contrary to the popular myth about a large cluster of levies occupying the centre of the line near the guns, no NNC companies were so disposed. Such bodies of NNC men as remained on the field, squatted behind the firing line, or sought cover in folds in the ground, under the watchful eye of their officers and NCOs, who in some cases stood over them with loaded weapons. Only the isiGqoza Zulus of No. 9 Company remained game. At various points on the left, some of the officers of the remaining NNC companies brought small parties of their NCOs and riflemen up onto the firing line, and disposed them in the intervals between the redcoats. Such parties did not interfere with the integrity of the position and might well provide some useful supplementary fire. Some of these colonial officers would survive the coming disaster and would confuse the history of the battle by referring to these irregular dispositions as if their entire commands were forward on the firing line. The hard reality was that the amaChunu and amaNgwane levies had absolutely no intention of dying for Queen Victoria. If at any point they were hard pressed by the enemy, they would be off like the proverbial greyhounds from the slips.

Allowing for about seventy rifles in the 1st Battalion companies and ninety in G Company, this means that, at this stage, there were about 440 Martini-Henrys on the firing line. The total frontage though was over 2,000 metres. In previous accounts of the battle, much has been made of gaps between men and gaps between companies. The firing line had no 'weight', we are told, surely a concept which belongs more rightly to ancient and medieval warfare. The facts bear closer examination. From Isandlwana to the guns was a distance of about 800 metres. This frontage was occupied by C, F and E Companies and half of A Company. These amounted to around 245 riflemen, or a man every three metres or four paces. In effect this means a rifleman at either end of the average sitting room rug. It is assuredly a tall order to run 400 metres in a straight line towards a sitting room rug with two riflemen firing at you and expect to live. It follows that if this was the situation to the left of the guns, then to the right there were 195 men spread over 1,200 metres: one man every six metres, or two sitting room rugs. The odds are better, but 400 metres is still a long way to run. This whole issue is another much debated red herring. In fact, H and G Companies would wheel back to the rocky ridge in such a manner as to reduce their frontage to about 700 metres, and Pulleine would shortly give the order that every man who could bear arms should be marched out of the camp to the firing line. This would bring forward the 2nd Battalion guard of twenty-two NCOs and men of A Company, anything up to thirty soldier-servants, the men left behind by the 2nd Battalion colour-sergeants, say a dozen or so, perhaps some N Battery men with carbines, and other miscellaneous parties, such as Chard's sappers. In effect, this amounted to the equivalent of another company fanning itself out along the firing line. Overwhelmingly, the reinforcement would have been in the direction of Pope, firstly because most of the men at issue were 2nd Battalion men, who would have instinctively gravitated towards their G Company brethren, but predominantly because the right was shortly to become the direction of the most significant enemy threat.

Even more fundamental to our understanding of the battle than cold ratios of men against frontages, is our grasp of what we now call the moral component of fighting power. One essential tenet is that men will not generally behave suicidally. Traditionally the Zulu warrior is portrayed as a savage automaton, a killing machine that knows no fear. Some 25,000 such warriors mounting a frontal attack amounts to a metaphorical juggernaut which, unless all the warriors can all be shot down, will steamroller everything in its path. In fact, nothing could be further from the truth. There is no doubting the formidable courage of the Zulu; they were and remain amongst the proudest and most courageous of all the African warrior tribes. In the age of the breech-loader, however, men cannot dash across hundreds of metres of open ground into an unrelenting fire, when all around them their comrades are being shot down. Rather the inescapable outcome of such a scenario is that an attack will be driven to ground. Men will seek concealment in the nearest natural cover or the smallest folds in the ground. Once they are down, it is next to impossible to get them moving forward again. In order to achieve this effect, the defending force has a number of important requirements: sufficient weapons with a sufficiently high rate of fire; well trained soldiers who can shoot straight and will stand their ground; good visibility; a clear field of fire out to the effective range of the weapon; and an adequate supply of ammunition. All of these the 24th Regiment had. The Zulu army was not made up of automatons, nor did it amount to a collective juggernaut. It was a flesh and blood army like any other. In summary, then, there is little relevance to the hoary old chestnut of frontages at Isandlwana. The firing line would not be penetrated, and the Zulus would do exactly what all flesh and blood must when faced with a storm of fire; they would get to their bellies and they would stay there.

At about the same time that Mostyn and Cavaye completed their withdrawal to the main firing line, there appeared from the British side of the battlefield to be a momentary lull. In fact, just behind the escarpment, the regiments of the Zulu chest were making their final preparations for the assault. It is difficult to say how long the lull lasted, but it was probably not much more than about five minutes. The Zulus above the notch, warriors of the uMbonambi and iNgobamakhosi regiments, had temporarily withdrawn out of sight to shield themselves from the fire of the 7-pounders. The guns had ceased fire. There had been no major pursuit down the Tahelane Spur. There was some distant rifle fire from beyond Amatutshane, coming from Durnford's withdrawal from the Qwabe Valley, but that apart, nobody else appeared to be heavily engaged. It was at this time that Pulleine apparently made the following remark:

> What a fool a fellow is; he only thinks of these things too late. Now if we had kept quiet in camp we should have coaxed these fellows on and given them a right good thrashing.*

---

* The remark is quoted in a letter of Lieutenant G. S. Banister of H Company, 2nd/24th, written five days after the battle. His source can only really be Gardner, or less probably, Higginson or Essex.

Up in the camp, Nevill Coghill took the opportunity presented by the lull to order Glyn's groom to pack his tent and equipment, which they would need to send forward to the colonel at Mangeni, as soon as the current action had drawn to a close.

Durnford Reaches Amatutshane

By the time Durnford's troops had fired half a dozen volleys each, they were back at the mouth of the Qwabe Valley near Itusi. The retreat had looked pretty enough, but it had slowed the left horn not a jot, nor had it done any significant damage. Perhaps four or five dozen Zulus at the most lay sprawled in the Qwabe Valley. Durnford had been looking anxiously for the rocket battery since commencing his withdrawal. He rounded the Itusi corner and galloped towards a few scattered figures to the east of Amatutshane.

The first indication that things had gone awry was when he rode up alongside the red-coated Private William Johnson, alone and helpless in the middle of the veldt. If Johnson's account of what ensued between them is wholly truthful, and there is no good reason to suspect that it is not, this might also be the historian's first indication that Durnford was beginning to come apart. 'Where is the battery?' demanded the colonel. Johnson replied that the battery had been cut up and Major Russell shot. 'You had better go back and fetch him,' said Durnford. This was sheer insanity and Johnson knew it. 'I then pointed out that the enemy had already nearly surrounded us,' he recorded politely in his statement. To his discredit, Durnford rode off and left Johnson where he was, notwithstanding the fact that his orderly was leading a spare horse at this time. Johnson was obliged to flee on foot. Davies's troop had meanwhile wheeled to the right, to chase off a few iNgobamakhosi skirmishers, who were exchanging shots with Nourse and his handful of stalwarts. Davies managed to rescue Nourse, and then sent some of his men to recover a stray mule and some boxes of rockets lying around in the grass. According to Nourse, Durnford rode across to enquire after the fate of Russell and the rest of the battery, in much the same way as he had of Johnson. When Nourse confirmed the worst, Durnford muttered something about 'not surviving the disgrace'. How telling a pointer to his psychological state; even in this dire situation, Durnford was still thinking only of his tarnished reputation.

As ever, there were four elements to Ntshingwayo's 'horns of the buffalo' battle drill and three were already in place. All the regiments of the right horn were now descending along the line of the Manzimyama Stream for the rear of Isandlwana. The reserve regiments were moving slowly west behind the line of the Ngedla Heights. The chest was poised in readiness just behind the escarpment. Only the left horn had still to come up and this was not significantly behind the rest of the army. As the sound of the Durnford fight drew near, the indunas on the plateau waved their men forward, and the Zulu chest surged *en masse* over the escarpment. Davies's order to the Edendale Troop to recover the rocket battery's abandoned kit had been an eccentric one in the circumstances, and the sudden descent through the notch of huge numbers of warriors forced them to give the job up as a bad idea. The retreat around the south side of Amatutshane was quickly renewed. At this point Durnford can have had no idea what he would find when he rounded the koppie, as he still had no knowledge whatsoever of Pulleine's plan or dispositions.

The Zulu Chest Breaks Over the Escarpment

Only a few moments after it was proffered, Pulleine's prayer was answered. He would, after all, have the opportunity to administer a 'sound thrashing' to the Zulu. As the *amabutho* rolled onto the forward slope of the escarpment, their close-order formations began to disperse into much looser swarms. To the observer at the foot of Isandlwana, the escarpment looks sheer in many places, but in reality nowhere along its length is it impassable. The attack poured over the lip all along the line of the Nyoni Ridge, but the big thrusts came down the two easy stretches, the Tahelane Spur on the left, and the notch on the right. Curling's 7-pounders barked once more from their position on the rocky ridge. Seconds later, the shells exploded in the notch amongst the men of the uMbonambi. Next, Pulleine's attention was drawn to the left, when C and F Companies commenced firing on the uNokhenke regiment, as it began its assault down the spur. On the other side of Mkwene Hill from the uNokhenke, the right wing of the umCijo was similarly attempting to push downhill. Raw and Vause confronted this advance from the head of the Nyogane Donga, opening fire at the same time as C and F Companies came into action to their left rear. For the time being, the native horse were squarely in Cavaye's field of fire, leaving him unable to join in the engagement.

Younghusband, Mostyn and their respective subalterns and NCOs were all steady hands, and the musketry of the men they commanded was amongst the best in the army. Nobody had yet made better use of the Martini-Henry than the soldiers of F Company, the veterans of the two big stand-up fights in the Transkei. The range was short, in places as little as 300 yards: under the direction of their officers, the men of C and F Companies shot the uNokhenke attack to pieces. It probably took no more than about seven or eight volleys. Dozens of warriors were hit and came crashing down the slope through the aloes and boulders. The fire was more than flesh and blood could stand. The surviving warriors at the forefront of the attack pushed to the rear. Those following behind sensed the fear of their comrades and dropped to ground on the safe side of the crest. A few dozen Zulus armed with rifles and muskets sought cover amongst the rocks and opened a heavy return fire. With the attack down the spur stalled, and at least temporarily defeated, Younghusband and Mostyn ordered no more company volleys. Here and there, the sergeants directed the individual fire of their best shots at the Zulu riflemen concealed on the spur: occasionally, when handfuls of Zulu brave-hearts once again tried their luck on the forward slope, they ordered section volleys.

The indunas of the uNokhenke knew that they had to do so something to dislodge the redcoats below the spur, if the regiment were not to fail the rest of the army. Large parties of the *ibutho*'s right wing were quickly directed along the reverse slope, to extend the attack further down the spur to the west. The western end of Tahelane was a blind spot to the firing line, and it was here that the uNokhenke would be able to make some quick headway. To the left of Younghusband's position, the ground sloped downhill through a series of hollows to the Manzimyama Stream. With the warriors slipping over the western end of Tahelane and down into these hollows, there was every danger that they might eventually constitute a serious threat to the British left. To prevent this causing problems later, Younghusband initiated a further short withdrawal of C, F and E Companies, until his own left flank was resting firmly on the scree slope of Isandlwana. The nature of the ground on the left would indicate that he must have sent one of his sections onto the lower slopes of the mountain, in order to anchor the flank securely. From its elevated position, the section had a good view into the hollows, and was doubtless able to inflict a significant number of casualties on the uNokhenke infiltrators. Some warriors diverted still further to the right, and began to drop down behind

Isandlwana into the Manzimyama Valley, to threaten the British rear.

Much to the trepidation of the NNC, the further withdrawal of the 24th had brought the front-line action uncomfortably close once more. Erskine's amaChunu now found themselves clustered just behind the point at which Mostyn's right met Cavaye's left. Stafford and his headman Ntini, held their amaNgwane together just to the rear of Younghusband's company. A hundred yards further back again, were the reserve companies of Krohn and Murray.

In the centre, the two 7-pounders continued to pound the uMbonambi and the iNgobamakhosi as they made their descent through the notch, but this was an insufficient weight of fire to stop or even slow the progress of the attack. This is why artillerymen like to fight their guns by whole batteries, not mere pairs. At 76.2 mm the 7-pounder was a small-calibre weapon; as a muzzle-loader it was capable of a maximum rate of fire of two to three rounds a minute. Although it was not a particularly deadly field piece, it could throw its 3.3-kg common shell to 3,660 metres, or just about two miles. It also fired a slightly heavier shrapnel round, which could achieve an airburst effect over the target but had a more limited range of 2,860 metres. Paying no real heed to the occasional shell exploding around them, the two *amabutho* poured downhill, the uMbonambi leading.

Halfway down the notch, the uMbonambi began to feel to their right, to effect a link up with the umCijo. Indeed, all the *amabutho* were fanning out left and right, to begin what they imagined would be an unstoppable charge. On their way downhill, the warriors were able to get their first good view of the enemy their king had spoken of. There were disappointingly few of them, spread out in a long thin line. They would be easy to kill. Many warriors worried that all the red soldiers would be dead, before they personally could draw blood.

Facing the uMbonambi from the right of the firing line, H and G Companies of the 24th waited patiently for the range to close. From the outset, Charlie Pope must have been concerned for his right. The lower slopes of Amatutshane provided a circuitous, but nonetheless ideal, dead-ground approach to the right rear of his current position. He would certainly have turned round quickly to survey the ground behind him and run through his options for withdrawal. His left flank rested on the Nyogane Donga, where it met Wardell's right. If he was threatened on his right, as now seemed likely, he would pivot on his left, fall back to the donga, and fight at a rough right angle to Wardell. If the enemy developed their attack in front of Amatutshane only, then all well and good. If on the other hand, they manoeuvred in significant numbers behind the koppie, then the line of the donga would be breached further down to the right, and his current position would be rendered untenable. In this scenario, it would be necessary to fall back all the way to the rocky ridge, and then quickly extend the company to the right. Such a move would leave George Wardell's right flank exposed, and would necessitate H Company falling back to the ridge in conformity. Unbeknown to Pope, Durnford had arrived on the far side of Amatutshane just a few moments earlier, drawing the left horn after him, a menace that was not yet visible to the officers of the 24th. The threat to G Company's right was even more pressing than Pope yet realised.

It will be helpful to our reconstruction to deal from time to time in numerical estimates of Zulu strength on the various sectors of the field, for only in this way can we ever hope to bring the battle properly to life. It must be clear, however, that the fighting strengths of the twelve *amabutho* engaged at Isandlwana have not been, and now never can be, satisfactorily established. We are forced to rely on only the roughest approximations. The regimental start states used in our reconstruction are summarised earlier in the chapter, and represent as good a start point as any. Where the source evidence would indicate that an *ibutho* split its efforts between two avenues of approach, we have no recourse but to divide the regiment's already approximate start state into two equal halves. With this caveat in place, let us consider what the 24th Regiment was now looking at.

There were fewer warriors between Mkwene Hill and Amatutshane than is often imagined, but that is not to say that the attack on this sector lacked momentum. Around 12,000 warriors had been assigned to the Zulu chest when it was launched from the Ngwebeni Valley. With the left wing of the iNgobamakhosi having drifted off the plateau to the support of the left horn, this left only 9,000 warriors above the escarpment. Then, having descended through the notch behind the uMbonambi, another 3,000 warriors, the men of the iNgobamakhosi's right wing, arrived at the foot of the escarpment to find themselves squeezed out of the line of battle. Instead of pushing up tamely behind the uMbonambi, the indunas led their men around the eastern side of Amatutshane, to re-unite with their regimental left wing out on the plain; beyond the koppie there was all the room for manoeuvre they could ever hope for. On the right side of the chest, the uNokhenke had pushed beyond Mkwene Hill to mount their attack down the Tahelane Spur. This means that only 4,000 warriors, the aggregated strength of the umCijo and the uMbonambi, made the main attack on the firing line between Mkwene Hill and Amatutshane. The assault would fall upon E, A, H and G Companies in their positions on either side of the guns. Younghusband and Mostyn were unable to bring their weapons to bear, and had to content themselves with keeping the uNokhenke in check on the spur.

The two key *amabutho* were soon united at the foot of the escarpment in a great arc of jogging men. Confident of brushing the red soldiers aside with ease, they swept on towards the seemingly flimsy British line. As the distance closed, the warriors spread themselves out in anticipation of being brought under fire, and began skirmishing from cover to cover. Confronted by such a fluid exhibition of open-order tactics, the younger men in the ranks of the 24th must have felt some anxiety. Even the old sweats looked worried. Unconsciously, the men allowed the all-pervading discipline of their regiment to suffocate their individual fears. Not a man moved. Everything now depended on the Martini-Henry. As the leading *amabutho* skirmished through the rocks and the grass, the right wing of the iNgobamakhosi could be seen beyond them, disappearing behind Amatutshane. The developing threat to the right of the line was now only too apparent. It would be surprising if Pulleine and his aides did not at this point ride down to speak to Pope about a withdrawal to the rocky ridge. From the G Company position on the extreme right, they would then have cantered back along the line, to warn Wardell to be prepared to fall back in conformity.

With anxiety about the right mounting by the minute, Pulleine now ordered that every man capable of bearing arms should be marched out of the camp to take post on the firing line. It seems most likely that it was Dyer, the adjutant of the 2nd Battalion, who is known to have been mounted on the firing line, and would certainly have been somewhere near G Company, who rode back to the camp to round up his battalion's rear details. Coghill may have gone with him, as the soldier-servants at the column headquarters were also turned out at about this time. Certainly Gardner was ordered back to the cavalry lines, where Pulleine knew there

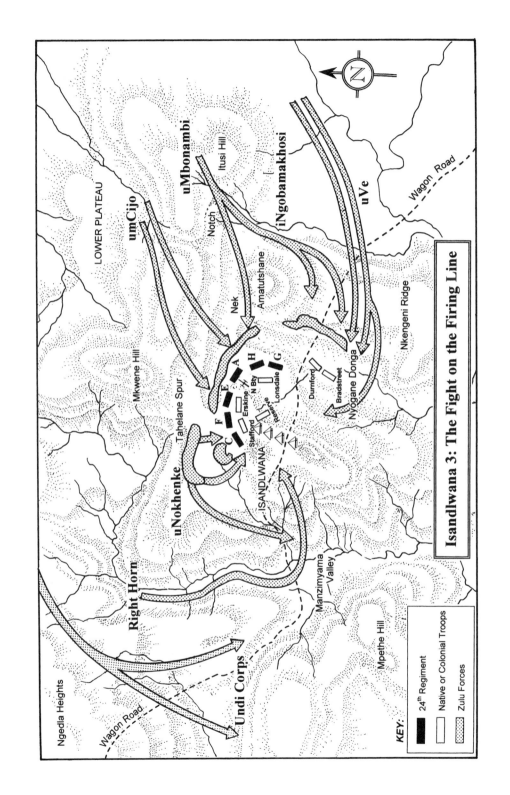

Ngedla Heights

Wagon Road

Right Horn

Undi Corps

uNokhenke

Mkwene Hill

umCijo

LOWER PLATEAU

Tahelane Spur

uMbonambi

Itusi Hill

Notch

Nek

Amatutshane

iiNgobamakhosi

uVe

Wagon Road

Nkengeni Ridge

Nyogane Donga

Bradstreet

Dumford

Lonsdale

N Bty

Erskine

Reserve

Stafford

ISANDLWANA

H

A

G

E

F

C

Manzimyama Valley

Mpethe Hill

Isandlwana 3: The Fight on the Firing Line

KEY:
24th Regiment
Native or Colonial Troops
Zulu Forces

was at least a section's worth of mounted infantry. Gardner was to bring forward all the mounted men he could find, and take them down to the right hand side of the rocky ridge, which when Pope fell back, would become the new right flank.

The Infantry Open Fire

On the firing line the junior officers and senior NCOs were pacing up and down behind the men, exhorting them to be steady and listen carefully for the words of command they knew to be imminent. The company commanders meantime were concentrating on judging and re-judging distance. One by one they shouted out a range setting, which the soldiers hurriedly clicked onto their rear-sights. 'At 600 yards . . . Ready . . . Present!' Everything changed when the infantry opened fire. The companies plied their skill at arms in the approved smooth and rhythmic fashion, volleying once – twice – three times. This was real killing range for the Martini-Henry and these first few volleys were extremely punishing; scores of Zulus were bowled over by them. Driver Elias Tucker of N Battery wrote that the volleys 'cut roads through them'. Fortified by their superior numbers, most of the warriors came on regardless. As the distance closed, the sergeants of the 24th bellowed out new range settings to their sections. At 400 yards, a fourth, a fifth, and a sixth volley scythed through the umCijo and the uMbonambi. With this, the sense of their unstoppable momentum was dispelled. It must be remembered that no living Zulu had ever heard a man-made sound as loud as a British volley, nor had they ever encountered or imagined such a murderous fire. The psychological effect of the thundering volleys, the billowing white smoke, and the horrible wounding of human flesh at every turn cannot be underestimated. In his memoirs Smith-Dorrien recalled the steadiness of the 1st/24th:

> Here was a more serious matter for these brave warriors for the regiment opposed to them were no boy recruits but war-worn matured men, mostly with beards, and fresh from a long campaign in the old colony where they had carried everything before them. Possessed of splendid discipline and sure of success they lay on their position making every round tell so that when the Zulu army was some 400 yards off it wavered.

From their position at the foot of Mkwene Hill, Vause and Raw attempted to contest the advance of the umCijo down the escarpment. They fired several hard-hitting volleys, but the downhill assault was remorseless and it was soon time to get out. Mounting up quickly, they galloped back through the infantry firing line, clearing Cavaye's fields of fire at last, and allowing him to come into action. E Company's volleys soon broke up the attack and drove it to ground. The warriors in the van dashed forward to take cover in the abandoned donga. Those caught on the escarpment fell back to dead ground. Reining in behind the gun-smoke on Cavaye's position, Vause realised that his men were just about out of ammunition, and quickly led them back to the camp to replenish. Uguku of the umCijo described this phase of the fighting:

> The engagement now became very hot between the amaNgwane and us, the former being supported by the infantry who were some distance in their rear. We were now falling very fast. The amaNgwane had put their horses in a donga, and were firing away at us on foot. We shouted 'Uzulu!' and made for the donga, driving out the amaNgwane towards the camp. The infantry then opened fire on us, and their fire was so hot that those of us who were not in the donga retired back over the hill . . . we then shouted 'Uzulu!' again, and got up out of the donga. The soldiers opened fire on us again and we laid down.

Uguku's account is of note because it conveys well the effect of the 24th's volleys on the *amabutho*. It also shows that well-disciplined fire control was in play. Over the entire frontage of their attack, the warriors of the chest realised they could take no more. Some sank down amongst scree boulders, some into long grass, some into folds and hollows in the ground. A man seeking cover has the choice of going forward or back; many hundreds of warriors were caught in the open, and had no choice but to keep going forward until they reached the Nyogane Donga or its feeder tributaries. Many dropped to their bellies short of the dongas, and over the next few minutes crawled towards them through the grass, trying hard not to draw fire in the process. Eventually, there may have been as many as 3,000 Zulus crammed into the dongas in front of Cavaye and Degacher. In places the warriors were now well within 200 metres of the firing line.

The attempts by Pulleine's aides to round up reinforcements were now paying a dividend. One party which responded to the call was a group of five soldier-servants, consisting of the GOC's three orderlies, and Privates John Williams and William Hough, Colonel Glyn's groom and cook respectively. These men ran out of the camp to the north, to take post on the left of Cavaye's company. Much more significantly, a party of forty to fifty men of the 2/24th were doubling down the slope towards the rocky ridge, in search of Pope. If they were not under Dyer's personal command, then it was probably young Sub-Lieutenant Griffith who led them at Dyer's behest. Gardner, meanwhile, had turned out Captain Bradstreet with about forty-five to fifty mounted men, at least half of whom were IMI. There were also about a dozen NMR, a handful of BBG men and the last few police and carbineers. Gardner led them downhill at the gallop.

Because of the threat to his right, Pope knew he could fight from his forward position for only a few minutes. He and Godwin-Austen probably prepared the ground for the withdrawal by moving in opposite directions behind the firing line and briefing the sergeant section commanders face to face. As they broke over the nek between Amatutshane and the escarpment, the uMbonambi had received a nasty shock from G Company's first few volleys. There was very little cover on the forward slope, and with each new thunderclap a couple of dozen men were sent reeling. Soon there was consternation and hesitation amongst the warriors. Some hit the ground; some ducked forward and kept running as if into a rainstorm; many slipped back over the nek. G Company now concentrated its fire on the foremost warriors, those courageous enough still to be moving forward; they were quickly shot down. Had it not been for the threat to his right, Pope might have held his ground all day. Ultimately though, the lie of the land was against him. After a couple more volleys, it was time to execute the anticipated pivot on the left flank. It must be emphasised that the withdrawal was hashed together by the officers and NCOs at great speed, only with the aid of plenty of shouting and running about.

Changing Front

Pope now gave the signal for G Company to retire. This was executed as a quasi-drill movement. In such a wheel, the extreme left hand man is going nowhere, and stands still. The extreme right hand man, on the other hand, has the furthest distance to cover and has to get a move on, if he is not to be left behind and killed. The two left flank sections, the men on the inside of the wheel, walked slowly backwards, pausing momentarily on the word of command to present, aim and fire; the right flank sections, the men with the most ground to cover, doubled back at a half-jog to make up the distance, ready at all times to turn on their heels and fire a volley if so ordered. Talking to Bertram Mitford after the war, a warrior of the uMbonambi simulated the regular rhythm of Pope's volleys by snapping his fingers. He recalled the fight around Amatutshane as follows:

> Here were some parties of soldiers in red coats who kept up a heavy fire on us as we came over. My regiment was here and lost a lot of men. They kept tumbling over one upon another . . . Then the iNgobamakhosi regiment . . . extended and swept round on the south of the conical koppie so as to outflank the soldiers, who seeing this, fell back and took cover in the donga and fired upon us from there . . . but we [the uMbonambi] could not advance because the fire from the donga was too heavy.

For a few minutes after the successful completion of the wheel, Pope kept the uMbonambi pinned down in front of Amatutshane. Although the account above has been translated in such a fashion as to suggest that at least a portion of G Company was positioned *in* the donga, it is clear from the lie of the land that Pope fell back *across* the donga, and deployed along the line of the home bank. Even from this new position, though, both of G Company's flanks remained problematical. On the left of the company, the main donga curved around the foot of the rocky ridge, where it then fanned out into the feeder tributaries. These had already been occupied by the umCijo, who were sheltering there from the fire of Cavaye, Degacher and Wardell. With H Company deployed on the scree slope behind the donga, there was nothing to prevent infiltration against G Company's left. With the iNgobamakhosi manoeuvring to the rear of Amatutshane, the position on the right was even more serious. Whilst Scott and his carbineers had ridden down in that direction, to confront the iNgobamakhosi when they appeared around the southern side of the koppie, a mere thirty carbines were unlikely to prevent a breakthrough.

Pope decided that he would now have to execute the second part of his withdrawal plan, and fall back onto the rocky ridge. He and Godwin-Austen ran up and down the line of the donga shouting the preparatory orders. George Wardell and Colour-Sergeant Wolfe were probably watching carefully for any imminent sign of the move. Undoubtedly Pope would have implemented a company fire and movement plan, the aim of which was to keep 'one foot on the ground'. Possibly he retired by half-companies alternately, commanding one himself and leaving the other to Fred Godwin-Austen. He may have retired by files, a manoeuvre in which the designated front rank men fire a volley, and then double back to take up a new position 15–20 yards behind the rear rank men. The old rear rank has become the front rank and now fires its volley ... and so on. However it was executed, the troops were faced with a rough scramble across the scree; no doubt men tripped, slipped and cursed as they ran. Amongst their number was one particularly distinguished veteran. Private William Griffiths 56 was the holder of one of the Victoria Crosses won in the Andaman Islands twelve years earlier. The uMbonambi had been hit hard and seem not to have pressed a very determined pursuit, for there were few if any G Company casualties at this time. Where parties of Zulu warriors did begin to skirmish forward, they were quickly driven back into the grass.

It was time for H Company to be gone too. When Wardell gave the word, Colour-Sergeant Wolfe barked at the section commanders to begin a rearwards wheel by the left flank. Being that much closer to the top of the rocky ridge, they were able to execute the movement in a quicker, more ordered fashion than G Company. Within a couple of minutes, H Company had completed a right-angled pivot which wheeled them back from the long forward slope of the ridge to its crest. Here they were able to fire over and around Pope's men as they came doubling back up the slope. On the crest, the winded G Company men ran through the new H Company line and then turned left behind it, to extend the position along the ridge to the right. No doubt Pulleine and his aides were on hand to direct the movement, to urge all possible speed, and to offer the men encouragement.

Although the G and H Company manoeuvres have been described in terms of the parade ground, their actual execution would have been nothing like as smooth. It was the individual soldier's comprehension of the fundamental military principles of the wheel, and of alternate fire and movement, that enabled Pope and Wardell to carry such manoeuvres through successfully. As ever, the sergeant section commanders were key men. Based on their long years of experience, they would have known instinctively what was required, even if their company commanders had no time to brief them face-to-face. They were able to keep tight control of every man in their twenty-strong sections by a combination of familiar voice and hand signals. For the time being at least, the situation on the right was now under control. Pulleine must have breathed a huge sigh of relief. It was to be a short-lived sensation.

By now Melvill had returned from the left, and riding along the firing line soon encountered his commanding officer. He was the bearer of dire news. When he reached the top of the spur, Cavaye and Mostyn reported that they had been firing on a large body of Zulus manoeuvring at speed for the rear of Isandlwana. Melvill was a sharp operator and knew as much about Zulu tactics as anyone else in the army; this was the right horn and it was already behind Isandlwana, he advised. Pulleine's last reserve, discounting the worthless NNC companies on the left, was even now galloping down the slope under Gardner, heading for the right flank. There was nothing left to cover the rear. In that awful moment of realisation, it must have dawned on Pulleine that defeat was now only a matter of time. Only a miracle could prevent the Zulu right horn from assailing the camp over the undefended saddle. Perhaps Pulleine prayed for one.

Durnford Decides to Hold the Nyogane Donga

As G Company was beginning its hasty withdrawal to the rocky ridge, Durnford's troopers appeared at the canter around the south side of Amatutshane, with the uVe and the left wing of the iNgobamakhosi in close pursuit. They had only narrowly avoided being cut off from the camp by the attack down the notch and the subsequent manoeuvre to the south of the koppie by the rest of the iNgobamakhosi. Durnford halted his command for one more volley. As his men dismounted, he looked around to take stock of the wider situation. For the first time he could form some impression of Pulleine's dispositions. He could see Wardell's men deploying along the line of the rocky ridge, and Pope's men scrambling back over the rocks to join them. Lonsdale's isiGqoza were just beyond the two companies of redcoats. Scott's troop of police and carbineers had taken position along the lower reaches of the Nyogane Donga, a few hundred metres to the rear. Behind Scott, another *ad hoc* troop of cavalry was galloping down the slope from the camp. Durnford could see that if he did not now make a stand, the 24th Regiment's firing line would be exposed to flank attack by the left horn. Durnford had ridden across the Nyogane earlier and knew that it was wide enough to provide good cover for the horse-holders. Importantly, the position also offered a clear field of fire back up the gentle slope of the Nkengeni Ridge, the relatively insignificant feature running south from Amatutshane. When the Zulu attack came across the ridge onto the forward slope, it would find itself caught in the open, with only long grass and a small cluster of abandoned beehive huts for cover. Durnford concluded that the donga would be the best position from which to protect Pulleine's right. The pressure though would be remorseless. If there were fewer warriors between Mkwene Hill and Amatutshane than is commonly imagined, it necessarily follows that there were many more to the south of the koppie. The uVe and the left wing of the iNgobamakhosi had advanced along the Qwabe Valley with as many as 6,000 men. Now, to the south of Amatutshane, they were reinforced by a further 3,000 men of the iNgobamakhosi.

Some writers have contended that it is uncertain whether Durnford made his stand in the Nyogane Donga, which is 1,700 metres from Isandlwana, or the Mpofane Donga, which is only about 700 metres out. A practised eye for ground will immediately identify that the Mpofane offers no decent field of fire and could not have been held. Most tellingly, some of the cairns marking places where men fell and were buried, on this part of the field G Company cairns for sure, are in front of the Mpofane. These two factors enable us to identify the Nyogane as 'Durnford's Donga' with certainty.

From the gun position at the left end of the rocky ridge, Major Smith saw Durnford's command ride into sight to the south of Amatutshane and decided, or was directed, to take one of the 7-pounders further along the ridge to the right, to give him covering fire. Instructing Curling to stay where he was with the left hand gun, Smith ordered the crew of the other to limber up. In less than a minute, the gun team was trotting off to its new position, but the scree-boulders along the top of the ridge were a significant hindrance, and progress to the south was necessarily slower than the norm.

The Firefight

In the centre, where the majority of the umCijo and the uMbonambi were now in cover in the Nyogane Donga and its tributaries, the battle quickly became a static close-range firefight. The luxuriant blanket of long grass brought on by the summer rains was three feet high in most places, and provided a significant impediment to the marksmanship of both sides. At the foot of the slope, the warriors were crouched below the banks of the dongas, or were prone in long grass. Surprising though it may seem, given that there were as many as 4,000 Zulus distributed along this sector, most were all but invisible to the British. The firing line lost much of its regularity, as men shifted back and forth in search of decent fire positions. One must imagine the soldiers of the 24th almost straining on tiptoe to see over the grass. The downhill gradient was in their favour at least, and provided a key advantage in checking the attack. With no massed target presenting itself, the heavy company volleying had stopped, and the men of F, E, A and H Companies were now firing independently at fleeting opportunity targets. Mostly these were presented when Zulu riflemen leapt out of the long grass to get off a shot.

It has been consistently overlooked that, with as many as one in four Zulus carrying a firearm, the 24th Regiment was significantly out-gunned in the battle. On this sector alone, the umCijo and uMbonambi may have fielded as many as a thousand firearms. Sure enough, there was no comparison between the Martini-Henry and the Zulu weapons at 600 yards, but at 200 yards many technically inferior weapons could be just as deadly. Only their poor marksmanship prevented the warriors from blasting gaps in the British line. Given the weight of fire brought to bear from the donga, it was just as well that the soldiers of the 24th were spaced several metres apart. Mostly the Zulu aim was wild and inaccurate, with many rounds being fired high. Such rounds are referred to by soldiers as 'overs'. The 'overs' fired from smoothbore muskets generally landed harmlessly enough a short distance to the rear, but those from rifled muskets and more modern rifles had sufficient velocity to sail right over the firing line and land in the camp area.

By now back with Captain Krohn, Higginson noted the unsettling effect of this fire on No. 6 Company, as it waited in reserve in front of the NNC lines. Here and there though, the Zulu fire was striking home on the firing line. A few men were hit and were helped to the rear by bandsmen detailed as stretcher-bearers. One of the men giving aid to the wounded was Private Edmund Wilson of the 1st Battalion Band. Surgeon-Major Shepherd must have been down on the firing line initially because Wilson recalled that, after ten minutes or so, Shepherd ordered the bandsmen back to the hospital tents, 'as he said there would be too many wounded for us to attend to'. It is not entirely clear what is meant by this, but it does point to the fact that the Zulu fire was very heavy. It seems likely that Shepherd established an aid post somewhere immediately to the rear of the firing line, but that Zulu fire soon compelled its abandonment in favour of the hospital tents. There was precious little point in Shepherd getting himself shot or running the risk of the wounded being re-wounded or killed in an exposed forward position. Far better to let the companies send their casualties back to a properly equipped medical focal point, safely out of the line of fire.

Seen from a Zulu perspective, the red soldiers at the top of the slope were difficult targets. Although the fire of the *amabutho* was quantitatively superior, the qualitative advantage lay with the infinitely more proficient marksmen of the 24th. When Zulu riflemen leapt up to fire they were guaranteed an accurate return fusillade. Thus they had next to no time to aim properly. Since the redcoats dropped back into the grass between shots, to eject their spent rounds and reload, it was difficult even to acquire a target.

There were, however, two groups of men on the British side, who remained exposed throughout the firefight. The officers of the 24th and the gunners of N Battery were unable to kneel and shelter from the fire, the former because they would not, and the latter because they could not. This was still a redcoat army, and it remained an unwritten rule that officers of the infantry would disdain to take cover. This was an ethic which had been perpetuated since the time of Marlborough. The boyhood heroes of the officers of the 24th were the men who had fought in the Crimea 25 years earlier. Technology had outstripped the tsar's army, which fought the war with smoothbore muskets of Napoleonic vintage. Thus for the British officer corps, the last 'real' war had been fought in truly heroic style. They stood in the open, clad gorgeously in scarlet and gold, in bearskins and kilts, they waved swords, they led from the front, and field officers frequently remained mounted under fire. 'Brother Boer' would bring these ways to an end in less than two years time, but for now the ethic was alive and well. Most of the field officers of the 24th had fought in the Crimea as young men. No doubt their war stories had been recounted often in the officers' mess. They were tales of great daring.

Now the younger blades of the regiment had been presented with the opportunity to emulate the brave deeds of their elders. Young officers such as Edwards Dyson, Charles Atkinson, and Thomas Griffith, none of them older than twenty-three, strode fearlessly up and down the firing line, encouraging their men with exhortations, smiles and quips. They sincerely believed that, without such a display of bravado, their men would be seriously unsettled by the ordeal of battle. Even worse, if they ducked, bobbed, or took cover, they would earn a reputation for being 'windy' under fire, and would be despised by the men; and there could be no worse fate for an officer. And so they remained fearlessly upright, as if the rounds cracking through the air around them were no more than some irritating but ultimately harmless insect. The enlisted men saw them from the corner of an eye as they passed and were proud of them. It would have required extraordinary luck for all seventeen of the regimental officers fighting on the firing line to have survived so galling a fire unscathed; perhaps one or two of them were hit. Standing in the open to serve their guns, Curling's men were similarly exposed. In the finest traditions of the Royal Artillery, they stood to their guns without regard for incoming fire.

Ammunition

One of the 24th officers on the northern side of the firing line, probably Cavaye, whose company had been first into action, now asked Essex to attend to the re-supply of ammunition. On his way back along the line of unit transport parks at the rear of the tents, he would have noticed Vause and his troop queuing to replenish their bandoliers from the No. 2 Column wagons; ample testament to just how wildly they had been firing when Essex had taken note of them on the spur. Essex made for the 2nd/24th's transport park, where he knew the heavily laden ammunition wagons of Quartermaster Edward Bloomfield were to be found. To assist him, Essex rounded up an officer, almost certainly his subordinate on the transport staff, Smith-Dorrien, and all the spare men he could find amongst the tents, including some 24th bandsmen, some cooks and a number of the N Battery drivers, smiths and saddlers. Bloomfield and Essex quickly formed these men into carrying parties and sent them out to the firing line, lugging a box of cartridges between pairs.

Another lengthy exposition on ammunition boxes at Isandlwana would be tiresome to many experienced readers, and probably mystifying to those reading of this battle for the first time. Suffice it to say that stories of incompetent quartermasters, impossibly difficult boxes, or a shortage of screwdrivers are without foundation and largely owe their prominence in the folklore of Isandlwana to Donald Morris's interpretation of Smith-

Dorrien's memoirs. This appeared in Morris's 1965 work *The Washing of the Spears*, which proved to be a bestseller and is still in print. Foremost amongst a number of erroneous statements advanced by Morris was that no fewer than six screws had to be undone to open an ammunition box. In fact, he is describing the screws in the copper banding, which served only to hold the boxes together; these were absolutely irrelevant in terms of access to the rounds inside. In 1879 Boxer cartridges came in the Mark V hardwood box, which contained sixty waxed paper packets each of ten rounds, and weighed close to eighty pounds. Access was through a sliding lid in the top of the box, held closed by a single two-inch screw. The boxes had rope carrying handles and were weatherproofed with a thin tin liner, which was pulled back sardine-can style, by means of a fixed handle. Whilst the hardwood lip could probably not be split by a single blow from a rifle butt, as has been suggested, a few sharp blows on the edge of the box with a hefty improvised tool would certainly splinter the wood and bend the screw, allowing immediate access.

Even better than improvised tools, of course, are the real thing. It has been wholly overlooked that the place of the regimental pioneer section in action was with the quartermaster and the ammunition. Right down to the modern day there are regimental pioneers in British infantry battalions, who continue to be employed under the quartermaster. The 1st Battalion section was certainly present at the battle, under the leadership of Corporal Henry Richardson. A 'team photograph' of Richardson and his men, taken in the Ciskei a little over a year earlier, shows ten magnificently bearded senior soldiers. Pioneers are the regimental artisans and artisans have tools. It is hard to conceive of Richardson's veterans struggling to shift a single two-inch screw. Whilst research for this current work has failed to turn up data on the 2nd Battalion's pioneers, it is clear that Henry Degacher took only his fighting companies and his bandsmen to Mangeni. G Company aside, another eighty men were left behind at the camp, and it seems certain that the pioneers would have been amongst them.

Clearly then, neither Quartermaster Pullen nor Quartermaster Bloomfield would have struggled to open ammunition boxes. Sadly Donald Morris really went to town on the posthumous reputations of both these gentlemen. He seems to have made full use of his imagination in doing so, for there is nothing in the sources to justify much of what he wrote. Morris's contention that Bloomfield refused ammunition to 1st Battalion runners is not only historically unsupportable, it is also militarily ludicrous. Quartermasters are great traders and regard themselves as a special brotherhood, who have to work together to keep their books straight. They are great mutual back-scratchers. Bloomfield knew full well that, if operational circumstance dictated that he should give ammunition to the 1st/24th, then he need only stroll over to his colleague Pullen after the battle to claim back the requisite quantity. This is how quartermasters work.

In short then, there was no difficulty opening the boxes, nor did the 2nd Battalion quartermaster refuse to issue ammunition to 1st Battalion runners, nor were the men of the 24th even short of ammunition on the firing line. Having dealt with what is not true, let us move on to describe what is.

In all, there were over 400,000 rounds in the camp. The 2nd/24th had departed in light marching order, with the customary seventy rounds a man. Quartermaster Bloomfield had an additional 200 rounds per man aboard his wagons. With an eighth of the stock left behind with B Company at Rorke's Drift, this means that he had in the order of 140,000 rounds available. In the 1st Battalion camp, with five companies in the field, Quartermaster Pullen had only marginally fewer. Eighteen thousand of Bloomfield's rounds (6 x 100 man companies x 30 rounds per man)* specifically constituted the first line reserve of the 2nd Battalion. In accordance with the elder Degacher's orders of earlier that morning, Bloomfield had loaded thirty boxes aboard a wagon, which he was now holding at immediate readiness for despatch to the 2nd Battalion at Mangeni. Smith-Dorrien recounts in his memoirs how he clambered aboard a wagon and started breaking open boxes. Looking up from his work on an adjacent wagon, Bloomfield snapped, 'For heaven's sake don't take that man, for it belongs to our battalion.' Smith-Dorrien tells us that he replied, 'Hang it all! You don't want a requisition now do you?' Smith-Dorrien, who was an old man when he wrote his memoirs, actually offers this anecdote as an example of the coolness of the 24th Regiment in action. It is, however, an anecdote without a punch-line, so to speak. It only makes sense when one deduces that Smith-Dorrien was aboard the wagon carrying the 2nd Battalion first line reserve.

Essex remained with Bloomfield to load ammunition boxes aboard a mule cart. The quartermaster was almost certainly standing high on a

---

* Though in fact, there were fewer than 500 men out with Degacher.

wagon, heaving boxes around, when he was hit by one of the 'overs' whirring across the firing line. He had been in the army since the age of eleven, and had worked his way through every non-commissioned rank in the army from boy-drummer to sergeant-major. Now, as a 43-year-old, he lay dead across his ammunition. It was a bad day for quartermasters: in the cavalry camp Quartermaster London of the Carbineers had also been hit and wounded. Essex continued with the task in hand and detailed somebody to drive the cart out to the firing line. He then rode on ahead, to tell the company commanders that plenty more ammunition was coming. (Although just because ammunition was coming, and that is all that Essex said in his statement to the board of inquiry, it does not follow that it was distributed in a timely fashion.) Bloomfield's number two, Quartermaster-Sergeant Davis, who would have been close at hand, no doubt took over his duties at this stage. On his way back to Cavaye's position, Essex noticed '. . . a number of native infantry retreating in haste towards the camp, their officer endeavouring to prevent them without effect'. It is impossible to know which of the NNC companies this was: probably all of them were suffering a significant number of desertions by this stage.

Durnford's Defence of the Nyogane Donga

The Edendale and Basuto troops made it safely back to the Nyogane Donga, where they dismounted as before and told off horse-holders. The Basutos took the right of the line, whilst the Edendale Troop were mixed amongst Scott's men on the left. Somewhat against the odds, Captain Nourse and Private Johnson also made it safely back to the donga. Durnford let it be known that this was not a temporary position; the line of the Nyogane was to be defended. The uVe and iNgobamakhosi were already charging over the Nkengeni Ridge. The colonel waited for them to get halfway down it before ordering his men to open fire. No longer breathless from hurriedly mounting and dismounting, and shooting now for their very survival, the standard of the men's musketry improved markedly. The first volley hit the leading ranks of the uVe and iNgobamakhosi hard, but just behind them more and more warriors were pressing over the ridge to support the attack on the donga.

Gardner and Bradstreet now galloped up to Durnford's support. The *ad hoc* troop strung out behind them must have cut a dash, as it rode down the long slope between Isandlwana and the donga. Importantly, all the men concerned had full bandoliers of ammunition. With these rounds they would sustain the defence of the donga longer than might otherwise have been the case. Bradstreet dismounted his men on the right of the Basutos, thereby extending the British right flank slightly further to the south. In all, there were now about 180 men defending the donga. It has been assumed by many historians that George Shepstone remained on the left of the camp with Raw and Vause, but in fact Lieutenant Harry Davies saw him on the right. He must have ridden down to the donga to rejoin his colonel at about the same time as Gardner and Bradstreet.

Having brought the mounted troops forward, Gardner did not tarry at the Nyogane, but made his way back towards Pulleine's position on the rocky ridge, as he and the other mounted aides were the colonel's only means of passing orders around the battlefield. A remark made by Charlie Pope on the firing line has come down to us through Captain Penn Symons's extensive enquiries into the battle. The one man who could have ridden through Pope's position, and would survive to report such a conversation to Symons, was Alan Gardner. Pope apparently remarked that he considered himself fortunate to have made it back from his advanced position, and that his company had been '. . . warming them well out there and they would get it hotter directly.' A moment or two later, the 2nd/24th rear details arrived on the ridge and were quickly absorbed into the G Company firing line.

The fire of the mounted troops soon took a heavy toll of the left horn. Mehlokazulu described the fight from the Zulu perspective:

> The iNgobamakhosi and uVe attacked on this side . . . on the side of this little hill [Amatutshane] there is a donga, into which the mounted men got, and stopped our onward move there: we could not advance against their fire any longer. They had drawn their horses into this donga, and all we could see were the helmets. They fired so heavily we had to retire; we kept lying down and rising again. The Edendale men were in the donga but we did not see the Basutos. The former were mixed with the carbineers.

Many warriors had taken cover in the long grass on the downhill slope, but many more had fallen back over the ridge. Several dozen men clustered around the huts of an abandoned kraal, where they were soon spotted by Major Smith. From his new position he had already dropped a few rounds onto the Nkengeni Ridge, but now he specifically brought his gun to bear on the kraal. With one of the first rounds they fired, Smith's gun-crew scored a direct hit on one of the huts, killing and wounding some of the warriors who had sought cover there and scattering the rest. Satisfied that the situation on the right was now stable, Smith limbered up again, and trotted back to rejoin Curling. Reunited on the left of the ridge, the guns came back into action as a pair. The toiling gun-crews remained vulnerable to the Zulu fire cracking overhead. In the course of the action on the firing line, one of the gunners was hit in the head and killed, another was shot in the ribs, and a third through the wrist. Smith himself was shot in the arm: four men hit out of twenty-two. Since nobody could be spared from serving the guns, the wounded were left unaided where they fell. Smith said nothing of his wound to Curling, and remained on the ridge to fight his guns. Perhaps it was the galling nature of the Zulu fire that drove Captain Degacher to order a thirty-yard advance down the slope in front of the guns.* His purpose can only have been to improve his field of fire. Such a bold manoeuvre is ample testament to the cool temperament and fighting spirit of the 24th. Eighty men stepped off together and advanced steadily and calmly on thousands. The short advance put Degacher's men on the forward slope of the rocky ridge, quite out of sight from the spectators amongst the tents and wagons.

Durnford meanwhile was fighting in what he imagined was heroic mode. He rode up and down the donga on his horse, 'Chieftain', barking encouragement and disdaining to dismount in cover. Several times he did dismount, but only to clear carbine stoppages for some of his troopers, a difficult proposition for a man with only one good arm. From a professional soldiering point of view, these episodes are damning to Durnford: the senior officer in the field should have better things to do in the middle of a battle than spend time wrestling with jammed carbines. Whilst the impressionable and devoted black troopers thought highly of the conduct of their colonel, some of the white officers did not. In probably the most condemnatory piece of prose ever written about Durnford, Lieutenant Alfred Henderson of the Basuto Troop said, 'If I had known what sort of man Durnford was, I don't think I would have gone with him. He was close to me during most of the fight and he lost his head altogether; in fact I don't think he knew what to do.' It is interesting to note

* Curling

also that, in the aftermath of the battle, Sir Theophilus Shepstone, a man of great intelligence and a keen judge of character, would remark that he had become nervous for the safety of his son George, the minute he heard that he had been appointed to Durnford's staff.

With the warriors immediately in front of the donga killed, wounded or driven to ground in the grass, there were few good massed targets to be seen. Some of the iNgobamakhosi thought they detected an exploitable gap between the men in the donga and G Company's right flank. Looking to his half-left, Lieutenant Harry Davies spotted their charge, and quickly directed a couple of volleys from the Edendale Troop in that direction. The crossfire stalled the attack and drove the warriors back to ground. All was not well in Durnford's command, however. The Edendale and Basuto troops had not been in the donga for long, before they started to run short of cartridges.[*] Noticing his men turning to call for ammunition, Durnford told Harry Davies to take a party of Edendale troopers and ride back to the camp, to find the No. 2 Column ammunition wagon. Had the indunas known just how short ammunition now was, they could have rushed the donga with ease, but having been driven to ground, the Zulus could be kept in check with a minimal amount of fire. If, however, they were to organise themselves and summon up the courage for a rush, there was little the native horse could do to stop them. In essence, the donga was now being held more by bluff than firepower: Bradstreet's white troopers, the only men with plenty of cartridges still in hand, now became the mainstay of its defence.

Having ridden away with fifteen members of his troop, Harry Davies was gone for what seemed like an eternity; the one-way trip alone was over a mile long. He was not the only man in search of ammunition. In the centre of the rocky ridge, just to the rear of the regular infantry, were Lonsdale's isiGqoza. With fewer than twenty men in all carrying rifles, the firepower of No. 9 Company was not essential to the defence of the perimeter, but it was nonetheless a useful adjunct. Presumably the Europeans shared a few extra cartridges around the half dozen isiGqoza armed with Martinis. Firing, like all the native contingents, at an unnecessarily rapid rate against a stalled enemy in cover, No. 9 Company rapidly emptied its bandoliers and was compelled to cease fire. A white sergeant rode back to the camp to get more rounds from Quartermaster McCormack, and returned with a box quite

---

[*] Harry Davies.

quickly. Like Lonsdale's men, Stafford's amaNgwane similarly shot their rounds away rapidly. Stafford felt compelled to go back to the wagons himself, and took Ntini with him. Whilst Harry Davies had no idea where No. 2 Column's wagons were to be found, or even if they had arrived yet, Stafford knew exactly where they were. He tethered his horse and set off to rejoin his company on foot, carrying a box of cartridges between him and Ntini. Back in the donga, with no sign of the return of Harry Davies, Durnford now sent Henderson back too. It has been suggested that the men in the donga were somehow left leaderless, but Durnford, Shepstone, Bradstreet, Cochrane, Nourse and Scott were all still present there. This situation would be tenable so long as the battle was static, but in a deteriorating situation a retreating soldier will instinctively look to rally upon his own officer, not to a stranger he does not know; if he turns and cannot locate his commander, there is every danger that he might lose his head.

In contrast to the fire of the native troops, that of the 24th was disciplined and well controlled. There had been some heavy volleying to bring the Zulu chest grinding to a halt amongst the dongas to the north and east of the guns, but since that time, with no massed target presenting itself, the company officers and NCOs had imposed strict fire control. Essex recalled how the men of the 24th were laughing and joking amongst themselves as they plied their skill at arms. By now the mule cart and ammunition carrying parties had arrived on the northern stretch of the firing line, to begin the replenishment of E Company. Elsewhere on the field, somebody had also put some boxes of ammunition aboard mules; almost certainly this was the work of Quartermaster James Pullen.

Try as he might, Davies could not find the No. 2 Column wagons. He eventually found an opened ammunition box with about twenty packets left inside, in a tent in the cavalry lines. Davies set off to ride back to the donga with the box across the pommel of his saddle. He may have left the troopers who had accompanied him back to the camp to continue the search for the wagons. He would not make it back to the donga in time for even this paltry number of rounds to be used in its defence.

The Flanks

To the west of Isandlwana, the uNodwengu Corps was completing its descent from the hills. Pulleine must have been pre-occupied by Melvill's conclusion that the right horn was now somewhere behind the mountain.

Ultimately there was very little he could do about it. He had been left holding the metaphorical baby; in this instance the sprawling camp that Clery had so thoughtlessly laid out. He had committed every man he had to holding the front of the camp and so far he had not done a bad job. His battle line was holding, but he had no reserve in hand with which to deflect a fresh threat from the rear. Clery had laid out a camp to house and be protected by over 4,000 men. Not least there should be twelve companies of regular infantry to defend it. Pulleine had only six. The omni-directional defence of the camp at Isandlwana was an impossible task for so small a force. Thinking the situation through, and in this he would have been aided by the shrewd and able Melvill, Pulleine can only have concluded that disaster beckoned. This was now a matter of survival; the tents, the wagons, the oxen and the stores no longer mattered. It was necessary to contract the perimeter, to pull everybody back into a fighting square. It was a daunting task, given the dispersed dispositions of the troops.

To make matters worse, things were now going badly awry on the right, where the indunas of the uVe had succeeded in regaining the initiative. Although many of their men were pinned down in front of the Nyogane Donga, many more were still sheltered in the cover of the Nkengeni Ridge. Eventually they were rallied and led along the reverse slope to the left. Five hundred metres down the ridge, they broke cover and attacked downhill *en masse*. Whoever it was that led these men won the Battle of Isandlwana, for this was its turning point. They were well out of range of Bradstreet's police and volunteers on the right of Durnford's position. Not only had the donga been comprehensively outflanked, but its defenders were just about out of ammunition. The position was no longer tenable and Durnford bellowed an order to withdraw. All about him men scrambled through the wet shale of the Nyogane, back to the line of horse-holders. The men heaved themselves into the saddle and galloped uphill in the direction of the mountain. It would be a mile-long ride. Behind them, the uVe and iNgobamakhosi leapt to their feet and hurled themselves at the donga. Scott's carbineers tarried for a few seconds, firing from the saddle by way of a rearguard. Two troopers fell to Zulu return fire. Then Scott called in his men and galloped away behind everybody else.

Horrified by the scene unfolding on the right, Pulleine sent Gardner to find out what Durnford thought he was doing, and then turned with his regimental aides to try and salvage something of a now dire situation.

Chapter 6

Rally on the Colours

Last Stand of the 24th

The final phase of the Battle of Isandlwana is one of military history's great enigmas, and its faithful reconstruction one of its greatest challenges. It has much in common with the Little Big Horn, for broadly the same obvious reasons. Unlike Custer's disastrous defeat at the hands of the Sioux and Cheyenne, though, there were something in excess of eighty European survivors of Isandlwana. Surely, then, there should be little that is mystifying or unknown. The first-hand accounts of these men, invariably fascinating, frequently hair-raising, sometimes embellished, have served, however, not to add clarity, but to obscure the true course of events. These men were not in fact survivors of the battle's final and climactic phase, but rather had remained on the field only as far as its penultimate one. Even so, their ordeal was bad enough. The striking thing about their accounts is how the fate of the 24th Regiment is glossed over. We are left to assume that all are slain, or on the very verge of death, somewhere to the rear. Not one survivor's account describes the destruction of any one of the six companies of redcoats – not even of Pope's, assuredly the first to be overwhelmed. Occasionally, a survivor will make a fleeting reference designed to justify his departure from the field. One good example is Essex: 'Few of the men of the 1st Battalion 24th Regiment had time to fix bayonets before the enemy was among them using their assegais with fearful effect.' Yet the last thing Essex did in the camp was speak to Durnford, as he arrived at the tents from the donga. This places him about 800 metres from the left flank companies and well over a kilometre from Degacher and Wardell. We know from mutually corroborating sources, much better placed to see, that at this time the 24th was 'retreating very slowly'.* It takes about five seconds to fix a bayonet: the Zulu may be

---

* Higginson. A similar reference was also made by Curling.

famously fleet of foot, but no man is that quick across the ground.

Essex wrote the words cited above in time for the board of inquiry, which sat at Helpmekaar within five days of the battle. For company at that time, he had the grieving officers and men of D and G Companies, 1st/24th. Little wonder, then, that Essex and others resorted to vagueness and obscuration in their testimony, designed to conceal the fact that the 1st/24th was still substantially intact when they fled the field. The ethics of flight and the honour codes of the Victorian army have a crucial bearing on how the survivors shaped their testimony, and will be examined in more detail later. Crucially, when Essex gave this early evidence, nobody had yet identified that the 1st/24th died for the most part in rallying squares in the saddle, or that Wardell, for example, retreated 1,300 metres in order to do so. Essex could never have imagined this. Indeed, his testimony becomes untenable, when the evidence garnered during the later returns to the battlefield is considered alongside it. The best that can be said about Essex's remark on bayonets is that it is a white lie. All such survivor's testimony must be seen in the context in which it was made, and in the context of the psychological phenomenon known today as 'survivors' guilt complex'.

Survivors' recollections are largely characterised by tales of guns and limbers flying across the saddle; by the story of their own desperate ride, and of the men they saw around them; and by accounts of the cruel despatch of wounded or unhorsed men. Always the same explanation for survival is proffered: the Zulus had not quite closed the horns of the buffalo; miraculously a narrow corridor of hope remained open between Mahlabamkhosi and the Manzimyama Stream. The truth is subtly different. The horns may not have closed on the men who would go down in history as 'the fugitives', but for the great majority of British soldiers fighting at Isandlwana that day the Zulu encirclement was executed to perfection and snapped firmly shut across their line of retreat. Most historians have been taken in by Essex and others like him, so that in their traditionally sequenced version of the battle, the men of the 24th are polished off in front of the camp, often with indecent haste, before the writer then embarks on a lengthy and compelling narrative of the fugitives' race for survival. In fact the sequence must be reversed, for the truth is that whilst the fugitives were being harried along the line of the Manzimyama to the Buffalo the 1st/24th was still fighting fiercely for its life. The recurrent appearance of the flying guns in survivors' accounts enables us to fix their flight as being within eight or nine minutes, at the most, of the bugles sounding retire. The majority were quicker even than that. Thus, it was not the destruction of the 24th that precipitated the flight of the fugitives, but a deteriorating situation, which suggested that such an outcome was likely.

Writing home in the wake of the disaster, a young officer of the 1st/24th* wrote to a friend that the 1st Battalion had fought well, but had been slaughtered in seconds; he did not imagine this for himself – the idea was firmly planted in his mind by the survivors. In fact, the resistance was much fiercer and more protracted than they could ever have imagined, and the last victims of the fight fell not on the 'Fugitives' Trail', but in the camp. Thus a period of around forty-five minutes has been largely lost to history, because no white man who fought in it lived to tell the tale. Yet the story of this last great fight can still be traced. The men of the 24th did not panic, they did not run, they were not scattered and they were not immediately swamped. Rather, they stood shoulder-to-shoulder and back-to-back, volleying hard so long as their ammunition lasted, and when at length it was done they closed ranks still further and presented a bristling hedge of bayonets that the Zulus were quite unable to break at close quarters. Yet these were not superhuman fighters, they were merely the embodiment of all that is best in the British infantry. They shared an instinctive unity that only an ancient and revered regimental system can convey upon a body of men. They were proficient in their skill at arms, experienced in war and physically hardened by protracted campaigning. Above all else they were stubborn. But theirs was not a unique stubbornness, rather it was that habitual stubbornness in adversity exhibited so often over the centuries by the British infantry; the stubbornness that had prevailed at Agincourt, at Waterloo, and at Inkerman – the same sort of stubbornness that had carried the guns at Chillianwallah.

Reconstructing the Last Stand

In attempting to reconstruct the last stand of the 24th, we have five principal tools with which to work. First, there is the position of the cairns

* Lieutenant W. W. Lloyd.

which mark the graves of the fallen;* second, there are the accounts of the men who visited and described the battlefield before the interments took place;† third, there is a handful of reasonably coherent Zulu accounts which describe this phase of the fighting;‡ fourth, there is Maori Browne's account of what he saw through his binoculars, from his vantage point behind the Zulu left horn; and fifth, there is military probability and soldierly logic. This fifth and last dimension may be the most critical tool, for if Isandlwana is an incomplete jigsaw, then it is military common sense that offers by far the best prospect of filling in the missing pieces. Of no use at all are the survivor's accounts – they were not there and did not see what happened.

Before proceeding with the reconstruction, it will be instructive to consider a number of the key parameters around which it is based. It will also be necessary to dispel some of the myths that dog this great battle. Much will unfold as we go, but at the outset we will need to reflect on four key issues. The first is the retention of tactical cohesion by the 24th and its crucial connectivity to ammunition; next we must dispose of the 'official' version of events, which is trite, misleading, and in most respects just plain wrong; third we should reflect on the nature of the fighting; and last we should consider the command style of Lieutenant-Colonel Henry Pulleine, not only because it is an important subject in its own right, but because so much else flows from it.

Tactical Cohesion and Ammunition

In establishing our key parameters the best place to start is at the end – with where the British died – for this will indicate where the fighting was at its most fierce, and constitutes the single most crucial element in any reconstruction. The positions of the cairns and the pre-interment source evidence make it quite clear that around half of the 600 officers and men of the 24th made it back from their forward positions to the saddle. A further 120 or so were cut off, and died split between three identifiable and

---

* But we must be clear that the cairns can provide only a broad-brush picture. Many bodies were buried and re-buried; many were disturbed by wild animals; and many were scraped up into piles and were interred only in the general area of the point at which they fell.

† Principally Major Black and the correspondents Norris-Newman and Forbes.

‡ Principally Mehlokazulu, Uguku, and un-named interviewees of Mitford.

significant stands which took place just short of the saddle. Add in a conservative estimate of thirty or forty men shot down by the Zulus during the course of the retreat, and a little under a quarter of the 24th remain unaccounted for. The evidence enabling this conclusion is summarised at the end of the chapter, and is a key pointer to the maintenance of tactical cohesion. Men who are scattered in front of a much more numerous and more mobile enemy are easy to kill and do not die in large clusters.

What, then, was the key to the maintenance of tactical cohesion? To take the case of the men who died in the saddle or beyond, it is simply not possible for them to have fought back across the distances in question with the bayonet alone. Regardless of any adrenalin surge, men would drop from sheer physical exhaustion long before they had covered even 300 metres. The distances at issue vary between three and ten times that far. We can safely conclude, then, that most men of the 24th were still reasonably well supplied with ammunition when the crisis broke, and that firepower was the key enabler to the maintenance of cohesion. (Any remarks on ammunition supply must, however, be qualified by the observation that the situation in Cavaye's E Company was probably markedly different, of which more in a moment.)

To illuminate the developing picture further, we must consider the part of the Zulus in all of this. It is quite clear that the soldiers of the 24th could not have got back to the saddle, even with a plentiful supply of ammunition, if thousands of Zulus had been hanging on their flanks, or were already across their line of retreat. Since the soldiers did get to the saddle, then the Zulus were somewhere else, and that can only mean that they were still in front of the troops – prevented from pressing the withdrawal too hard by the same sort of fire that had held them in check earlier. It follows that, if the Zulus were checked in front, then the 'official' version of the battle cannot be true.

What then of the quarter of the 24th which remains unaccounted for within the arithmetic outlined so far? Where should we search for them? It is to study of the ground and military logic that we must turn. After the battle, there was no way in which the bodies of the 1st Battalion men and those of their 2nd Battalion comrades could be told apart. Their badges and other regalia were identical. There are, therefore, no clues in the conventional pre-interment sources, principally the accounts of news-papermen, as to which battalion died where. Only those who had known the men in life, and were capable of post-mortem identification of named individuals, could have thrown any light on the subject. Yet the two battalions fought on markedly different quadrants of the battlefield and it should not be surprising to find that their fortunes varied accordingly – for a time at least. The five 1st Battalion companies were engaged on the left and centre-left with the uNokhenke, umCijo and uMbonambi regiments. The men of the 2nd Battalion were engaged on the far right, with the uVe and iNgobamakhosi. It was on this side of the field that the crisis first broke and that the Zulu break-in took place. Once the donga had been abandoned, it was over the ground beyond G Company's right flank that the Zulus were able to manoeuvre unchecked and thus make rapid progress for the camp. If one stands on Charlie Pope's far-flung position, imagines the scenario with which he was confronted, and then turns around to look back across the huge distance to the saddle, it becomes immediately clear that the men unaccounted for in the big stands in the saddle, or elsewhere, simply have to be 2nd Battalion men. A recently unearthed source has now lent definitive collateral to this contention. The Royal Regiment of Wales Museum at Brecon has obtained the pocket book of Corporal John Bassage of the 2nd/24th's C Company, who was present in June 1879 when the regiment was finally able to bury its dead. It contains the following crucial notation: 'G Company 2nd/24th with the exception of a few men, was found lying in the place where they were posted the previous night as an outlying picquet.' We know that this location was along the general line of the Mpofane Donga. There were 176 2nd/24th men in the camp at the start of the battle, of whom approximately 145 were fighting on the firing line. This sort of figure almost exactly mirrors the quarter of the men so far unaccounted for. Thus we arrive at the key point in respect of the retention of tactical cohesion. The 1st Battalion was engaged in a distinctly separate fight from that of the 2nd Battalion contingent, and was able to retain its tactical cohesion virtually wholesale. It had sufficient time, albeit only a few short minutes, to reconfigure itself to deal with the deteriorating situation. By contrast, the 2nd Battalion contingent was left cruelly exposed by Durnford's retreat and was cut to pieces in that same brief period.

Taking as read the inescapable conclusion that the men of the 1st/24th volleyed their way back to the saddle, a digression to consider rates of ammunition expenditure up to this point may throw some further light on the issue of cohesion. As we have seen, the 24th had gone into action with seventy rounds a man. Based on the ammunition expenditure of regular infantry companies in the other major battles of the war, and assuming that the officers and NCOs of an experienced battalion like the 1st/24th would have exercised strict fire control, it is difficult to imagine the men firing more than about thirty-five rounds each on the firing line. Two months later, at the Battle of Kambula, Evelyn Wood's infantry would fire about the same amount in an action which lasted between three and four hours. At Ulundi, only ten rounds would be expended in half an hour's firing. In the case of Isandlwana, even thirty-five rounds would be fairly extravagant expenditure against an enemy who had been pinned to the ground within two to three minutes of being brought under fire, and held in check with only intermittent fire for a further twenty-five minutes at the most. In order to arrive at a worst-case calculation, let us assume a maximum of four minutes firing at the relatively rapid rate of three volleys a minute, and one round a minute thereafter for twenty-five minutes. This computes at thirty-seven rounds expended. At the time of the crisis, then, the majority of the infantrymen probably had around thirty-three rounds left in their pouches. It was this ammunition that would enable them to fight their way back as far as the saddle.

But what of the men who had been fighting on the spur? The rate of fire that Cavaye and Mostyn would have used on a passing target posing no immediate threat is debatable – it may have been as low as a round a minute, or as high as two a minute – but assuredly no more than that. It is relatively easy to calculate F Company's expenditure, as we know they were in action on the spur for about five minutes. Hence Mostyn's men had fired either an additional five rounds, or an additional ten rounds – leaving them with either twenty-three rounds or twenty-eight rounds in hand at the time of the crisis. It is rather more difficult to calculate the situation in E Company. If Mostyn was sent out to Tahelane as soon as Cavaye came into action, and allowing a ten-minute transit time for a company moving 1,000 metres at the double, then Cavaye was in action for fifteen minutes in all. This is far too long a pass-time for a body of 3,000 Zulus moving at a jog-run, however, and there would, in addition, undoubtedly have been a significant tactical bound between the two *amabutho* concerned. Let us estimate that Cavaye ceased firing for a period of around three minutes, meaning that the pass time for each of the roughly 1,500-strong regiments was a much more realistic six minutes each. Such an assumption would mean that E Company fired either twelve rounds or twenty-four rounds on the spur, and at the time of the crisis had either twenty-one rounds left, or as few as nine. If we assume the worst, and accept that it is distinctly possible that Essex's mule cart and carrying parties had insufficient time to effect a full scale replenishment of Cavaye's men before the crisis broke, then E Company could have been 'rounds expended' not long after the withdrawal began. Of course these are all rough order calculations, but they do serve to aid our comprehension of the battle.

On balance it seems likely that Cavaye's company would have fired at two rounds a minute on the spur, and when one breaks down Essex's movements and actions into their individual components, it is unlikely that twenty-five minutes was sufficient time to effect full-scale replenishment. First, Cavaye had to gather in Essex and speak to him; then Essex had to ride 500 metres back to the 2nd Battalion camp; next Essex had to interact with Quartermaster Bloomfield; then he had to organise Smith-Dorrien and the ammunition carrying parties; then he had to find and load a mule cart; then the heavily-laden carrying parties and mule cart had to transit the 500 metres back to Cavaye's position; then some boxes had to be smashed open; and finally the ammunition had to be distributed quickly and effectively along a company frontage of around 250 metres. In this reconstruction then, it will be assumed that, through no fault of his own, Essex's efforts were insufficiently timely, and that E Company was down to its last ten rounds when the bugles sounded retire.

Dispensing with the Official History

To continue delineating our critical parameters, we must now dispense with the most misleading but sadly still dominant interpretation of the battle. The *Narrative of Field Operations*, the official history of the war on which most writers have based their texts, is quite erroneous in its interpretation of the decisive phase. In essence it describes how a large body of NNC positioned in front of the guns broke in panic, opening a gap in the line through which the Zulus charged, quickly overwhelming the regular companies left and right of the gap. It is plainly apparent, however, that, if this had been the case, then the tactical disintegration of the 1st Battalion would have been immediate and there could have been no large-scale stands in the saddle. Furthermore, standing orders insisted that native troops were to be kept well out to the flanks, and we can account for the movements and paths of all the NNC companies. Barry never saw his men again after they fled from the plateau; Nourse never saw his again after they fled from the eastern side of Amatutshane; many of Erskine's men ran with Barry's; and Stafford, Murray and Krohn were all on the left of the camp, some 500–600 metres from the gun position. The only remaining company, Lonsdale's isiGqoza, is known to have been fighting alongside Wardell's company some time after the crisis broke on the right. In order to manufacture the mythical NNC contingent in front of the guns, some writers click and drag Barry's and Erskine's 'rallied' companies from the Tahelane Spur to the gun position. But real men do not behave like icons on a computer screen; on the real piece of ground, this is an utterly illogical line to trace, requiring the badly shaken NNC to move on a right rearwards oblique of well over a kilometre, away from the camp, and into the very jaws of the Zulu attack. In fact their only possible sanctuary was to be found on a left rearwards oblique towards the saddle. There is no question, therefore, but that the official history is quite incorrect on this point. More than anything else, its version of events constitutes the contrivance of an embarrassed and bewildered imperial army; an attempt to account for the unaccountable – the wholesale slaughter of a regular battalion by a 'primitive' native foe – by shifting the blame for it onto unreliable black allies. Sadly, the feeble official interpretation has been picked up and proliferated by successive generations of writers, most of them marching idly in the train of Donald Morris.

The Nature of the Fighting

The nature of the fighting at Isandlwana is another key area and one which is little understood. Most visitors to the battlefield imagine the great Zulu host sweeping forward in a single overpowering wave of humanity, the metaphorical juggernaut of the last chapter. They see in their mind's eye, a close-order assault conducted at great speed. In fact, within the overall confines of the army level scheme of manoeuvre, the indunas of the individual *ibutho*, and those of their component companies, were free to manoeuvre as the nuances and subtleties of the ground dictated. It had been widely recognised by the Zulu that firearms had brought a new dimension to warfare, and they had not been slow to adapt the classic battle tactics of Shaka's era. So, although an advance to contact was conducted in old style close-order columns and phalanxes, in the final approach such formations would quickly fan out into open order. When they were actually brought under fire, the warriors would resort to what are now regarded as the classic skirmishing tactics of the modern age. Having initially taken cover in long grass or folds in the ground, warriors would suddenly leap to their feet, dash forward ten or twenty yards, and then throw themselves down in the next available piece of cover. Thus they presented only the most fleeting of targets; typically a rifleman had only six or seven seconds to acquire his target, aim his weapon and get off a shot. Only marksmen of the very highest quality can consistently achieve hits on such targets. The battle was fought at the height of the sub-equatorial summer, a time of year characterised by extremely hot days and late afternoon or early evening downpours. The rainfall had been exceptionally heavy in December 1878 and January 1879 so that, by the time of the battle, the countryside was blanketed in luxuriant long grass. Such vegetation is ideal for the skirmishing tactics practised by the Zulu. If the British fire became too heavy even to move forward in bounds, then the warriors could continue to make forward progress by crawling slowly through the grass. Thus, the fighting must be imagined as looser, more fluid and, perhaps most importantly, much slower-moving than has traditionally been portrayed.

Pulleine's Style of Command

One final subject that warrants contemplation before we proceed with the reconstruction is Pulleine's command style. No single piece of source evidence pins down exactly how he commanded his battle. On the face of it, the missing details of his movements around the field are a critical gap in our knowledge. It is possible, however, by garnering clues, by applying military logic, and contemplating the ethical and doctrinal norms of the Victorian army, to deduce a strong set of probabilities. If an action or movement can be shown to be the most militarily logical one in the circumstances, and cannot be excluded by reference to the sources, then we are probably as close to the truth as we can ever be. If we can narrow Pulleine's movements down, then some of the other issues around the battle may fall into place.

There can be no doubt that Henry Pulleine has been done a disservice by successive generations of historians. All previous accounts have imagined him commanding his battle from some elevated viewpoint at the foot of Isandlwana. This is a huge distance from the firing line, so that he comes across accordingly as an ineffectual and rather lame commander at the tactical level. There is no evidence to substantiate such a view. The fact that not one of the fugitives saw him as they galloped through the tents, should be enough for us to conclude that he was almost certainly not on that part of the field. If he was not with the men at the rear, then he must have been with the men at the front, exactly where the ethics of the British officer corps required him to be. At one point James Brickhill actually looked for him, unsuccessfully scouring the 1st Battalion camp, the cavalry lines, the N Battery lines and the 2nd Battalion camp, just beyond which the front-line battle was raging. Donald Morris tells us emphatically in his *Washing of the Spears* that an officer killed writing in his tent was Pulleine. There is not a single shred of evidence on which to base such a pronouncement, and it is so bizarrely off-course in terms of military probability that not a single writer should have followed Morris's lead. Yet many did. More recent writers timorously advance that we cannot be certain how he died. Yet there are a number of strong clues. Maori Browne saw his body on the morning of the 23rd. His memoirs even contain an artist's impression of Browne saluting Pulleine's corpse. The two men knew each other well, and although the sighting took place early in the morning it was broad daylight nonetheless, so that there can be no doubt over the identification. At the time, Browne was on his way back from his wrecked tent in the 1st/3rd NNC encampment, to the saddle. This enables us to fix a general bearing along which Pulleine fell. Coupled with Brickhill's fruitless search in the opposite direction, along roughly the same bearing as Browne, then we have an excellent rough fix for the place at which Pulleine died. He died in the gap between the encampments of 2nd/24th and 1st/3rd NNC. He was shot; at least two fugitives heard Coghill say so. Pulleine was therefore far from being the ineffectual figure that historians have portrayed. He was right on the front-line, commanding a masterfully-conducted withdrawal, in an appallingly difficult tactical situation, and no doubt inspired the men of his battalion with his personal example and his courage. He paid for the steadiness he inspired with the early sacrifice of his life. An entirely new portrayal of the 1st/24th's commanding officer will emerge from this reconstruction. Let history think again about Henry Pulleine.

As we have seen, Pulleine would have been mounted, with Melvill and Gardner acting as his aides and gallopers. We know that Coghill was also mounted and dashing around the field, his knee injury notwithstanding.[*] Since he held a staff appointment, but was first and foremost an officer of the 1st/24th, it is almost certain that he was acting as a third mounted aide to Pulleine. Dyer may have been a fourth. So much for the men around him, but where was Pulleine when the crisis broke? If he had been to the left of the line, somewhere behind C, E and F Companies, he could not have seen the fight on the right; the right half of H Company and all of G Company would have been out of sight. Crucially, the entire fight in the donga would also have been invisible to him. The most logical place for Pulleine to be was on the rocky ridge to the right of the guns, just behind Wardell's company, for only from there could he see the whole battlefield and still be close enough to the troops to issue timely orders. This location also marked the rough centre of the battalion line and it is at the centre that the battalion commander is customarily to be found. The pivot of Wardell and Pope back onto the rocky ridge had been the most recent manoeuvre of importance, and was bound to have attracted the attention of the battalion commander. It seems a racing certainty, therefore, that Pulleine was in the general vicinity of the rocky ridge when the crisis broke on the right.

The Reconstruction

With these critical parameters established, let us now proceed with the reconstruction. Since there was no Zulu breakthrough in the centre of the firing line, then the British withdrawal was a deliberate act, not a spontaneous one. Penn Symons's researches established that at least two of the survivors he interviewed heard the infantry bugles sound 'retire' at this juncture. A warrior of the umCijo named uMhoti recalled, 'Then at the sound of a bugle the firing ceased at a breath and the whole British force rose from the ground and retired.' Often writers fail to connect the bugle call with Durnford's abandonment of the donga, but the linkage is absolute. Symons concluded that the bugles sounded on the British left, where Younghusband and Mostyn were positioned, and indeed they may

[*] Private Williams said that Coghill 'galloped up' to order Glyn's tent packed – *ergo* he was mounted and riding about, not observing the battle from the area of the headquarters tents.

well have done, but he also says that the call was relayed along the line. In fact, it is clear that the call must first have been sounded on the right, and was relayed in the opposite direction. Because of the lie of the land, the lower reaches of the Nyogane Donga cannot be seen from the positions to the left of the guns. Younghusband, Mostyn and Cavaye would all have been completely oblivious to the abandonment of the donga – in fact they would not even have known it was being held, only that the firing line ran to their right as far as the guns, and then disappeared into dead ground along the line of the rocky ridge. These officers were fully preoccupied with the fight in front, a fight which, as far as they were concerned, they were winning hands down. Cavaye may have had some anxiety about ammunition, but by now Essex's mule cart would have been on his position, in the process of being unloaded. None of them had any reason whatsoever to sound retire. Neither did they have the authority to do so; they were fighting on a battalion firing line, and as such only the commanding officer himself could give such an order. The job of the company commanders was to hold their ground and control the fire of their men, not to shape the strategy of the battle. The fact that the line was able to withdraw in good order shows that the call to retire was sounded promptly, when the crisis first occurred on the right.

Pulleine Battles to Keep Control

From his vantage point in the centre, Pulleine must have viewed Durnford's abandonment of the right flank with profound dismay. Aware of the presence of the enemy right horn somewhere behind Isandlwana, he would have sensed at once that things were coming unstuck on a grand scale. As we have seen, he immediately sent Gardner to find out from Durnford what he was playing at. He might have hoped briefly that the flamboyant sapper had some master plan in hand for dealing with the looming crisis, but as the flight of the mounted troops continued past Pope's right flank, such hopes would have been quickly dashed. The firing line was compromised – within minutes the Zulu left horn would be threatening its right and rear. There would have to be a withdrawal to a fresh defensive position. When an infantry battalion finds itself in desperate straits, and is about to engage in a difficult manoeuvre which could easily collapse into tactical disintegration and rout, and this was indisputably the predicament now confronting the 24th, then it is crucial

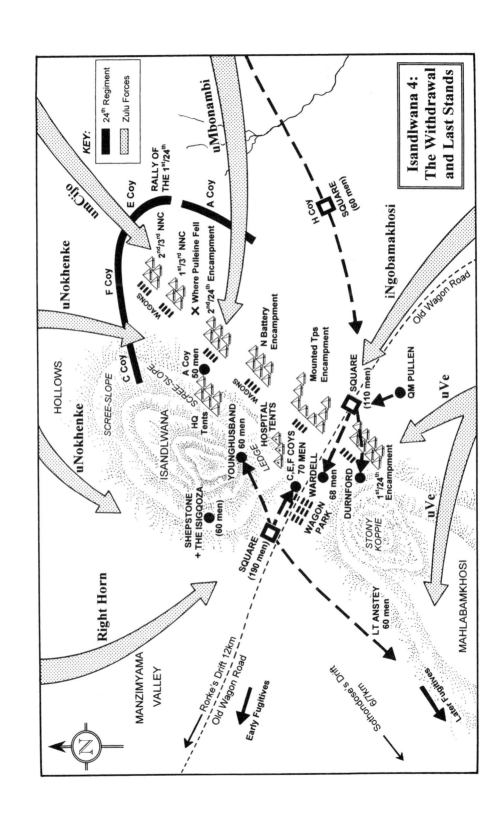

Isandlwana 4:
The Withdrawal
and Last Stands

that the commanding officer maintains firm control of the situation and, just as importantly, that he is seen by his men to be in control. He must make his presence felt and dominate events by his force of personality and resolve. What exactly Pulleine did next can only be a matter of conjecture, for he would be dead in less than ten minutes and none of the men with whom he interacted in this crucial period would survive the battle. So many things happened concurrently in that same short period of time that their recounting will take considerably longer than the events themselves. With the caveat that the movements and actions of Pulleine and his immediate staff officers are reconstructed purely on the basis of military logic, let us start the clock on the last ten minutes of Lieutenant-Colonel Henry Pulleine's life.

The first thing he had to do was to convey his intent to withdraw to the company commanders, at least three of whom would not have been able to see the reason for doing so. He had to do this in a clear and unmistakeable fashion and, above all else, he had to do it quickly. The bugle would be the best option for achieving this. Pulleine and his aides rode across to the nearest drummer, probably one of George Wardell's, and told him to sound retire. The only viable tactic for dealing with the unfolding crisis, would be to withdraw the companies back to a central rallying point, where the battalion could form a 'receive cavalry' square. Since the right flank was now wide open, the obvious thing to do would be to rally on the left, where the flank was still anchored, where there was some prospect of Isandlwana providing rear protection against the as yet uncommitted right horn, and where there was sufficient ammunition stockpiled to sustain a protracted defence.

It would be necessary for the CO clearly to mark the point on the ground where the rally was to occur. The very reason that a battalion had colours was to act as a clearly visible rallying point above the hubbub of battle. Pulleine therefore ordered Melvill to gallop back to the tents to fetch the 1st Battalion's Queen's Colour from the guard-tent, which was located just behind the 1st/24th encampment. The adjutant would have been a very natural choice for such a task. Traditionally he was responsible for the care and safe custodianship of the colours, and was also a key authority figure, a man deputed as a matter of course to speak and act with the commanding officer's authority. Probably the plan was not much more sophisticated than rallying as many men as possible in one place, ideally around the ammunition wagons. 'Rally on the colours' was one of the great heroic clichés of the era, but it still had real military validity; everybody knew what was meant by it.

The adjutant set off at the gallop, on a left oblique, in the direction of the saddle. Melvill would soon have realised that he was in a race against time and the Zulu left horn, part of which was even now pushing rapidly uphill in pursuit of Durnford's men, and another part of which was wheeling inwards to attack Pope's company. The scene unfolding on the right would have compelled Pulleine to write off any idea of salvaging G Company, and to concentrate his attention on saving as much of his own battalion as possible. Pulleine would have wanted to snatch a few words with each of the company commanders in turn, in order to confirm his intent and allay any confusion. He probably now turned to ride back along the firing line towards the camp, in order to do so. Already other company buglers had picked up the call he had initiated, and the order to retire was on the lips of everybody in authority.

In order for the infantry to command the dongas in front of the guns with fire, it was absolutely necessary for them to occupy the forward slope of the rocky ridge. As soon as A Company fell back onto the reverse slope, there would no longer be any means of keeping the warriors below in check. When Degacher and his men came shuffling back on either side of the guns, Stuart Smith knew that it would be only a matter of time, before the Zulus came charging over the low crest in front of him. Keen to give the infantry a little breathing space, he barked out the order to load with case-shot. Sure enough, as the deadly charges were being rammed home, a hubbub from the dongas indicated that the umCijo were on their way. When a band of them crested the rocky ridge, they found themselves staring into the barrels of the 7-pounders; with the last fire order he would ever give, Stuart Smith blew them to eternity.

A letter from Pulleine's groom, a young Merthyr soldier called Thomas Parry, who was not at Isandlwana, but back on the lines of communication, probably at Helpmekaar,* would suggest that Pulleine had a horse killed

---

* Parry claimed, in a letter to his parents written from Helpmekaar on 14 February (reproduced in the *Herefordshire Times* of 12 April 1879), to have been at the Defence of Rorke's Drift. He does not, however, appear on the defenders' roll and most scholars are inclined to dismiss his claim. Some extend this further to disbelieve everything he said in his letter. This is perhaps a little harsh – certainly there is nothing overtly suspicious in the rest

under him during the battle. How this snippet of the action on the firing line came down to Parry is unclear, but he might have heard it from one of the NNC Europeans who survived the battle. Pulleine was popular and well thought of: Parry is certain to have asked around the survivors for news of his late master. Since Gardner did not report so noteworthy an event as the unhorsing of the battalion commander, this enables us to pinpoint it as occurring either at the time Gardner was away leading Bradstreet's men forward to the donga, or more probably now, at the critical and vulnerable juncture at which Pulleine and Coghill set off along the rear of the companies to confirm the order to retire and rally on the colours. No doubt there was a hard fall for Pulleine. He would have kicked himself free of his horse, clambered to his feet, and immediately cast about for a remount. Coghill, of course, could not yield his own horse to the bruised and winded commanding officer due to his knee injury. Most probably the remount would have come from a potential cast of Degacher or Wardell, who as senior company commanders might well have been mounted, or Dyer, the adjutant of the 2nd Battalion, who certainly had a horse on the firing line but seems to have fallen back with H Company on foot.

Saving the Guns

As soon as the guns had discharged their deadly hail of canister, Smith and Curling bellowed the order to limber up. In a trice, the gunners had lifted the trails clear of the ground and began heaving the 7-pounders over the

---

of it. He had become separated from Pulleine when one of the colonel's horses went lame, presumably on the way up from Pietermaritzburg, a journey with plenty of potential to injure one of the animals. It seems probable, then, that Pulleine left his groom at Helpmekaar and went on with his second horse. Parry might have marched on Rorke's Drift with the Helpmekaar companies on the night of 22 January, and got to within earshot of the battle; thus it would be a relatively short hop to telling a white lie to his parents about his role in the proceedings. On the other hand, one of the worst honour-code crimes a soldier can commit is that of staking a false claim to having been in a particular engagement. A stray officer's batman is exactly the sort of man who might have been missed when compiling the rolls, especially if, as a 1st Battalion man, he had been sent back within a few days of the battle to join the remnants of his unit at Helpmekaar. By the time he wrote his letter, Parry was parading with D Company, 1st/24th. Such a man *might* have been forgotten about and he *may* really have been at Rorke's Drift. His tale of Pulleine being unhorsed would be so bizarre a thing to make up a story about that I am inclined to believe that he did hear of it from one of the non-commissioned survivors.

intervening ten yards to the limbers. It was a frantic race against time. As their first duty was to serve the guns, the men of Curling's division were only lightly armed for self-defence with sabres and revolvers. No doubt some of them felt compelled to draw their revolvers now. As the cry went up to 'save the guns', Degacher's infantrymen stepped up their rate of fire, to keep the ground around them clear of the enemy. In twenty seconds the guns were limbered. As the drivers whipped up their animals, some of the gunners were still afoot, and were forced to scramble hurriedly for seats on the limbers and carriages. One courageous and fleet-footed Zulu survived being shot down by A Company and stabbed one of the gunners to death as he was in the act of climbing into an axle-seat on one of the guns. Soon the teams were in motion and before long they were pulling away at a sharp trot. Not all the men clambered aboard in time and a number of them were forced to run after the guns on foot. The Zulus raised a great roar as they saw the British retire: no doubt Smith, Curling and the two gun-sergeants had to battle to control their frightened horses before they were able to haul themselves into the saddle.

G Company's Plight

From Charlie Pope's position, the situation already looked grim. A minute or two earlier the battle had been static and the only Zulus in plain view were the ones lying maimed or dead on the forward slope of the Nkengeni Ridge. Now that same slope was alive with warriors. There may have been as many as 2,000 men of the iNgobamakhosi surging over the crest in front of Pope. They were almost a mile away and would take five or six minutes to close on the firing line if left unchecked. As many as a thousand more warriors were considerably closer. These were the men who had been caught on the forward slope by Durnford's volleys and sought concealment in the long grass. Now they were back on their feet and skirmishing forward once more. Pope brought them under fire at a range of about 600 yards, but was unable to prevent them occupying the Nyogane Donga.

If there had been nothing else to command the attention of the 2nd Battalion contingent, it might have been possible to blunt this renewed attack along the general line of the donga, but even bigger problems were now burgeoning on the far right. Beyond Pope's right flank, there was now nothing but a mixed and disorderly crowd of riders – police, carbineers,

NMR men, Edendale Christians and Basutos – all galloping back up the slope towards the tents. Behind the long string of riders, the warriors of the left horn were hastening up the slope in pursuit. Furthest forward were the men who had broken over the ridge to Bradstreet's right, but echeloned behind them at varying distances were thousands more warriors that G Company had no hope of stopping. In a matter of minutes, many of these men would begin wheeling in to roll the company up from the right. It probably did not take Pope long to confront the ugly fact that there was no viable tactical solution to his predicament, and that the annihilation of his command was now only minutes away. For want of any better plan, he stood his ground.

From his position further along the ridge, Captain George Wardell had also witnessed the abandonment of the donga and was similarly grappling with its dire implications. He was quick to perceive that G Company was living on borrowed time, that the wholesale collapse of the British right was imminent, and that his own predicament was only marginally less serious than Pope's. All along the rocky ridge, the cry to 'fix bayonets' was raised. A British soldier is trained to know that when this order is given by his officers, he is about to experience the supreme human ordeal, a hand-to-hand fight, in which the man who can unleash the most primeval aggression is the man who will prevail. The order to fix bayonets invariably causes an adrenalin surge. Men steel themselves to the fray; they know there will be no rules, that it is kill or be killed; their vocal cords raise an involuntary and guttural growl; their faces harden to the scowling and ferocious features of demons. There are few things on this earth as terrifying as a British infantryman with a levelled bayonet.

Withdrawal of the 1st Battalion

The deteriorating situation on the right was not visible to the companies on the left, which, in response to the bugles, began to retire on the camp, unaware for a minute or two that the situation was as serious as it was. Zulu oral tradition would have it that an induna of the umCijo called Mkhosana kaMvundlana was responsible for the forward movement made on the Zulu centre-right at about this time, which, it is claimed, drove the British line in on the camp. The senior Zulu commanders had assembled on the top of the Nyoni Ridge, just above where Isandlwana Lodge now stands, from where they had an outstanding view of the battle below.

Mkhosana was sent forward from here, to re-energise the stalled attack. Arriving amongst the men of his own *ibutho*, he berated them furiously for cowering in the cover of the dongas. Many of the umCijo responded to his challenge and leapt to their feet with a roar. As he turned to lead the charge, Mkhosana was shot in the head and killed. He rightly deserves his place in the Zulu pantheon of heroes, for he reinvigorated and revitalised a stalled attack, a notoriously difficult thing to do on a battlefield. But to overlay oral tradition with military reality, there were also more practical reasons why many more warriors than could possibly have seen or heard one man railing encouragement surged forward from their cover at this point.

As we have seen in discussing the withdrawal of the guns, only the original forward slope positions could command the upper reaches of the Nyogane Donga; within a few paces of making a retrograde movement, F, E and A Companies would be on a reverse slope, unable to hold the Zulus in check. It was evident that the assault would be given renewed momentum once the line had fallen back onto this slope. The same principle was true for Wardell and Pope on the right – withdrawal from the rocky ridge would leave them unable to keep the Zulus pinned down in front of Amatutshane. Freed at last from the deadly fire of the 24th, the Zulu surged forward, first by the score, then by the hundred, and then in thousands. The British were broken – it was time to kill them all as they fled. But the 24th Regiment was made of sterner stuff, and was about to play a cruel trick on the warriors at the forefront of the renewed assault.

The immediate problem for F, E and A Companies would be to hold the determined rush of the umCijo in check, when it broke out of dead ground at relatively short range. On the extreme left, Younghusband would be less hard-pressed as his flanks were secure, the mountain shielding his left, and Mostyn's company his right. Additionally, his immediate foe, the uNokhenke regiment, had dissipated its effort by splitting its attack between the hollows and the Manzimyama Valley. In all four of the companies on this side of the field the officers and sergeants battled to keep control, striving to contract the extended company frontages in on the centre, and exhorting their men to remain steady. Crucially, they knew the importance of maintaining a bold front – to turn and run would be to invite disaster – the same precept that is applied in the bush to an unexpected encounter with a lion – keep calm, walk slowly backwards, look as untroubled as possible and, above all else, do not run, for this is sure to trigger a charge.

In stark contrast to the steadiness of the 24th, at the first sign of a retrograde movement the NNC companies collapsed into a panic-stricken rabble. Many levies cast aside their weapons as they ran; others ripped off the red rags customarily worn around the head or the upper arm to identify them as 'friendlies'. The European officers and NCOs each made their own personal decision to fight or fly; most commonly the decision was governed by whether the man was mounted or not. Higginson remembered the disintegration of Krohn's company:

> When my company saw them coming on, nothing could stop them; they all jumped up and ran and though I knocked a man down with my rifle it was no use. I then saw the men of the 2nd Batt NNC running and looking for the 24th men. I saw that they were retreating also, but very slowly. All the mounted men were riding past as fast as they could.

Higginson's account is of importance because it contains a *bona fide* glimpse of the 24th companies on the centre-left at the time of the crisis: they were 'retreating . . . very slowly', a remark wholly corroborated by Curling's testimony. The mounted men referred to by Higginson were Zikhali's Horse who, like the NNC, abandoned their positions on the British left as soon as the 24th began its withdrawal. As he rode past F Company, one of the European officers noticed Lieutenant Pat Daly smile and wave farewell to him. There was one notable exception to the wholesale disintegration of the levies: the isiGqoza Zulus of Lonsdale's No. 9 Company kept their nerve and stood firm on the rocky ridge near H Company.

The last place a man should be caught on a battlefield is standing upright on an open slope, seventy yards from the enemy. The umCijo regiment scrambled out of the dongas, surged over the abandoned British positions and charged boldly onto the reverse slope. F, E and A Companies were waiting and primed in a rough but resolute two-rank battle line. In the preceding forty seconds or so, they had contracted into close order and fixed bayonets. As an inevitable consequence of closing ranks, there were now significant gaps between companies. Suddenly the redcoats disappeared into clouds of billowing white smoke, as three thunderclap company volleys mowed down the Zulu pursuit. Without waiting for the smoke to clear, the company commanders volleyed again. Almost all the rounds fired in these deafening and terrifying salvoes would have struck home amongst the umCijo's leading wave. No man could remain upright in the face of such a fire. The surviving warriors threw themselves flat amongst the dead and maimed, giving the men behind them the impression that the slaughter of the leading ranks was wholesale. Perhaps more bravehearts rushed forward in a fresh assault wave, regardless of the heavy losses in front, but if they did, then they too were swept away by the fire of the 24th. Everywhere the mangled corpses of once magnificent specimens of a proud and noble warrior race lay strewn in the grass. The big 0.45-inch Boxer round was a fearsome man-stopper which could leave an exit wound the size of a saucer in a man's back. The agonised suffering of the wounded was no doubt terrible to behold. After Isandlwana, the old hands would say, the *amabutho* never came on in quite the same way. On that bare and gentle slope, old Africa met its death at the hands of the Martini-Henry.

On the right, Alan Gardner had intercepted Bradstreet and some of the mounted volunteers as they galloped back towards the camp. Challenged on the inadvisability of the retreat, Bradstreet replied that it was Durnford himself who had ordered it. A moment or two later, the colonel came riding up the slope and remarked that the position had been 'too extended'. Everyone rode on for the saddle. Completely powerless to influence events, Gardner kicked up his horse and rode after them.

Keeping the head of the impassable Mpofane Donga to their left, Smith and Curling led the gun-teams towards the camp at a brisk canter. As Smith scoured the ground ahead for a new gun position, he could see the uVe and iNgobamakhosi charging uphill for the 1st Battalion tents in the mouth of the saddle. There was every danger they would be in amongst them before the guns could get through. Smith concluded that there could be no question of halting this side of the mountain. He decided to aim for one of the intervals between the encampments, probably that between the 2nd/24th and N Battery. In their anxiety to break through the closing trap, the drivers whipped their wild-eyed teams into a gallop that was altogether too fast for the rocky terrain. It is distinctly possible that some of the men seated on the limbers and guns would have been jolted off.

Panic Breaks Out

There were still a great many men watching events unfold from amongst the tents and wagons. From the elevated ground at the foot of Isandlwana, they had a commanding view of the battlefield and could see the rot of tactical disintegration setting in. Looking to the left, they could see around 400 black levies fleeing through the tents in the direction of the saddle, with their European officers and NCOs scattered amongst them. Barton, Raw and Vause had similarly lost control of Zikhali's Horse, who were to be seen cantering along the foot of the mountain behind the tents. It looked very much as if they had no intention of reining in again until they were safely back in Natal. Beyond the routing native troops, the main body of the 24th was falling back slowly in the face of a great arc of skirmishing warriors, but it would have been obvious to the observer that no matter how well the regiment was bearing up, it was doomed ultimately to be assailed on all sides. Looking to the front, the observer would have seen the two guns and their accompanying outriders galloping back in the direction of the tents. On the rocky ridge, Wardell had just broken clean with H Company and was doubling down the reverse slope in the direction of the Mpofane Donga. Strangely, a small party of his men was still on top of the ridge. Lonsdale's isiGqoza were near H Company and falling back in conformity. G Company, meanwhile, was under acute pressure in front, and from the right, but was nonetheless standing its ground on the rocky ridge and volleying into the iNgobamakhosi.

Looking hard right, our observer would have seen Durnford and the last of the men from the donga arriving back at the tents. Some of the European troopers were dismounting, but many others were riding hard for the saddle. Around half the black horsemen on this side of the field galloped clean through the encampments without stopping. Another large group reined in around the ammunition wagons in the 1st/24th lines. Further down the long glacis slope as many as 6,000 warriors of the uVe and iNgobamakhosi were now in plain view. Some had only just broken over the Nkengeni Ridge; others were skirmishing through the grass and boulders against Pope's position; but out on the open flank, a great mass of warriors was rushing forward completely unchecked. It was this awe-inspiring sight that decided our observer, and most others like him, that the situation was irredeemable. With the mounted troops failing to rally in any substantial numbers, they were right.

Panic quickly set in amongst the civilian drivers and *voorloopers*, some of whom had mistakenly inspanned earlier in the day and now tried to drive their teams away along the old wagon road. The ox-wagon does not make the best of getaway vehicles, and it seems certain that the first few to move would have run into each other in the first 200–300 yards, preventing others from getting under way. The snarled wagons would have been quickly abandoned; at least one overturned in a donga. Everywhere men seemed to be running in search of horses. In the N Battery lines, Sergeant Costellow helped himself to Stuart Smith's charger Black Eagle. Curling's servants, Driver Tucker and Gunner Green, mounted spare battery horses and rode away bareback.

The urge to quit the field was not entirely unanimous, however. Charlie Raw spotted the Honourable William Vereker on foot and quickly rounded up a horse for him. Vereker was about to mount, when a trooper of Zikhali's Horse appeared and protested that the horse was his. With the consummate gentility of his kind, Vereker immediately handed the animal over. Raw and the trooper rode away, leaving the hapless Vereker to reflect that his luck had finally run out.

Amidst all the panic James Brickhill decided to look for Quartermaster Pullen, presumably to seek guidance on what he should do. On his way to the 1st Battalion camp, he passed a civilian wagon conductor of his acquaintance called L. P. Dubois, who asked him in Zulu how things looked. 'Ugly', said Brickhill bluntly. 'Yes, the enemy has scattered us this day', replied Dubois. The splendidly be-whiskered Major Francis White, the 49-year-old paymaster of the 1st/24th, had no intention whatsoever of quitting the field, though he certainly had every opportunity to do so. He had served with the 24th continuously since 1850 and was a veteran of its service in the Mutiny. White strode not away from danger, but into it, making his way through the tents to join in the fighting as a combatant officer.

Quartermaster Pullen Holds the Right

From his wagons behind the 1st Battalion camp, Pullen had a grandstand view of the flight of the mounted troops. As they raced uphill towards him, he could see that the British right was now completely unhinged.

Like the old soldier he was, he decided to do something about it.* He would round up some men to try and hold the left horn on the glacis slope, short of the saddle. Leaving a boy-soldier to guard his ammunition, Pullen made his way on foot into the stream of refugees, bellowing, 'Come on men. Rally here. Follow me. Don't be running away like a parcel of women! Let's try and turn their flank.' In the confusion he spotted Brickhill approaching and called out to him, 'Mister Brickhill; do go to Colonel Pulleine and ask him to send us help, as they are outflanking us here on the right.' Brickhill further recounted that Pullen then led a party of 'soldiers' to 'the front of stony koppie'. 'Soldiers' is a colonial euphemism for regulars, and the 'stony koppie' is how people referred to Mahlabamkhosi. It seems improbable that Pullen went alone into the stream of refugees and was successful in persuading panic-stricken men to dismount alongside him. Much more probably, the soldiers who went to the right had been with the quartermaster all along. Given the geography, it was almost certainly Pullen and his men who initiated what history would record as 'Durnford's Last Stand', for it was in front of Mahlabamkhosi that this took place. We know that some red-coated soldiers were found amongst the men who fell with Durnford. Historians have traditionally accounted for the presence of these men by describing them as remnants of Pope's company but, as we have seen, there is huge difficulty around any suggestion that G Company men could have got back that far. Much more probably then, these were men of the 1st/24th's pioneer section – whose place of duty had been with Pullen in the camp – plus a few orderlies and bandsmen who had also been helping out with the ammunition. This would explain how the 1st Battalion ammunition wagons, which must have been a hubbub of activity

---

* Private Bickley, who had been posted during the first alarm to guard the officers' mess tent, says in his statement that QM Pullen ordered him to saddle a horse for him. The impression is given that this is a precursor to flight. In fact, Pullen showed no inclination whatsoever to leave the field, and it seems certain that this incident occurred prior to the collapse of the perimeter. Pullen may have wanted to ride out to the firing line to superintend the distribution of ammunition. Brickhill's statement makes it clear that, after the collapse, Pullen was engaged in rounding up all the men he could. Had he got his hands on Bickley at this time, rather than earlier, he would have taken him off with the rest of his party to oppose the left horn. Unfortunately, and no doubt unintentionally, Bickley left on record a sequentially jumbled version of events, which serves to cast an unwarranted slur on Pullen's undoubtedly courageous conduct.

up to the point when the perimeter collapsed, came to be so suddenly deserted by all but a lone boy-soldier.

Flight of the Native Horse

Much nonsense has been talked and written about the NNMC, suggesting they were some sort of elite amongst the native troops. Perhaps it is true that the men of the Edendale Troop were a cut above the rest. The native horse could ride and, importantly, the British had armed them well, but ultimately they were a ragtag and bobtail outfit, just like the rest of the levies. They were poorly trained, ill-disciplined and drawn from the same tribal stock as the rest of the NNC. They were no more resolute in adversity than their brothers and no more willing to die for Queen Victoria. When the British began their withdrawal, the native horse fled the battlefield *en masse*. Notwithstanding the scale of the disaster, there were tellingly few casualties amongst these men: less than thirty out of 260.

From the British left came the troopers of Zikhali's Horse, whose flight over the saddle reduced the hesitant men amongst the tents and wagons to panic-stricken ones. Simultaneously, the Basuto and Edendale troops galloped into the encampments from the direction of the donga. The Basutos took one look over their shoulders and fled the field. By contrast, Sergeant Simeon Kambula kept most of the Edendale men in hand and made for one of Pullen's ammunition wagons to replenish his bandoliers. The boy-soldier left to guard the wagons refused to give Kambula any ammunition. There were a few cartridges lying around in the grass, and some of the Edendale men dismounted and scrambled around on their hands and knees to pick them up. Kambula tried to persuade the boy to climb up behind him, but he was insistent that he could not leave his post. After briefly contemplating the disaster developing around him, Kambula concluded that he could be of no further service to his British masters on this side of the mountain. Instead, he led his men over the saddle into the valley beyond, where the troop would continue to do some good service in the British cause.

Pope Stands Firm

With apparent disregard for the deteriorating situation, the 2nd Battalion contingent was still standing its ground along the line of the rocky ridge. In fact, given the huge distance back to the camp, Charlie Pope could come up with no practical alternative. On the forward slope below, the right wing warriors of the iNgobamakhosi were striving to press home a strong frontal attack, but the G Company volleys were as punishing as ever, so that forward progress remained risky and could only be achieved by means of short rushes from cover to cover. Any check Pope's fire may have imposed could only ever be fleeting, however, as the left wing warriors were now wheeling in to roll up the firing line from the right. With each passing second the danger became more pronounced.

When the assaulting warriors were within striking distance, the soldiers on the right fell back from the crest of the rocky ridge to the reverse slope, in an attempt to refuse the line in the direction of the threat. It is impossible to know for sure whether Pope and Godwin-Austen co-ordinated this, or whether it was a largely instinctive recoiling movement; probably it was the latter. The reverse slope descends gently to the Mpofane Donga, and it is between the rocky ridge and the donga that the G Company cairns are to be found. They are roughly linear in distribution and run parallel to the ridge, about 150 yards back from the crest.

Although at first glance it is not immediately apparent, the linear distribution of the cairns does not in fact define a firing line being driven in frontally as it retired down the reverse slope, but rather a line of retreat parallel to, and between, the rocky ridge and the Mpofane Donga. In other words, Pope's men fell back not in the direction of the saddle, but towards Wardell's position. This was an entirely involuntary line of retreat, dictated by the onset of the enemy from the right. The 'Humblers of Kings' were young, fearless and fleet of foot, and their assault was mounted in overwhelming strength. This time they were not to be denied. The sections on the right did their best to stem the rush with the most rapid rate of fire they could manage, a shot every six or seven seconds, but it was impossible for such diffuse firepower to stop so massive and determined a charge and it quickly came to a hand-to-hand brawl.

From the outset the men of the 2nd Battalion stood little or no chance, but they were proud and disciplined professionals and did not go down without a stiff fight. There was no time for the men on Pope's right flank to coalesce into the larger bodies that would at least permit the sort of protracted resistance seen elsewhere on the field. The best that could be managed was to come together in threes and fours and sixes. One such band was a four-man group from C Company, 2nd/24th. Three privates rallied around Sergeant William Shaw: one was Private Benjamin Latham, a 21-year-old Newport lad; the second was Private Thomas Jones 976 from Brecon; and the third was Private James White, whose home town is unknown.* No doubt they died hard, for the snuffing out of even such little stands as these was no easy proposition for the iNgobamakhosi. The combined length of rifle and bayonet was six feet. This gave the redcoats a far superior reach to that of the *iklwa*. Many Zulus fell to a lightning quick thrust, as they came to close quarters. Some soldiers had their lunge deflected by a cowhide shield, and had to be quick to regain their balance and so avoid the ensuing counter-thrust. Not all succeeded in doing so. By and large, with the Zulus attacking in overwhelming numbers against a thinly spread skirmish line, the mêlées were one-sided combats and ended in seconds. Within two or three minutes, the right flank of G Company was no more.

In the fleeting breathing space bought by their comrades, the men in the centre and on the left were able to rally on Pope and Godwin-Austen, and fall back before the onset of the enemy. But now the rocky ridge had been ceded and with each passing second dozens more warriors were pouring over it to enter the fray. Under massive omni-directional attack, the remnants of G Company were broken up into ever-smaller knots of men. In one place around fifty soldiers managed to coalesce and form a rallying square. Their cohesion enabled them to sustain a fierce but brief resistance and bought time for other men to scramble away. Hemmed in on all sides, and without any supporting fire from other elements of the British force, they were soon cut down where they stood. With their assault gathering momentum in proportion to the weakening resistance in its path, the iNgobamakhosi pressed the extermination of the 2nd/24th along its line of retreat. Here and there, a last few men stood at bay over wounded comrades, to defend them briefly in their helplessness. In six or seven minutes, it was over. Somewhere in the fray, Griffiths VC met his end; no doubt it was a fitting one.

Enquiries by 2nd Battalion officers after the war established that Pope and Godwin-Austen were distinctly remembered by the Zulus. They stayed together to the end and died back-to-back, blazing away with their revolvers. When one of them was shot down by a Zulu rifleman, an induna hurled himself forward to attack the other. The officer fired three shots at

---

* Notebook of Corporal Bassage, Royal Regiment of Wales Museum.

him: the first grazed the right of his neck, the second hit him in the left ribcage and the third wounded him in the leg. The induna recoiled in pain but had sufficient strength and presence of mind to hurl a throwing assegai into the officer's chest. The officer staggered but did not fall; he had almost extracted the assegai from his body, when the induna fell upon him and finished him with his *iklwa*.

It is highly improbable that a single G Company man made it back to the saddle. Those who had been left badly wounded were quickly despatched, as excited warriors ran from corpse to corpse stabbing them repeatedly, a practice known as *hlomula*, ordinarily resorted to in the hunt to celebrate the slaying of dangerous game animals. During the war this practice greatly angered the British who in their cultural ignorance viewed it as nothing more than needless mutilation of the dead. In fact it constituted high tribute by the Zulu to the worthiness of their foe. After being subjected to *hlomula*, the 2nd Battalion corpses were rolled onto their backs and slashed open along the length of the abdomen. This was a Zulu ritual practice known as *qaqa*, conceived of as releasing the victim's spirit. It was believed that if a warrior failed to carry out *qaqa*, his own stomach would swell like that of a corpse left to rot in the sun. Worse, he would be haunted by the imprisoned spirit of his victim and by the *umnyama* or evil forces, of which every Zulu lived in mortal dread. After *hlomula* and *qaqa* had been performed, the pouches of the butchered G Company dead were rifled for cartridges by those warriors quick enough to pick up a Martini-Henry.

H Company's Plight

In the centre, Captain George Wardell and the men of H Company found themselves in a similarly desperate predicament. When the bugles sounded retire they were the best part of a mile from the saddle and the sanctuary of a battalion rallying point. In the donga in front of their sector of the rocky ridge, the uMbonambi regiment and elements of the iNgobamakhosi were waiting for the slightest opportunity to dash forward and renew the assault. There may have been as many as 2,000 warriors in front of H Company. Like the company commanders left and right of him, as soon as Wardell fell back onto the reverse slope, he would lose the ability to suppress the enemy by fire. If H Company was to cover the great distance back to the camp, it would need some form of head start. There was

probably a hurried consultation with Colour-Sergeant Wolfe, the outcome
of which was that Wolfe would remain on the rocky ridge with one of the
company's sections, to act as a rearguard, whilst Wardell rallied the other
three into a square and fell back on the camp. If all went well, the
rearguard would break clean and dash back to the square under the
covering fire of its volleys. It was a plan born of desperation; no doubt it
was Wolfe himself who suggested it.

As Wardell looked to his right, he could see G Company falling back
from the ridge to face the seemingly inevitable prospect of being engulfed
by the left horn. To the left, the umCijo were charging out of the dongas
to press the companies of the centre-left. To the rear, the guns were
bouncing away at a canter. Wardell knew he had only seconds to play
with. Seeing no viable alternative he gave his assent to the plan, and Wolfe
moved onto the firing line to detail men to the rearguard. Moments later
Wardell bellowed the order to fall back. As speed was of the essence, there
was nothing of the parade ground about the ensuing manoeuvre.
Signalling to Lieutenant Atkinson and the three section commanders to
follow his lead, Wardell jogged away in the direction of the camp. Nearby,
Captain James Lonsdale took his cue from Wardell and led off his isiGqoza
in the direction of the Mpofane Donga.

In front of Wolfe and his twenty riflemen, the uMbonambi had been
seized by the sense of renewed bravado coursing through the *impi* at the
sight of the British withdrawal. In an instant, they were up and out of the
dongas and came charging up the rocky slope in their hundreds. In that
moment, Wolfe must have known that there would be no dash back to the
company main body. He probably ordered one or two controlled volleys,
before yelling to the men to load and fire as fast as they could. Knowing
that the rearguard could buy only a limited amount of time, the other three
sections instinctively coalesced around Wardell as they jogged along. They
had probably not covered much more than about 200–300 metres when
the frantic firing from the rocky ridge caused them all to look back. One
moment the men of the rearguard were kneeling and blazing away; the
next, they rose to their feet as one, and instinctively backed together. It was
the cue Wardell had been watching for; he stopped at once and roared the
order to form square. The enlisted men quickly clustered around their
officers and sergeants and jostled themselves into a two-deep ring, which,
whilst it bore little resemblance to a geometric square, fulfilled the crucial

tactical requirements of having no flanks or rear. Sixty men were crammed into an area of ground perhaps ten or twelve yards across. Behind them, the uMbonambi poured over the rocky ridge in a great black tidal wave. For a few seconds the wave seemed to break around a tiny island of red … and then the red could be seen no more. Further to the right, Pope's men were now locked in the savage hand-to-hand fight that would bring about their destruction. From here on in, every step of the way would be a dogfight for H Company.

Flight

Edward Essex made his way back through the tents amongst the NNC fugitives. In the saddle he met Durnford, who asked him to bring some men to hold the left horn in check. The two men quickly parted company but, realistically, there was nothing Essex could do. There was nobody to bring forward; the infantry were still fighting in front of the tents and everybody else was making their way out of the rear of the camp. For Essex, the writing was on the wall. He cantered off amongst the rest of the fugitives. Alan Gardner had arrived at the same conclusion a minute or two earlier. Cochrane, too, had been quick to cross the saddle, in company with the native horse.

We would do well to reflect on the ethics of flight from the battlefield, as this is an important issue in the context of Isandlwana. Men have always run away from battlefields. Most commonly they do so as a panic stricken rabble. There can be glory in defeat though – Leonidas and his Spartans, the whitecoat infantry at Marston Moor, the Texans at the Alamo, the Legion at Camerone, the 24th at Isandlwana. These actions have a common bond: the *esprit de corps* of the vanquished precluded any question of flight. They believed themselves to be better men than the enemy; they disdained the normal human instinct for self-preservation; in a sense they could not bring themselves to recognise the reality of their defeat. Isandlwana was no different from any other defeat – men ran away. The thing that makes Isandlwana difficult in ethical terms is that one part of the British force was a disciplined body of professional soldiers, well imbued with *esprit de corps*, whilst the rest of the force was made up of hastily raised and poorly motivated levies, or part-time units of colonial stake-holders. It should not be surprising that the conduct in defeat of these two groups of men lay at opposite ends of the spectrum. It is not a crime not to behave like Leonidas, or Bill Travis, or Captain Danjou. These are examples of exceptional gallantry. So too was the stand of the 24th. By all normal standards, the 24th should have collapsed in panic. The fact that it did not do so is remarkable. It also quickly became a problem for the Isandlwana survivors, particularly after the battlefield was re-visited and the bodies of the 24th were found clustered in rallying squares.

Many of the fugitives fled when all normal men would have fled, and at a point when they were perfectly entitled to do so. A man is only a coward if he runs when the issue is still in the balance; when defeat is not yet certain. There was a very brief moment when the situation in front of the camp could have been saved. Had Durnford's command rallied *en masse* in the saddle, and ammunition had been brought up quickly, then the right might have been held, enabling much of the 24th to complete its withdrawal in good order, though G Company was doomed in any scenario. The fact is, though, that Durnford lost control, and most of his men fled the field. These early fugitives behaved reprehensibly, for the issue was not yet settled beyond doubt. From the very instant that Durnford's men failed to rally, however, defeat became inevitable.

Nobody in the succeeding waves of fugitives, the likes of Smith-Dorrien, Smith, Curling and so on, can be considered to have behaved improperly. Those lucky enough to survive would, however, be personally compromised by the extraordinary steadiness of the 24th and the supremely demanding honour codes of the Victorian military. The infantry behaved as the British public expected its infantry to behave – rather death than dishonour. They lived up to a romantic ideal. The fact that some men present on the field did not do so does not make them cowards, though in the immediate aftermath of the battle this was an inference that the surviving professional soldiers lived in dread of.

The men who found themselves most embarrassed to be alive were the five regular officers who would survive the day: Gardner, Essex, Cochrane, Curling and Smith-Dorrien. Whilst an instinct for self-preservation might be readily condoned by the public today, such an unworthy motive was not at all in line with the code of honour which governed the conduct of the Victorian officer corps. Whilst the public and the army had low expectations of colonial officers, regulars were a different matter. They held the Queen's Commission, an honour which singled them out as a special breed, men who were prepared to die for queen and country. So long as one enlisted man fought on, it was the duty of a regular officer to stand by him. This onus was absolute in the case of regimental officers. Indeed, it is part of the regiment's oral tradition that, as the crisis worsened, the mounted officers of the 24th turned their horses loose. Regardless of how fair or unfair this whole precept was to officers who found themselves in impossible situations, it was what was expected; it went with the territory. As a result, the five regular officers who survived Isandlwana would purposely resort in their accounts to vague language designed to obscure the fact that the 24th was still fighting hard in front of the camp when they left the field. They could not afford to let the real time and space equations become common currency, for then they would assuredly face the cheaply levelled accusation of cowardice, and consequent dishonour and ruin. Skin of the teeth survival was one thing, and in an extreme situation like Isandlwana might just teeter on the brink of acceptability, but crowing about it was another. People like Edward Essex were sensible enough to keep their heads down, grateful merely to be alive. Alan Gardner, though, made a serious mistake. It seems that he attempted to portray his role in the battle in altogether too heroic a mode. Thereafter the whispering began, until eventually it broke into open ridicule and became the talk of the army. In due course, the derision found its way into the colonial newspapers. Gardner may have survived the battle, but to all intents and purposes, he was finished.

It is often mistakenly believed that all the survivors had to run the gauntlet on the Fugitives' Trail. In fact, there was a golden window of about five minutes duration, when the route to Rorke's Drift lay pretty much wide open. After clearing Cavaye's killing area, the reunited right horn regiments, the uDududu, the iMbube and the iSangqu, had faced an awkward scramble along some narrow and rocky defiles during their descent along the line of the Manzimyama Stream. Their journey coincided almost exactly with the duration of the fight on the firing line. Prior to their arrival there were only a few parties of the uNokhenke in the Manzimyama Valley, the men who had slipped down from the hollows at the north end of Isandlwana. These groups picked off some of the early fugitives in the area of the stony drift, but they were insufficiently strong to deal with larger bodies of fugitives, such as the Basuto troop. When such groups appeared, the uNokhenke bands slipped back into the grass and let them pass unhindered.

One of the first men to flee the camp was the NNC officer Gert Adendorff. He would travel the direct route back along the wagon road to the ponts at Rorke's Drift, where in due course he raised the alarm with John Chard. So incomplete was his report that Chard at first refused to believe that there had been a disaster; with good reason – Adendorff had not seen one, he had merely sensed it coming. The first sizeable group of fugitives to cross the saddle were Hlubi's Basutos, led by Lieutenant Henderson, now riding in the company of a civilian meat contractor called Bob Hall. The Basutos were followed by substantial parties of Zikhali's Horse. The rocket battery survivors, Grant, Trainer, and Johnson, also got out along the road at this time, but were amongst the last to do so.

In the time that it took Simeon Kambula to rein in at the 1st Battalion wagons, implore the boy-soldier to come away, and distribute the cartridges his men had picked up from the grass, assuredly not more than about four minutes, the situation in the Manzimyama Valley changed completely. As Henderson and the mounted natives were galloping uphill from the Manzimyama Stream, the warriors of the vanguard regiment of the right horn began to emerge into the open behind them. The main avenue of approach was along the narrow re-entrant through which the stream flowed down from the hills. The drift and the road were within thirty metres of its mouth, so that within seconds of the first warriors completing their descent, the direct route to Rorke's Drift was severed as a line of retreat. Although the deployment of the right horn was hindered by the narrowness of the defile, the leading parties of warriors were quick to attack towards Isandlwana. From the stream to the saddle was a distance of about a mile. It was a steep uphill slope and the going was difficult; scree-boulders provided their usual nuisance underfoot, and there were a number of moderately deep dongas running down off the south-western corner of Isandlwana. In the centre, the old wagon road climbed tortuously up the slope to the saddle.

In the six or seven minutes it took the Zulu vanguard to get up the slope, many fugitives were able to evade their onset by diverting along the eastern side of the Manzimyama Valley at a left oblique. It was this treacherous downhill oblique that would define the line of the 'Fugitives' Trail'. After a two-mile angled descent to the Manzimyama, the route crossed over the stream and began to rise again onto the equally difficult southern slopes of a hill called Mpethe where, to add to the misery, there were also a number of bogs. Then it was a steep downhill to the point on the Buffalo known as Sothondose's Drift, the difficult and seldom-used native crossing soon to bear the new designation 'Fugitives' Drift'. When the river was in spate, as it now was, the drift was impassable – to all but men in mortal fear of their lives. The very rocks that enabled the locals to hop across the drift in the dry winter months were now treacherous underwater obstacles. In addition there were literally thousands of sub-surface boulders, jumbled together along both banks of the river; it is difficult to imagine an obstacle more likely to break a horse's leg. Depending on the course steered by the individual rider, the Fugitives' Trail was five to six kilometres long.

For about five minutes, men crossing the saddle were able to flee unopposed along the left oblique. Thereafter, parties of warriors were in a position to give chase to those who had gone ahead or to harry those still leaving the camp. There were, then, four kinds of Isandlwana fugitive: those who were quick enough to get out along the road to Rorke's Drift with Henderson's Basutos and Zikhali's Horse, and who thus got away without significant hindrance; those who were able to divert unopposed along the Fugitives' Trail; those who were able to divert down the trail unopposed, but sufficiently late to be chased along it; and those who experienced the full nightmare of running the gauntlet at the mouth of the saddle, being chased along the trail, and harried over its course by parties of warriors already ahead of them. Few of this last category would survive.

From his aid post at the hospital tents, Surgeon-Major Shepherd sensed the looming disaster and quickly instructed Lieutenant Arthur Hall and his ten Army Hospital Corps medics to load the wounded aboard an ambulance wagon. Next, he told the bandsmen helping at the hospital that they could be of no further use. Band-Sergeant David Gamble told his lads to make their way to safety as best they could. Private Edmund Wilson and another man, possibly one of the Hospital Corps men as Wilson does not seem to have known his name, took a stretcher and ran across to the rocks at the foot of Isandlwana. A passing carbineer advised them to clear out all together. They dropped the stretcher and fled over the saddle on foot. Wilson was lucky enough to catch a riderless horse in the Manzimyama Valley. Although he would be unhorsed in crossing the river, he met with Private James Bickley on the far bank and one of the colonial volunteers brought him a spare horse. In due course Wilson and Bickley got separated, but Wilson would make it to Helpmekaar just as the sun was setting, in company with Sergeant Naughton of the mounted infantry. On the high ground on the Natal bank of the Buffalo, Bickley fell in with Captain Essex; they would likewise make their way to Helpmekaar by nightfall. No doubt Shepherd had intended the ambulance wagon to trot out along the old wagon road, but on crossing the saddle the driver would have seen the warriors of the right horn lining the banks of the Manzimyama below. The wagon had to be abandoned. At some later point, the wounded men in the back were dragged out and butchered. For many weeks after the battle the ambulance could still be seen from the area of Rorke's Drift, silhouetted against the skyline in the mouth of the saddle.

H Company Falls Back

Having watched his colour-sergeant and the brave little rearguard go down in a flurry of flailing bayonets and rifle butts, George Wardell prepared to blunt the exuberance of the uMbonambi. 'Ready . . . Present!' – up came the H Company rifles. The volley punched hard into the regiment, bowling a couple of dozen warriors over, and driving hundreds more to ground in anticipation of the next salvo. Wardell did not disappoint them. For the next few minutes he continued to sweep the ground around his square with deadly volleys. Realising the futility of pushing directly against the square, the warriors edged left and right of it, dashing from cover to cover as they went. In between volleys Wardell kept making ground in the direction of the saddle. H Company now found itself in its own private fight, in the very centre of the battlefield. Now and again, the uMbonambi's return fire found its mark amongst the clustered redcoats. Men who went down wounded were dragged into the centre of the square and helped along by a mate.

Before long H Company found itself at the Mpofane Donga, a significant obstacle to its further retreat. The isiGqoza crossed ahead of H Company. They had remained faithfully alongside their British allies much longer than the rest of the native troops, but now the situation was so serious that they too bolted for the saddle. For all his amateur status, Captain James Lonsdale was a man who knew what it meant to be an officer. With the crisis deepening around him, he dismounted, gave his horse to his headman, Malindi, and turned back on foot to join the 24th. For the men of H Company the scramble across the donga was frantic; the imperative was to get across as quickly as possible and re-form on the far bank, before the Zulus could exploit their vulnerability. Fortunately the company's musketry had bought it a short breathing space and the wary respect of the uMbonambi. They were able to cross the donga without serious loss and quickly huddled back into square. Wardell ordered another volley and continued the withdrawal in the direction of the saddle. Stung by H Company's fire, many of the uMbonambi took cover in the Mpofane Donga and stayed there.

Defence of the Right

In front of the 1st Battalion tents, James Pullen and his party opened fire on those elements of the uVe and iNgobamakhosi which had bypassed the G Company fight and were continuing the charge uphill for the tents. Given his background as a former sergeant instructor of musketry, we can be sure that Pullen exacted a high personal toll of the enemy. About now, Corporal Richardson of the pioneer section was badly wounded in the arm. Somebody seems to have helped him onto a horse, to join the stream of fugitives. No doubt he was a poor horseman in any case, but the serious extent of his injury and the extremely difficult going cannot have helped his equitation. Just a little way into the Manzimyama Valley, he was seen to fall off his horse. With only one good arm, Richardson found he was unable to haul himself back into the saddle. He was soon caught and killed by warriors of the right horn.

Durrant Scott and his party of police and carbineers had their blood up, as they came galloping back up the slope to the tents, the last group of riders to do so. They had fired on the *impi* all the way from Mabaso Ridge; they had fought in the notch, fought from Pope's flank and fought from the donga. They had loitered behind all the other mounted men to cover the withdrawal from the Nyogane. They came up the glacis slope well behind everybody else, riding in the very teeth of the enemy, and looked on in disgust as the rest of the mounted troops fled the field. Now, in a heroic act of defiance, these resolute men threw themselves from the saddle beside Pullen's twenty-strong party of redcoats, and turned their horses loose. From somewhere nearby, Durnford cantered up, dismounted and took command of the combined group. For a while the left horn was held on the slope below and prevented from breaking into the saddle.

At the joint Anglo-Zulu 125th Anniversary Commemoration of the battle, held on the field itself, the warriors of the modern-day Isandlwana *ibutho* sang many of the old songs. I listened to them in the company of my friend Lindizwe Ngobese, a descendant of Sihayo and a fine singer-songwriter in his own right, who was good enough to translate the gist of them for me. At one point Lindizwe turned and said with a puzzled expression, 'Now they are singing about fighting the zebras at Isandlwana. I don't understand what they mean by that.' It came to me at once: 'They are singing of the carbineers, Lindizwe.' 'Ah . . . of course,' he said. The uniform of the Natal Carbineers was a dark tunic faced with white collar and cuffs, with a broad white stripe down the outside seam of their trousers. Durrant Scott and his men would have been proud to know that their fight was destined to be so long remembered.

The Right Horn Prepares to Attack

In the Manzimyama Valley the indunas of the uNodwengu Corps were raging amongst their warriors to restore discipline and order. Whilst they had lost control of the first few hundred men to emerge from the hills – the warriors who were now harrying the fugitives – it was imperative that the rest were brought under control quickly. There was still a serious fighting role for the right horn to fulfil. When the *amabutho* were properly formed, they would attack the British rear over the saddle. The narrowness of the defile through which they were emerging into the valley, was an aid to the indunas in their attempts to regain control. Whilst some of them did the necessary railing and gesticulating, others began to form the regiments along the line of the Manzimyama as each successive group came up. More parties of the uNokhenke were also dropping down into the valley from the hollows at the north-west corner of Isandlwana. The charge of the umCijo had cut across their front and pushed the redcoats back on the tents, so rather than lead their warriors into the camp behind the umCijo, some indunas decided to move down to the Manzimyama and attack the British from the other side of the mountain.

The 1st Battalion Coalesces

Aware that their dreadful volleys had again checked the umCijo, the officers of the left flank companies seized the opportunity to retire towards the tents at the front left corner of the camp. The soldiers walked slowly backwards, locking themselves into a rough line between the shoulders of the men left and right of them, striving always to keep formation and retain their cohesion. The sergeants raged up and down the line, holding things together with commands bellowed above the din of battle. In F Company, for example, it was Colour-Sergeant James Ballard and Sergeants Thomas Cooper and George Upton who provided this crucial level of leadership. Bodies of the uNokhenke, the umCijo and the uMbonambi continued to press the 24th, but were less bold than formerly, skirmishing from cover to cover towards the troops. Where the instinctive coalescing of the men had opened gaps between companies, the warriors of the chest pressed hardest. Every now and again, though, one of the bands of redcoats raised its rifles in unison and swept away those warriors who had erred by pressing the withdrawal too hard.

Some of the Zulus continued to put their rifles and muskets to good use. By now the range was short and the clustering effect amongst the British made them a much easier target than formerly. Each time the companies took a few steps back, there now seemed to be one or two of their number on the ground at their feet. Rather than leave a comrade behind, the men left and right of a casualty would haul him up roughly and help him to the rear. Here and there a man was too badly injured to help himself and had to be left to his fate. A string of red-coated bodies sprawled in the grass now marked the line of the retreat. Where they could press close enough, bands of warriors filled the sky with showers of throwing assegais. By now the retreat had reached the tents and shelters of the NNC battalions. As the Zulus pushed through the camps behind the 24th, they stabbed furiously at every living thing they encountered. Maori Browne's Hottentot groom was too slow to get away and was assegaied behind his master's tent. In their frenzy, the warriors slew both of Browne's spare horses too. Then to cap the scene of desolation that would greet his eyes the following morning, a Zulu went into the tent and pinned his devoted setter to the ground.

Over the next 200 metres of the retreat, the paths of C, F and E Companies converged until there was a solid mass of redcoats clustered between the front left corner of the 2nd Battalion camp and the mountain. A Company had furthest to come, on a left rearwards oblique from the gun position, and was still slightly separated from the other three companies. Allowing for casualties shot down in the withdrawal, there may have been

270 officers and men in the general vicinity of the rally point. Pulleine and Coghill had ridden the length of the firing line as it fell back, and were now at the centre of this large body of men.

Pulleine Orders the Colours to Safety

Since 1879 it has been part of the regiment's oral tradition that, when all was lost, Henry Pulleine ordered Melvill to carry the colours to safety. Regardless of the absence of a primary source that can verify this particular piece of interaction between the two men, we in the regiment know that it occurred. As Chelmsford himself said, Melvill was simply too good an officer to have left the field without a direct order to do so: as the adjutant such an order can only have come from the commanding officer. Nor could the colours ever leave a battlefield except by the express permission of the commanding officer or, if he had been killed, at the direction of the next senior officer. Today there is a lamentable trend amongst a small clique of revisionist historians to write cynically of the high drama of 22 January with the apparent aim of undermining this and all the other great deeds of the day. There is no room for heroism or sentiment in their world it seems.

The revisionists will hint to the effect that Melvill took the colours, without orders, in order merely to save his own skin. It is quite clear from the sources, however, that such people spout not only a low form of cynicism, but also extremely bad history. In fact, it can be shown that Melvill made it back from the guard-tent to the left front of the camp, where the 1st Battalion was attempting to rally; it can be shown that this is where Pulleine was; and finally, it can be shown that Pulleine was still alive when Melvill went on his way. Close examination of Private Williams's statement reveals that he was back in the area of Glyn's tent when he saw Melvill ride past in the direction of the saddle with the Queen's Colour. This tent was part of the column headquarters encampment at the centre of the mountain. Although he was still using his rifle to good effect, Williams had wisely kept one of the colonel's horses tethered within arm's reach. Moments after Melvill passed Williams, Coghill rode up and told him to save himself. The Queen's Colour had been kept in the guard-tent, which was located on the saddle. Melvill *must*, then, have brought the colour from the guard-tent back into the heart of the fray on the left of the camp, in order to be seen by Williams going back in the opposite direction. Later, on the Fugitives' Trail, we know that Coghill would report to Melvill that Pulleine had been shot – clearly then Pulleine was unharmed when the adjutant departed the field. As we have seen, Maori Browne would pass and identify Pulleine's body the following morning, as he rode back towards the saddle from examining his wrecked tent on the left of the camp – exactly where it should be for the paths of Melvill and Pulleine to have coincided in the manner of the legend.

It is clear, then, that Melvill did succeed in bringing the colours to the commanding officer at the left corner of the camp. The colours represent the heart and soul of a regiment; they are emblazoned with its bloodily won distinctions; they epitomise its proud record of service; they are consecrated by clergymen at first presentation; they are the personal gift of the sovereign, venerated by officers and men alike, who are universally sworn to defend them with their lives. Their loss to the enemy is the ultimate disgrace. As the adjutant rode up with the colours, Pulleine must have cast about himself and recognised that the situation was utterly hopeless. Those parts of the battalion that could rally in one place had now done so at this left corner of the 2nd Battalion camp. The likely course of the battle and its certain outcome were clear for all to see. All that remained was to die with honour.

Pulleine turned to Melvill and ordered him to cut his way out with the colours. Almost certainly this was coupled with an injunction to warn the garrisons at Rorke's Drift and Helpmekaar. It was a moment of supreme drama in the lives of these men. It would be nice to think that they had time to shake hands. As Pulleine turned back to the fight, Melvill pulled his horse about and galloped away along the rear of the regimental encampments, passing Private Williams at the headquarters tents a few moments later. Probably for a brief moment or two, the colonel railed encouragement at the men of his battalion. Then a round fired from amongst the pressing Zulu host sent Henry Pulleine reeling from the saddle. Almost certainly it killed him instantly. With the man he was serving as aide now down, and quite unable to play a vigorous role in the fighting because of his injury, Coghill judged that the best thing he could do was to ride after the adjutant and assist him with the salvation of the Queen's Colour, and in raising the alarm with the nearby garrisons. On his way past the headquarters tents, Coghill reined in and told Williams to save himself.

The Manzimyama Valley

In the mouth of the saddle, Smith and Curling reined in to make a hasty assessment of the situation. Only at this juncture did Curling realise that the major had been shot in the arm. The gun teams had gone on ahead, now crewed only by the drivers mounted on the limber horses.[*] A few moments earlier, Brickhill had noticed some of the N Battery gunners jumping from the limbers at the right-rear corner of the 2nd Battalion camp. They may have done so as a result of the bone-jarring ride back from the rocky ridge, during which they would have been compelled to hang on for grim death. Clearly the ride was not going to get any easier or safer on the other side of the saddle. Probably they intended to look for spare saddle horses in the battery lines. Curling had witnessed the death of one of his gun-sergeants during the dash through the camp. As the artillery officers pondered what to do, Coghill appeared from the left and reined in beside them. Smith asked whether a stand could be made in the saddle, but Coghill replied that he did not think it could be done. All three turned to ride after the guns and were amongst the last to break out of the camp.

As they emerged from the saddle into the valley, Coghill's horse was struck in the rump by a throwing assegai, but galloped on without faltering. Further down the slope, Coghill remarked to Curling that Colonel Pulleine had been shot. Before long the three officers caught up with the gun-teams, which had been forced to leave the road and divert cross-country. The going was impossibly difficult. Some of the *voorloopers* and levies were running alongside, clinging to the harness of the offside horses. A few hundred metres down the slope, a deep donga drained off Mahlabamkhosi to the Manzimyama. When Commissary Hamer and four other riders had hit this obstacle some minutes earlier, they had come under attack from the high ground to the left, and were forced to turn downhill to the right in search of a viable crossing point. Hamer said that he and his companions were obliged to use their revolvers 'very freely' during this diversion.

The donga was a wholly different proposition for the gun-teams. As the

---

[*] Curling later commented that only one 'gunner' remained with the guns at this time. This is often misinterpreted to mean only one member of the RA. There was, however, a very clear distinction between gunners and drivers, which Curling would have taken as read. He means that only one gunner remained seated on the limbers or guns. The number of drivers is unknown.

ground opened up before them, the artillery drivers knew instinctively that it was too late to stop; it was all or nothing. One of the teams crashed down over the bank at speed, badly damaging the limber on impact. Try as they might, the drivers were unable to get the terrified, tangled and possibly injured animals, to haul the gun out again. In an act of desperation, the lead driver of the second team must have whipped his horses up and over a low shelf of rock or some other immovable object, because when the wheels of the limber came into contact with it the whole team came to a dead stop. Such an impact must have thrown the driver from his stumbling horse into the donga below. Flailing around on the bank of the donga in shock and terror, one of the lead-pair fell from the edge and dragged its companion with it. The Zulus were on the guns in an instant.

As Curling galloped past, he saw one of the unfortunate drivers being pulled from the saddle and done to death. He did not see anybody else, suggesting perhaps that the other drivers were lying stunned or dead at the bottom of the donga. The warriors quickly turned on the horses, no doubt thrusting behind the forelegs for the heart, as they did when hunting game. The lead-pair of the gun stuck on the rocks were left suspended over the edge of the donga by their harness. In the confusion, Coghill and the two artillery officers became separated. A little way down the valley, Coghill caught up with Melvill, who was riding at this time with Private Bickley. As the trio cantered on, Bickley overheard Coghill report Colonel Pulleine's demise to the adjutant.

James Brickhill had done his best to find Pulleine and pass on the quartermaster's message about the right flank. He rode across the road from the 1st Battalion camp into that of the mounted troops, and from there into N Battery's lines. Continuing through the tents, he arrived in the 2nd Battalion camp. It was here that he saw one of the gun-teams come through at the gallop. Looking along the line of the tents, Brickhill could see that the infantry were being driven in from the north. He was now very close to the front-line; for a man enjoying civilian status to tarry here any longer would be nothing short of foolish. Though he could not have known it, the man he sought had only just been killed. Brickhill was a cool customer. He had already remained in the camp longer than most mounted men, and even now he decided to ride back through the tents to find Pullen. When he got back to the saddle he could see no sign of the quartermaster, who by now would have been fighting on the forward slope in front of the 1st Battalion tents. Already there were Zulus pushing into the encampments and, unarmed as he was, Brickhill had no option but to kick up his horse and ride away over the saddle. Not far down the trail, he grabbed the bridle of a riderless horse and led it down the slope to a soldier on foot. It was to no avail; the man was shot dead in the act of climbing into the saddle. A little further on, Brickhill passed and recognised Band-Sergeant Gamble, who was 'tottering about amongst the stones'. 'For God's sake give me a lift,' he implored. With candid honesty, Brickhill admitted in his account that he spurned Gamble's frightened plea with, 'My dear fellow it's a case of life and death with me.' Moments later Gamble too was done to death.

Recap

Not one of the men still fighting in the camp at this point was destined to survive the battle and so, as our reconstruction approaches its denouement, it becomes increasingly difficult to deal in absolute certainties. What follows is a best estimate of how the final stages of the fight unfolded. It will be as well at this juncture to stop the clock in order briefly to recap the situation as best we can. Falling back from the 2nd Battalion camp to the artillery lines, moving parallel to the rows of tents, were four significant clusters of redcoats. These were the main bodies of C, F, E and A Companies which, allowing for the attrition caused by Zulu rifle fire, were each sixty to seventy men strong.

Younghusband's C Company, still largely intact by virtue of its secure flanks, was falling back in the gap between the encampments and the eastern scree slope of Isandlwana. One of the C Company sections remained at the top of the slope, falling back parallel to the company main body just below. Parties of the uNokhenke were pressing the section back across the rocks, but so far the soldiers had been able to hold them at bay with rifle fire.

Amongst the unit wagon lines and the rearmost rows of tents were Mostyn's men, firing to the north on the uNokhenke and the umCijo. Cavaye's company was on Mostyn's right, amongst the front rows of tents, similarly attempting to keep the umCijo in check. Given their particular ammunition problem, it is likely that parties of E Company men were sent back to Bloomfield's wagons to pound some boxes open. They would have had to work quickly as, within a few minutes, the withdrawal was certain to cede the 2nd/24th encampment to the enemy.

Degacher's A Company was refused at a rough right angle to Cavaye's men and was fighting along the front of the camp, with the tents immediately to its rear. Fighting on two fronts, Degacher had been under acute pressure throughout the withdrawal; A Company had probably taken quite heavy casualties as a consequence. Now, as the umCijo continued to press the company in front, the warriors of the uMbonambi were threatening its open right flank from the area of the Mpofane Donga. Perhaps 300 metres beyond Degacher's right, Captain George Wardell was falling back towards the 1st Battalion tents with around sixty of his men. Lieutenant Henry Dyer, adjutant of the 2nd Battalion, had also made his way back with the H Company square. On the far right, many of the left horn warriors had closed in on the men standing firm around Durnford, Bradstreet, Pullen and Scott. Their situation was becoming more hopeless by the minute, but thus far they had denied the saddle to the Zulus* and kept alive H Company's slim chance of joining up with the rest of the 1st Battalion.

Notwithstanding the loss of their commanding officer, more than three-quarters of the 1st Battalion men, say 340 in all, were still alive and fighting for survival. By stark contrast, the 2nd Battalion contingent had been all but annihilated on the reverse slope of the rocky ridge; only a few bandsmen and pioneers, whose place of duty had been in the camp, remained alive.

The fugitives were long gone and were now battling their way at speed across the painfully difficult ground from the Manzimyama to Sothondose's Drift. Parties of the uVe had pushed south of the Durnford fight, and had driven on over the southern extremity of Mahlabamkhosi, to effect a junction with the right horn in the valley beyond. Men of both horns had given chase along the Manzimyama and been involved in the slaughter of the dismounted and unhorsed fugitives.

On the western slopes of Isandlwana, a party of NNC levies had rallied around George Shepstone who, for some reason, had been unable to break out along the Manzimyama with the rest of Durnford's officers;

---

* Mehlokazulu: 'When the Carbineers reached the camp they jumped off their horses and never succeeded in getting on them again. They made a stand and prevented our entering the camp . . . '

perhaps he had been unhorsed in the attempt. It seems certain that the men around him were isiGqoza Zulus, who would have found all escape routes closed to them by the time they crossed the saddle. Some way down the slope the main bodies of the uDududu, the iMbube and the iSangqu were now formed up in a holding position above the banks of the Manzimyama, from where they hurled insults and blood-curdling death threats at the isiGqoza. The heavy firing from the other side of the mountain indicated that there were still plenty of red soldiers left to kill. Knowing that their indunas would release them to the assault at any moment, the warriors worked themselves into a state of frenzy.

The A Company Fight

The indunas of the uMbonambi had rallied their men in the Mpofane Donga to protect them from the heavy fire laid down by the 24th during their withdrawal. Now, they judged the time to be right for a renewed assault. Leaping into the open, they whipped up a charge against the front of the camp. The assault came surging in well over a thousand men strong. With only fifty or so rifles available, there was little A Company could do to stop it. Seeing the uMbonambi rushing in from their left, parties of the umCijo leapt to their feet and also pressed an assault against Degacher's men. The soldiers of A Company realised immediately that they were the focus of the enemy's attention. There was no longer any point in carefully husbanding the cartridges they had left, so they loaded and fired as fast as they could. Although a few dozen men of the uMbonambi were shot down, the regiment's frenzied charge proved remorseless. When the racing warriors got to within a hundred yards, the redcoats looked around for their company commander and ran in to rally around him in a cluster that would pass for a square. In its terrifying isolation, A Company steeled itself to make an end. The uMbonambi charged in from all directions, flailing assegais, knobkerries and shields. The momentum of the assault drove the fight back into the 2nd Battalion tents. No doubt Paymaster White did sterling service with his revolver, but it was in this fight that he fell. Some men rallied again in a small knot just behind the ammunition wagons; they held their ground for a minute or two, until at length their pouches were empty. After a savage and supremely violent flurry of hand-to-hand fighting, this last remnant of A Company was also annihilated. The rifles of the slain were quickly looted and the bloody business of ritual disembowelment begun. Coupled with the loss of the 2nd Battalion weapons, something around 200 Martinis were now in the hands of the Zulu. It is difficult to say how quickly these might have been brought into action against the 24th. There were very few cartridges left on the British dead, but even so the looted rifles must have had an effect. Given their simplicity of operation, the only real obstacle to their immediate use was the wave of warriors who pushed past the looters into their line of fire. Those warriors who had not yet achieved a kill, pressed on through the tents in search of their own victims.

Uguku described the fighting amongst the tents and the destruction of A Company, from the perspective of the warriors of the umCijo; his account has been overlaid with some explanatory notes to aid its coherence:

> The whole of my regiment charged the infantry, who formed into two separate parties – one party standing four deep [bunched] with their backs [left flank] towards Isandlwana [C, F, & E Companies] – the other standing about 50 yards from the camp [Degacher's somewhat isolated A Company] in like formation [also bunched]. We [the umCijo's right wing] were checked by the fire of the soldiers standing near Isandlwana but [the regiment's left wing] charged on towards those in front of the camp, in spite of this very heavy fire on our right flank. As we got nearer we saw the soldiers were beginning to fall from the effects of our fire. On our left we were supported by the uMbonambi [indicating a twin-pronged assault on Degacher] . . . As we rushed on, the soldiers [A Company] retired on [were driven into] the camp fighting all the way and as they got into the camp we were intermingled with them [indicating a hand-to-hand fight]. It was a disputed point as to which regiment was first in the English camp but it was eventually decided that the uMbonambi was first [meaning that Degacher was driven in from the east]. One party of soldiers came out from amongst the tents and formed up a little above the ammunition wagons [on the slope behind Bloomfield's wagons which were at the rear of the 2nd Battalion tents]. They held their ground there until their ammunition failed them when they were nearly all assegaied.

Whilst the A Company fight was raging through the 2nd Battalion camp, the other three companies were able to fall back through the artillery lines into the saddle. Somewhere amongst the overrun encampments, a warrior called Maqeda pulled back the flap of a tent to reveal an unknown officer sat at his desk, writing a few last lines to a loved one. The officer raised his pistol and fired a shot which went straight through Maqeda's cheeks. Notwithstanding the shock of his injury, he sprang forward and stabbed the man to death.

In common with most of the other officers who marched with Chelmsford that morning, Lieutenant Berkeley Milne had left his servant in the camp. Signalman William Aynsley found himself cut off, alone amongst the tents, with Zulus all around him. He dashed across to a wagon, where he put his back to the rear wheel and defended himself with his naval cutlass. He slashed around to such good effect that one of his assailants peeled away from the fight, crawled under the wagon and stabbed him in the back through the spokes of the wheel. Aynsley was the only member of the Royal Navy to die in action in the Zulu War. Near the hospital tents, an NNC European put his back to a boulder and over the course of the next few minutes was able to get off dozens of shots from his revolver. He died with his pistol in one hand and his bloodied bowie knife in the other. It is said that Private James Williamson, Chelmsford's 24th Regiment orderly, died defending the Union Flag which customarily flew over his lordship's tent.

The Fighting in the Saddle

In front of the 1st Battalion tents, Durnford and his men were still battling hard to deny the saddle to the Zulus. Many warriors had fallen before their volleys, but crazed with the excitement of the fight, still more pressed forward over the bodies of the slain. As the pressure intensified, Durnford's men instinctively sought the sort of comfort in combat that only the close physical proximity of comrades can bring; their firing line slowly converted itself into an embattled cluster. With Durnford fighting from the front of the tents and Wardell's H Company falling back towards them, there was a sufficient volume of fire to keep the ground between the two groups clear of the enemy. Meanwhile C, F and E Companies, by now reduced to about 190 men, fell back through the saddle to Durnford's left, separated from him by about 150 metres and four or five rows of parked wagons – the wagons of the deferred morning convoy.

It was no mean testament to the tactical skill of Captain G. V. Wardell, that he now found himself back in the mouth of the saddle, where he was able to effect a junction with Durnford. The unified command jostled itself into a rough square of around a hundred men, with the carbineers and police mostly on the right hand side, and the infantry mostly on the front face and the left hand side. A hundred yards to the rear were Pullen's ammunition wagons, to which the quartermaster and others might well have returned, to smash open some boxes. But the mere act of opening boxes was no magical panacea; to distribute cartridges effectively was far from easy in the midst of such mayhem. From the centre of the square, Wardell bellowed out the orders for volley fire. For what seemed to the Zulus to be 'a long time', but was probably in reality no more than about five minutes, the volleys crashed out with their usual deterrent effect: most warriors stayed down on their bellies or sheltered behind tents and wagons. Then the iNgobamakhosi and the uVe attempted to press a series of heavy frontal attacks. These coincided with attacks across the wagon road, from the area of the 2nd/24th encampment, by elements of the uMbonambi and the umCijo.

Over the next few minutes, literally thousands of Zulus pressed into a few crowded acres, so that the attacks on the square became omni-directional and increasingly costly to the British. Showers of throwing assegais now came raining in with much more deadly effect, causing the number of casualties to rise sharply. Quartermaster Pullen probably fell about now. Under relentless pressure, the men in the square began to give ground and fell back through the tents, perhaps with the idea of finding hard cover amongst the wagons to their rear. The retrograde movement broke up the cohesion of the square, dividing it back into its two original constituent groups. The Zulus pressed them back through the tents, and then, through the row of wagons as well. Wardell and his men fell back parallel to the road in an attempt to keep in touch with the rest of the 1st Battalion, whilst Durnford and the colonial troopers were driven back towards the foot of Mahlabamkhosi. The Zulus closed in, pressing though the tents and wagons at a crouched run, firing rifles and hurling throwing assegais as they came.

The Fugitives' Trail

Both Teignmouth Melvill and Nevill Coghill were fine horsemen. Even so they needed every ounce of their skill to remain in the saddle over the dreadful ground between the Manzimyama and the Buffalo. At one point, they were riding in the company of a civilian wagon conductor called Martin Foley. Then the path of these three intersected that of a party which included Brickhill. His account of the flight along the Fugitives' Trail is one of the most vivid:

> No path, no track, boulders everywhere. On we went, borne now into some dry torrent bed, now weaving our way amongst trees of stunted growth, so that unless you made the best use of your eyes you were in constant danger of colliding against some tree or finding yourself unhorsed at the bottom of some ravine. Our way was already strewn with shields, assegais, blankets, hats, clothing of all descriptions, guns, ammunition belts, saddles which horses had managed to kick off, revolvers and belts and I don't know what not. Whilst our stampede was composed of mules with and without pack saddles, oxen, horses in all stages of equipment and flying men all strangely intermingled – man and beast apparently all infected with the danger that surrounded us.

Periodically the little group of riders came under fire from pursuing Zulu riflemen. In the approach to the Buffalo, they found themselves on a treacherous and narrow ledge, with a sheer precipice to their left. Melvill dismounted to lead his horse down through the rocks. It was no easy proposition with the unwieldy Queen's Colour to impede him. Brickhill dismounted behind him and blocked the way with his horse, so that Melvill would not be knocked over the edge by men pushing past on horseback. Other riders also dismounted. Coghill, at the back of the little group, and quite unable to see what was going on, called out, 'Get on your horse there Mr Brickhill; this is no time for leading a horse. Get on your horses you fellows in front!' Somebody in the group called back, 'You get off yours. This is no place to be riding one!' Coghill of course was quite unable to dismount, even if he had wished to do so, but nonetheless made the descent safely. A little further on the rest of the group remounted, but then had to slither their animals down a steep embankment. Carried forward fast by the momentum of its descent, Melvill's horse slammed him into the branch of a tree, almost unseating him. Brickhill caught the backlash before it could do him any serious damage beyond tearing his coat. Then they came to a grassy morass that scattered the group somewhat, as each of them sought a way through it.

Trooper Muirhead of the Carbineers was riding hard for Sothondose's Drift in the company of Trooper Macleroy,* when the latter was hit and wounded by a throwing assegai. Muirhead spotted Surgeon-Major Shepherd riding down the valley and implored the doctor to attend to his comrade. It says much for Shepherd's sense of duty that he agreed to stop. A cursory examination revealed that there was no hope for the badly wounded Macleroy, but even this short delay proved fatal to Shepherd, who was struck and killed by a throwing assegai in the act of remounting his horse.

Trooper Hayes of the mounted police was just congratulating himself on getting across the Buffalo, when he managed to get himself stuck in the mud and reeds. His frantic cries for help soon attracted some assistance. He was helped out of his predicament by his mate Trooper Dorehill, Sergeant Costellow of N Battery and Private Gascoigne of the IMI. Whilst they were busy with the rescue, one of the NNC levies crept up and stole one of the horses they had tethered nearby. Spotting the man out of the corner of his eye, Gascoigne gave chase, dragged him out of the saddle, and brought the animal back to its owner. Although they came under fire from the far bank at this juncture, all four men were unhurt and duly made their way to safety.

The heavily flooded Sothondose's Drift was as perilous to the fugitives as was the Zulu pursuit. Not least it took a heavy toll of the NNC, most of whom were poor swimmers, if they swam at all. Some of the luckier Europeans owed their survival to their horses. Trooper Richard Stevens of the NMP owed his to a riderless animal he encountered midstream:

> Well now about myself, I got out of camp somehow, I don't know how, and went through awful places to get to the drift, where my horse was taken away from under me and I was as nearly drowned as I could be. I just happened to catch hold of another horse's tail which pulled me through.

Stevens was a recent immigrant to Natal and is not likely to have been a greatly experienced horseman. He had been lucky. Lieutenant Harry Davies of the Edendale Troop was an accomplished rider, but even he struggled to keep his seat in the approach to the river. He had a narrow scrape when a Zulu grabbed hold of his bridle. He slashed at the man with

---

* Usually misidentified as Trooper Kelly. See Julian Whybra, *England's Sons*.

the knife fitted to his carbine, but had the weapon wrenched from his grasp. Just then his horse reared and bolted, which served to get him away from danger, at least temporarily. He had only just drawn his revolver, when another group of Zulus appeared in his path. He rode straight at them, singling out the man at twelve o'clock for what might prove to be his last shot. He hit his man in the neck, though Stafford, who was nearby, thought he hit him between the eyes. Either way, it was a fine shot, and it enabled Davies to burst through his assailants unharmed. A shower of throwing assegais was hurled after him, one of which wounded his horse. Further down the trail, in the final approach to Sothondose's Drift, he was thrown, but made a swift recovery:

> The ground was so stony that I was going over, and I soon came to grief; but as there was no time to think, I was soon up and away again, and took the river in front of me. Many were then escaping but not being accustomed to take horses across rivers they fell and rolled over, as the current was strong. I have had a good deal of experience in swimming horses, and I kept mine from falling, and directly he was in the water I threw myself off and caught hold of the stirrup. The Zulus followed down to the river and fired at us crossing. Some of them took to the water after us, as our natives stabbed two Zulus just as they reached the Natal side.

In the absence of Davies, it was Sergeant Simeon Kambula who led the Edendale Troop to safety. He alone amongst the leaders of Durnford's mounted natives managed to keep his troop in action as a formed body of men, their cohesion and numbers enabling them to travel the Fugitives' Trail in relative safety. When they reached the river, Kambula dismounted the troop for a minute or two and laid down some covering fire for the scattered bands of fugitives. Ammunition was in extremely short supply; almost immediately they were obliged to pull out and swim their ponies back across the river. On the Natal bank, they made their way to the top of the high ground, from where they fired off the last of their cartridges at the groups of Zulus infesting the valley. When his ammunition was finally done, Kambula led the troop away to safety.

Private Sam Wassall was a member of the 80th Regiment's IMI section. When he reached the riverbank, it was to see a regimental comrade, Private Westwood, being swept downstream, clearly on the point of drowning. Disregarding his own best interests, Wassall tethered his horse to a tree and jumped in after Westwood. He was able to pull him ashore some way downstream, but still on the Zulu side of the river. After gathering their breath, the two men sneaked back through the undergrowth in the direction of Wassall's horse; much to their relief they found it still in situ. Wassall mounted, hauled the distressed Westwood up behind him and rode into the river. Notwithstanding the sudden arrival of a large party of Zulus who fired on them and hurled throwing assegais after them, the pair made it across to Natal safely and were able to ride on to Helpmekaar without further mishap. Wassall's selflessness would duly be recognised by the award of a VC.

Smith-Dorrien, meanwhile, had reached a precipitous slope high above Sothondose's Drift. Here he came upon a badly wounded mounted infantryman of the 24th called Private McDonald, who had been assegaied in the arm and was bleeding severely. Smith-Dorrien dismounted to assist him, quickly applying a tourniquet with his handkerchief. McDonald had been taken into the 24th just over three years before, after being apprehended as a deserter from the 86th Regiment; his first spell of service in his new regiment had been eighty-four days in detention. Smith-Dorrien helped him down the slope, but soon heard a warning shout from behind, 'Get on man; the Zulus are on top of you.' The voice was that of Stuart Smith. Smith-Dorrien described him as being 'as white as a sheet and bleeding profusely'. A few seconds later a strong party of Zulus attacked; McDonald and Smith were quickly done to death and Smith-Dorrien lost his horse, but managed to get off a few wild shots with his revolver before running headlong for the edge of the cliff. Miraculously, he was at exactly the right place to drop safely into the river below. As he splashed around, he was able to grab the tail of a riderless horse which pulled him safely across the river. On the far bank, he was unable to bring the animal under control before it galloped off.

Although there were a number of levies and mounted natives around, James Hamer was the only European Smith-Dorrien could see. He was lying on the riverbank, seemingly incapacitated by a fall from his horse. Smith-Dorrien was able to catch another animal and helped Hamer into the saddle. Somewhat ungraciously Hamer then rode away, leaving his young rescuer to shift for himself. Smith-Dorrien scrambled his way up the hillside behind some NNC men, some of whom were bowled over by fire from across the river. Just downstream, a party of Zulus crossed to the Natal bank in pursuit, but by judicious use of his borrowed revolver cartridges, Smith-Dorrien was able to keep ahead of them over a three-mile chase. At sundown he made it to Helpmekaar, having walked every step of the way from the Buffalo. Thirty-five years later, as a corps commander, he would give his country reason to be grateful for his survival. For the time being he was a devastated and utterly exhausted twenty-year-old subaltern.

Given his preoccupation with the loss of his guns, it was as well that Henry Curling had a relatively easy descent to the river. He seems to have witnessed Smith-Dorrien's leap, so cannot have been separated from Stuart Smith by too great a distance. Although he was riding a distinctly second-string battery horse, the animal had behaved well throughout the dramas of the day. Now, at the river, it proved to be a strong swimmer, too. Despite the four unhorsed fugitives who grabbed hold of its tail and saddlery, it carried all five men straight across the Buffalo without faltering. On the far bank, Curling wished his passengers the best of luck and quickly rode on for Helpmekaar. The only other survivor of his division was one of his sergeants. Later he would be greatly relieved to find that both his orderly and his groom had survived their bareback ride and were amongst the ten N Battery survivors. Another artillery survivor was young Trumpeter Martin, for whom South Africa had yet more drama in store. Two years after Isandlwana, Martin would find himself besieged at Potchefstroom, the only siege of the Transvaal Rebellion to be pressed determinedly by the Boers. Martin would survive this second nightmare too. So much for the fugitives; back at the camp the denouement was fast approaching.

Durnford and the Carbineers

At the foot of Mahlabamkhosi the police and carbineers were nearing the end of their tether. By now they had been reduced to a mere score or so. Death was beckoning. Amongst these embattled men were Durnford, Scott, eleven carbineers, including Troopers Swift, Tarboton, Lumley, Moodie, Dickinson, Davis, R. Jackson, and F. Jackson, plus a handful of police and 24th men. They were now too few to give the Zulus pause about coming to close quarters. Worse, the volunteers were feebly equipped to meet them: there was a fitting on the barrel of the carbine which enabled a hunting knife to be fixed, but such a weapon was of little use against a fit young Zulu, wildly flailing shield and assegai. The only option was to shoot such warriors down, but by now all the carbine ammunition was spent. Zulu sources record that the troopers threw down their carbines and blazed away with their revolvers. The revolver has to be carefully aimed and does not have the same stopping power as a carbine: once emptied it is impossible to reload its six-shot chamber very quickly; it is far from being a weapon of first choice in a dire situation. As the Zulus came charging in, some of the carbineers threw their empty revolvers in their faces. Then they drew their hunting knives in a desperate attempt to sustain their resistance for a few seconds longer. It is recorded that stones were thrown and that men fought with their bare knuckles.* Well did the carbineers deserve the zebra praise-song. One last flurry of violence and it was over. Anthony William Durnford sank to the ground, where his body was stabbed repeatedly. At last he had found the military repute he so longed for. Sadly, he must have known when he died that it would be for all the wrong reasons. At least he had the consolation of a soldier's death. Ironically, he fell in the company of the men who had reviled him most, the Natal Carbineers. Perhaps after Bushman's River Pass, they too had something to prove; at Isandlwana they could have done no more.

The Right Horn Enters the Fray

The officers and men of C, F and E Companies had fallen back into the saddle for the want of anywhere else to go. It was not evenly remotely realistic to think of falling back on Rorke's Drift, even though the Oscarberg was at least visible from the rear of the saddle. Under such heavy attack, the intervening distance might as well have been a thousand miles. They had begun the day fighting for Queen, Country and Empire; now they were fighting for life itself. Theirs had been one of the most disciplined fighting retreats in the history of warfare – the ferocity of their resistance was all the more remarkable for its hopelessness. As the British infantryman does at such times, the men of the 24th had placed their lives in the hands of their officers, and concentrated their minds on their own small part in the fight. It was a terrible burden for the officers to bear. What were they to do now? Where were they to go? To survive they had to put some formidable obstacle between their men and the enemy, and then

* Mitford

hold back the maddened host with fire. To do this, they would need to have an uninterrupted supply of ammunition. They could fulfil neither requirement. There was no redoubt, no last bastion, and the ammunition wagons had fallen to the enemy. The situation could not have been worse. And yet so it now became.

How the hearts of these brave men must have sunk at the sight of the right horn surging uphill from the Manzimyama. The enemy may have been 500 metres away when the remnants of the 24th arrived at the rear of the saddle. Although several hundred warriors had taken off in pursuit of the fugitives, the indunas still had well over 3,000 men in hand. Certain death had stalked the men of the 24th for a terrifying mile; now it stood squarely in the path of their retreat. As the great wave of jostling, enraged humanity pushed uphill, it spooked the remaining trek-oxen like an approaching grass fire. Dozens of the frightened animals trotted in front of the right horn. We have no clue as to whether Mostyn and Cavaye were still alive at this juncture; Captain Reginald Younghusband and Lieutenant Edgar Anstey certainly were; Lieutenant George Hodson probably was. As for the other subaltern officers, Edwards Dyson could have been alive or dead; wherever it was that he fell, he did so a day short of his twenty-first birthday; Pat Daly was probably already dead, for he would not have been easily separated from his friend Anstey. Whoever the surviving officers were, they were widely separated and, because of the tumult, were unable to communicate effectively with one another. Faced with an utterly hopeless situation and with only a split second to make a decision, it is not surprising that they pulled in different directions. Anstey decided that the best thing to do was to attempt a break-out along the eastern side of the Manzimyama Valley. Shouting at the men nearest to him to follow his lead, he doubled down the slope at a left oblique. As many as sixty men went with him. A string of slaughtered bodies and dead horses indicated the fate that had befallen many of the men who had preceded them.

Assailed now from all quarters, and with no viable line of retreat open to them, the remainder of the 24th formed square where they stood. They were probably somewhere between 130 and 150 strong. Again the square had no recognisable geometric shape, but the redcoats clustered shoulder-to-shoulder and back-to-back, to brave it out as best they could. Most still had a few cartridges in hand, and opened fire on the right horn to good effect. The frightened cattle shied away from the noise and smoke and ran in all directions. Such was the Zulu bloodlust that some warriors ran at the animals and brought them down with their assegais. In their rage, they stabbed every living thing they came across – oxen, mules, dogs and human corpses. Colonel Henry Degacher's Dalmatian dog was stabbed, but ran away from danger over the koppies.

A few hundred outermost warriors peeled away from the charge of the right horn, to pursue Anstey and his men along the Manzimyama Valley. A running fight developed. Some of the men at the rear were caught and killed quickly. The remainder did their level best to hold their pursuers in check, by turning periodically to fire on them; no doubt they bowled a few of the leading warriors over, but with cartridges now in desperately short supply, this could only ever amount to a harassing fire. The redcoats scrambled down through the rocks, bushes and aloes as best they could. Occasionally, an individual or a small party would be caught and compelled to fight it out with the bayonet. At the foot of the slope, the remnants were confronted by large parties of warriors returning along the Fugitives' Trail, having become aware, perhaps from the slopes of Mpethe Hill, of the parties of redcoats in the valley behind them. In a state of physical exhaustion, and with their ammunition all but spent, Anstey's soldiers stood no chance of fighting their way through. He quickly called a halt and tried to rally the survivors around him. There were about forty men in the general area, but they had become well spread out in the chase and were not able to close into as tight a formation as before. Instead, they prepared to meet their end in fours and sixes. As the pursuit closed round, they fired off the last of their cartridges and braced their bayonets. Three or four minutes of desperate hand-to-hand fighting and it was over. Again the dead were stabbed repeatedly and then disembowelled. Anstey was the only officer of the 24th whose body would eventually be recovered to England. His grave is to be found in Woking Cemetery.

For a while the main body of the 24th, if it can be so called, for it now amounted to only about a third of the battalion, kept up a heavy fire that prevented the warriors of the right horn from breaking into the saddle. With the last remaining cartridges dwindling fast, the stalemate could not be kept up for long. Sergeant-Major Gapp was probably here. Perhaps one or more of Colour-Sergeants Ballard, Brown, Edwards or Whitfield were with him. Whichever senior NCOs were present, they jostled the men around the square so that they were evenly distributed, and the human walls had no gaps or weak points; perhaps then they supervised the dragging of the wounded to the centre of the square; perhaps they bent over them to give them aid or consolation; perhaps they found time to comfort the handful of teenaged army orphans, the boys of the Band and Drums, who thus far had been shielded by the older men. For all their youth, the boys knew full well how to handle a Martini and no doubt most had picked one up by now. You need to be strong to fire a fouled Martini; probably their young shoulders were bruised, and their cheeks and lips bleeding. The boys had come of age and would die as men. Perhaps Sergeant-Major Gapp and his colleagues pulled them back from the walls of the square into the transitory protection of its centre.

Then, when the ammunition was all but done, and the firing had tailed away to intermittent single shots, the indunas of the right horn whipped up a charge. The men of the 24th knew the end was at hand and lowered their shoulders to receive the shock on their levelled bayonets. The warriors crashed into the front of the square, stabbing and clubbing wildly as they came. Men on both sides were spitted, slashed or brained. Mostly the rush was driven back at the point of the bayonet. Everyone seemed to have one last cartridge in the breech and chose his own moment to fire it to deadly effect. Where a group of warriors carved a gap in the human wall, they were met by officers wielding swords and firing revolvers, and by the sword bayonets of the sergeant-major and the colour-sergeants, and by last gasp shots from the boys. On the ground, the wounded passed up the last of their cartridges to the men fighting to defend them, or grabbed for the ankles of the enemy to trip them, or tried to stab them from below. It was a hellish brawl.

The indunas raged amongst their warriors and quickly whipped up a new rush. Throwing assegais rained in at the last moment. Again the assault fell like a hammer blow on the front of the square. This time the Zulus cut down enough men to carve a significant gap. On both sides of the breakthrough, men recoiled. The momentum of the assault forced the 24th to fall back in divergent directions, yielding the ground where the wounded lay to the enemy. They were quickly stabbed to death, or despatched with skull-shattering blows from knobkerries. Younghusband and his subaltern George Hodson and many of the C Company men were driven back against the scree slope of the mountain. In all maybe sixty men recoiled in this direction, flailing about themselves with bayonet or rifle butt. The length of rifle and bayonet continued to stand the 24th in good stead. Quickly gaining the scree slope, Younghusband's men coalesced into a rough square and began to scramble uphill, with the rearmost men prodding at and pushing back the warriors at the forefront of the pursuit. Another seventy men fell back deeper into the saddle. Wherever they went, it was out of the frying pan and into the fire. It was on the site of the 24th monument that they re-formed their square. Here they came under attack by hundreds of warriors who had bypassed the Wardell fight.

The H Company Square

Two hundred metres away, at the eastern mouth of the saddle, Wardell's men were hemmed in on all sides by the warriors of the chest. The men who closed in on H Company found no easy way of satisfying their blood lust. There were sixty men in the square. It occupied a tiny area and could easily have been shot down, but the Zulu riflemen were rendered ineffective by the heaving mass of warriors who sought to kill with the *iklwa*. Few of Wardell's men still had cartridges. Maybe a box or two of ammunition had been dragged out of Pullen's wagons and had been pounded apart in the middle of the square, but the men on the outside of the scrimmage dared not even release a hand from their lunging rifles to receive a handful of cartridges. The men on the inside, loaded and fired over the shoulders of their comrades, but the Zulus were now at the height of their killing frenzy and no matter how many were shot down others continued to press the assault over the broken bodies of the fallen.

H Company was similarly raging with the lust of battle and plied the bayonet to bloody effect. The men remained grimly resolute, firmly locked in shoulder-to-shoulder and back-to-back. Working together to cover each other's backs and sides, they presented a bristling and formidable hedge of bayonets, which, try as they might, the warriors were quite unable to break. When a Zulu was spitted on one of the long lunger bayonets, the warriors nearby would dart in to try and stab the soldier wielding it, before he could recover his blade from the skewered flesh and bone of his victim. Commonly the soldiers thrust a boot onto the throat or chest of the fallen Zulu in order to do so. It was a gruesome and terrifying scene for all concerned in it. It was far from easy for the Zulus to pick off the redcoats however; the soldiers of the 24th knew how to fight as a team, and there always seemed to be another pair of bayonets prodding the warriors away from their chosen target. Inevitably though, men were falling dead and wounded at the feet of those who fought on. So fierce was the defence that, here and there, groups of Zulus picked up one of their own dead and advanced on the square using the corpse as a shield. When they were within a yard or two of the hedge of bayonets, they would heave the dead man forward in the hope of dragging the points down, thereby opening an exploitable gap in the human wall. At some point in the fray, Lieutenant Henry Dyer was stabbed in the heart. Now, Zulu riflemen pushed to the front of the mêlée and fired at point-blank range. Throwing assegais were hurled in with deadly velocity from only four or five yards. In this way, the Zulus began the final slaughter of H Company. First it was reduced from sixty to forty, then from forty to thirty. The carnage at Wardell's feet, where the wounded lay groaning and screaming in pain and anguish, was dreadful to behold. The men wielding bayonet and rifle butt above, stepped round them, over them and on them. Perhaps it was an H Company man that uMhoti of the umCijo grappled with:

> I then attacked a soldier whose bayonet pierced my shield and while he was trying to extract it, I stabbed him in the shoulder. He dropped his rifle and seized me round the neck and threw me to the ground under him. My eyes felt as if they were bursting, and I was almost choked when I succeeded in grasping the spear which was still sticking in his shoulder and forced it into his vitals and he rolled over lifeless. My body was covered with sweat and quivering terribly with the choking I had received from this brave man.

Before long H Company was a mere twenty. Then there was a final concerted rush and it was no more. The Zulus had taken a bloody ten-yard square of ground and quickly passed over it, despatching the last of the wounded redcoats. 'Ah those red soldiers at Isandlwana', remembered one warrior, 'how few they were and how they fought. They fell like stones, each man in his place.' Three other regimental officers fell with the admirable Captain Wardell. One was certainly Dyer, but the other two were unidentifiable when they were found and noted five months later; more likely than not, one of them would have been the 23-year-old Lieutenant Charles Atkinson, Wardell's only subaltern, the man who had broken the second Xhosa assault at Centane.

Last Stand

With the troublesome redcoats in the mouth of the saddle cut down at last, the Zulu assault swung against the men who had formed square where the 24th monument now stands. There can be no certainty that there were any officers present, but it is possible that Cavaye, Mostyn, or both, were leading these men. Many warriors were exhausted by the fighting up to this point and hung back to gather their strength, but there were plenty more men behind them who had not yet washed their spears in British blood, and who now came pushing to the forefront of the fight.

Both colours of the 2nd Battalion had been left in the camp in the care of the battalion guard. The silks were never seen again, but a length of pole, a golden lion, and a colour case were all eventually tracked down in the local area. It is known that the case was found in the Manzimyama Valley. On his 1921 visit to the battlefield, Brigadier-General Mainwaring (a subaltern in the 2nd/24th in 1879) climbed Mahlabamkhosi to take a photograph; he found the climb much harder than in his youth. In his account of his visit, he recalled that it was there on the koppie, over forty years earlier, that he had found the length of pole. It may be a romantic notion, but perhaps the 2nd Battalion colours flew defiantly over the last stand of the 24th; perhaps the artist C. E. Fripp was right to include them in his famous portrayal of the scene.* Nobody can say that it was not so. Whether the colours flew defiantly overhead or not, the embattled men of the 24th braced their bayonets and stood stoically at bay. Resoundingly defeated and outnumbered by fearsome odds, they fought on, as if by some miracle victory might still be theirs. The air was filled again with showers of throwing assegais. Mehlokazulu described the scene:

> The resistance was stout where the old Dutch road used to go across. It took a long time to drive back the English forces there; they killed us and we killed them, and the fight was kept up for a long time. The British troops became helpless because they had no ammunition and the Zulus killed them ... some Zulus threw assegais at them, others shot at them; but they did not get close – they avoided the bayonet, for any man who went up to stab a

---

* The original painting may be seen at the National Army Museum, Chelsea.

soldier was fixed through the throat or stomach and at once fell. Occasionally when a soldier was engaged with a Zulu in front with an assegai, another Zulu killed him from behind.

At the height of the fight in the saddle, the sky faded to grey, as if a heavy bank of cloud had arrived overhead. Few men gave the matter any thought, or had time to look up, but the cause was a partial eclipse of the sun. If the Great Redeemer so beloved of Victorian Britain was accustomed to watching over the faithful, then it was now that he turned away. The 24th Regiment met its supremely violent end under an eerie and prophetic shadow.

Melvill and Coghill

Down on the banks of the Buffalo, Brickhill had become separated from Melvill and Coghill. Spotting some Zulus running hard in his direction, he immediately put his horse to water. He was able to swim it safely to the Natal bank and to survive the heavy fire directed at him. Melvill and Coghill rode into the river a little further upstream than Brickhill. Coghill managed to get across safely to Natal, but on looking back saw that the adjutant had been washed out of the saddle and carried away downstream. There were many Zulu riflemen on the hillside who now concentrated their fire on the red tunic that marked Melvill out as a soldier. Gamely he was still holding the Queen's Colour aloft, as he splashed around to avoid drowning. The current carried him in the direction of a large flat-topped rock breaking the surface midstream. A few moments earlier, Lieutenant Higginson had also been unhorsed in the river but had managed to gain a handhold on the rock. Melvill called out for assistance and Higginson tried to haul him in by grabbing at the colour case. Melvill's momentum was such that Higginson was pulled away from the rock and swept downstream with him. They soon came to calmer water and began to kick hard against the current.

Seeing the Queen's Colour in peril, and his comrade in serious trouble, Coghill quickly turned his horse about and, in an act of great gallantry, rode back into the river to attempt a rescue. The Zulu riflemen above the drift poured in a heavy fire; a round struck and killed Coghill's horse almost immediately. Possessed of a profound sense of duty and an abundance of determination, the adjutant retained his grip on the colour.

Thrashing clear of his dead horse, and hindered by the damage and pain in his injured leg, Coghill swam across to assist Melvill. Bullets threw up spouts of water all around them as they struggled together for the Natal bank. Halfway across the inevitable happened – the sodden silk of the colour had become impossibly heavy and the current quickly filled its leather case – Melvill could keep his grip no longer and the precious banner was washed away downstream.

Cursing their wretched luck, all three officers arrived on the Natal bank in a state of heaving exhaustion. Still the Zulus were firing on them. Higginson was first to his feet and ran off in search of horses. Melvill threw an arm around Coghill and hobbled him away from the riverbank towards the side of the valley. They were fortunate to find the old native path down to the drift, but it was steep and the going was difficult. Parties of Zulus were already across the river and soon responded to the cries of the riflemen on the hillside opposite, who directed them through the rocks and undergrowth towards the two officers. They made an extremely game attempt to scale the side of the valley, but it soon became clear that the crippled Coghill was never going to be able to outstrip the pursuit. Yet again that day, members of the 24th Regiment lived up to a heroic ideal. Melvill could have abandoned his comrade to his fate; no doubt Coghill urged him to do so. The suggestion was scorned and Melvill stuck faithfully to the herculean task he had set himself.

Some considerable distance ahead of them, Higginson turned to see how they were getting on, and was just in time to shout a warning as two Zulu pursuers closed in. The pair staggered apart, raised their revolvers into the aim, and both dropped their man. Melvill quickly shouldered Coghill's body weight once more, and resumed his struggle with the hill. About two-thirds of the way up, the adjutant's strength finally failed him. He could go no further. The exultant cries of the Zulus indicated that the pursuit was closing in again. The two officers put their backs to a large boulder and prepared to defend themselves with their revolvers. The end was not long in coming. Higginson witnessed it from the top of the hill, where he had fallen in with some of the mounted natives. In his formal report on the incident, Glyn observed that, 'Several dead bodies of the enemy were found about them, so that they must have sold their lives dearly at the last.' In the Regiment it remains a matter of great pride that within a few minutes both of these officers took the decision to lay down his life for his friend. Teignmouth Melvill left behind him his wife of four years, Sarah, and two baby sons.

Defiance

Back at Isandlwana, this most extraordinarily savage of fights was about to end in a truly remarkable fashion. Younghusband and his men had rallied on the rocky shelf halfway up the south-eastern slope of Isandlwana, with the high crag of the hill just to their rear. Here, the steepness of the slope made it difficult for the Zulus to get at them. Where they pressed an assault, they were blown and off balance when they met the darting hedge of bayonets. The terrible points came over, under and, in some cases, clean through the cowhide shields. Spitted, shot, or brained, many warriors came tumbling back down the slope with terrible injuries. Younghusband's men were crazed with adrenalin. The ferocity of their resistance was without parallel in all the fights the veterans of the *impi* had ever seen. The Zulus modified their tactics. Some scrambled up the lower scree slopes on the flanks of the British resistance, so that they could gather their breath before pressing an attack. The warriors directly in front of the soldiers pushed only halfway up the slope, from where they hurled throwing assegais or fired rifles, many of them now looted Martinis. It was the same technique that had whittled down the squares in the saddle, and without ammunition there was no answer to it. Under this intense pressure, and with their casualties mounting fast, the last of the 24th were driven back from the edge of the shelf to the very top of the upper scree slope. Here the southern crag of Isandlwana rose vertically behind them. There could be no retreat from here. The Zulus pressed onto the shelf in huge numbers and quickly began their assault on the final British foothold.

Younghusband knew that the annihilation of this last remnant of his regiment was only minutes away. He raised a word or a roar that caused the survivors to look around at him. The fire of battle burned in their eyes. It was probably not necessary for Younghusband to speak; his eyes, his demeanour and his sword would have communicated his intent. There were no fine speeches. The men turned back to their front, briefly settled affairs with their Maker, levelled their bayonets and braced themselves for the off. Younghusband raised his sword high above his head and filled his lungs. The order to charge was answered with a furious roar of aggression from the men, as they spilled down the slope behind their leader.

Younghusband was seen to be wheeling his sword over his head as he ran. Stunned by such impetuosity, the closest warriors recoiled in surprise. The soldiers' momentum carried them thirty yards into the great host, but within seconds the Zulus had closed around them and hemmed them in. After an excessively violent struggle, this last heroic remnant of the 24th was cut down and butchered.

Victory

The Zulus exulted wildly in the scale of their victory. Not a single living red soldier was to be seen. With scarcely a pause the warriors began to loot the camp, running excitedly from tent to wagon to corpse in search of plunder. Only the necessity to ritually mutilate the dead distracted them. There were other more ghastly mutilations, perpetrated by men crazed with bloodlust. Those who had killed were required by superstition to remove and wear an item of their victim's clothing. Mostly they settled on the bloody red tunics, which they pulled on over their nakedness. Some men decapitated British corpses. A boy-soldier was hung up by his heels from a wagon wheel: then his throat was cut. Perhaps it was an act of posthumous mutilation, not one of murder; let us hope so. Here and there, the odd man was hidden in the debris of the camp, or feigning death amongst the slaughtered. One apparently dead redcoat suddenly leapt to his feet and shot down a warrior intent on his mutilation. The soldier took to his heels, but was quickly caught and killed. A black wagon driver concealed himself high up on Isandlwana, where he would remain undetected and in due course make his escape. At the front of the mountain a tall white man with a clean-shaven chin made a sudden appearance from inside a covered wagon. Although he is frequently misidentified as an officer of the 24th* on no stronger evidence than the fact that he was wearing gaiters, it is much more probable that he was a NNC European who had sought cover when the fight swept through the encampments from the north. Jumping to the ground, he started loading and firing at so rapid a rate that the Zulus fell back around him. Mehlokazulu said that anybody who tried to close with him was at once knocked over or bayoneted. He fought so long and hard, that many Zulus stopped their looting to watch him fight. Eventually somebody shot him down.

---

* Often specifically as Younghusband, for which there is no evidence whatsoever.

Such was the tumult of the looting of the camp, including perhaps the celebratory discharge of firearms, that for a while nobody noticed that there were still shots coming from the south face of Isandlwana, and that warriors were still being dropped. Eventually it was realised that the firing was coming from a tiny cave at the foot of the southern crag. One of the indunas rallied a handful of men armed with looted Martinis and led them uphill to the shelf. The next time the lone redcoat appeared at the mouth of the cave to fire, the warriors returned a ragged volley. There was no more firing after that. It was appropriate that the last member of the 24th to die at Isandlwana did so in an act of supreme defiance.

Now that the battle was over the killing rage of the Zulus began to subside. The warriors of the *amabutho* packed into the saddle now dispersed as the whim took them. Some set out to disembowel or mutilate the most recently slain; many went to the aid of the huge number of Zulu wounded; most went to loot the bodies, tents and wagons. Not a single man of the six 24th Regiment companies trapped in the camp remained alive. If Zulus waved the looted 2nd Battalion colours overhead in triumph, then there was no disgrace in it. When the exultant crowds had thinned a little, it could be seen that the ground between Isandlwana and Mahlabamkhosi was literally carpeted with corpses. It is impossible to know the precise extent of the loss of human life but it was probably well in excess of 3,500 souls. The number of Zulu wounded was also enormous. From Ulundi to Brecon there would be weeks of heart-rending lamentation ahead.

Corroborating the Reconstruction

The locations of the large concentrations of the British slain are a mainstay of this reconstruction of the battle's final phase. It will be as well to summarise them here. There are a number of key sources. Major Wilsone Black took a scouting party back to the battlefield on 14 March and recorded his findings. There was a major expedition on Tuesday 20 May, with the principal aim of recovering serviceable ox-wagons for the second invasion of Zululand. At the same time, all the bodies, less those of the 24th, were given rough interment. The war correspondents Charles Norris-Newman and Archibald Forbes were present, as was Trooper Symons of the Natal Carbineers, all of whom recorded what they saw. The 24th bodies were left untouched at the request of Colonel Glyn. The expedition was a mounted one, leaving the infantry unable to participate. Glyn was understandably anxious that the 24th be allowed to bury its own dead. It was Wilsone Black who returned to Isandlwana on 20, 23 and 26 June with 2nd/24th work parties to bury the regimental dead.

• Fifty men of the 24th were found on the British right, in an outlying position between the Mpofane Donga and the rocky ridge. These men were certainly G Company/2nd Battalion men. Their presence was recorded by Forbes and is a key pointer to early attack on G Company by the left horn, and the consequent improbability of any of the 2nd Battalion men making it back to the camp.

• Twenty men of the 24th, including Colour-Sergeant Wolfe of H Company, were found on the firing line just above an abandoned kraal. Such a kraal is shown on the Intelligence Branch Military Survey of Isandlwana, between the Nyogane Donga and H Company's position on the rocky ridge. Since Captain Wardell, the officer commanding H Company, made it back across the huge distance to the saddle with sixty men (*see below*) of a company whose original strength was eighty, it seems certain that Wolfe covered the retreat of the company main body with a section-strength rearguard.

• Fifty men of the 24th were found in the 2nd Battalion camp. Since the Zulus decided that the uMbonambi was the first regiment to break into the tents, then the main body of the 1st Battalion was pressed not only from an arc north through north-east, by the uNokhenke and the umCijo, but also from the east by the uMbonambi. The men at the critical corner, and thus most likely to have been cut off from the rest of the main body, belonged to the company on the right – Degacher's A Company. This group of bodies is mentioned in a letter written by Inspector George Mansel of the NMP. He does not state if any officers were found, but other sources indicate that Paymaster White fell in the 2nd Battalion camp.

• Four officers and around sixty men of the 24th, including Captain George Wardell, were found behind the 1st Battalion tents. There were also a few bodies from 'other arms' so that sixty-eight corpses were counted in all. Since the miscellaneous men were not with Wardell on the firing line, they must have joined him in the saddle. The only men still in the saddle by the time Wardell got back there were the men with Durnford – police and volunteers. This is a pointer to a probable junction between Durnford and Wardell. Norris-Newman records the existence of this cluster of bodies, and bases his report on Major Black's return to the battlefield on 14 March 1879. Black's report of 28 June further identified that there were three other regimental officers with Wardell, one of whom was Lieutenant Dyer. He believed the others were a lieutenant and a captain. He can only have based this on decomposing tunics and may have been mistaken about the captain; it is difficult to conceive how Mostyn or Degacher could have married up with H Company, whilst Younghusband was found elsewhere.

• Colonel Anthony Durnford and Lieutenant Durrant Scott of the Natal Carbineers were found at the foot of Mahlabamkhosi. They were surrounded by eleven troopers of the carbineers and a few policemen and 24th men. Since this is neither in the right place, nor is it a strong enough party, to have held the mouth of the saddle in the manner described by Mehlokazulu and other Zulu sources, then this was not the original position or composition of the group which did. Durnford and the men with him must have been driven back to Mahlabamkhosi from a position in front of the 1st Battalion tents, which would suggest that they acted in concert with Wardell's H Company, before the combined stand was broken up into two parties and driven back through the 1st Battalion tents. The number of carbineers found with Durnford is recorded in a letter written by Trooper Symons. Norris-Newman suggests that Captain Robert Bradstreet of the NMR was also near Durnford.

• Seventy men of the 24th were found in the saddle, where the 24th Monument now stands, and were eventually interred beneath it. No named officers were identified in this group. This group is the second of the large regimental clusters reported by Black following his June visits.

• Three officers and sixty men of the 24th, including Captain Young-husband, were found under the southern crag of Isandlwana. This group is the third of the large regimental clusters reported by Black following his June visits.

• Sixty or seventy NNC men were found around Captain George Shepstone on the western, or rear, scree slope of Isandlwana. They attract little attention in the sources as the corpses were naked and may have been mistaken by many for Zulus. In fact the Zulu dead were overwhelmingly removed from the battlefield.

• Lieutenant Edgar Anstey and about forty men of the 24th were found two miles down the Fugitives' Trail, where they were brought to bay on the banks of the Manzimyama. Since this was a running fight and individual redcoat bodies were found along the trail, the original strength of the Anstey breakout has been estimated within this reconstruction as about sixty strong. Time and space analysis shows that they must have moved down the trail well after the fugitives.

In total, of the 600 24th Regiment men in the field that day, over 360 died in identifiable and coherent stands. Over 310 of them were men of the 400-strong 1st Battalion. When further allowance is made for the men shot down during the 1st Battalion's withdrawal, say thirty or forty, and the twenty or so men who were killed as individuals at the rear of Anstey's running fight, it can be seen just how well the 1st/24th retained its tactical cohesion. The 2nd Battalion contingent, centred on G Company, was more exposed in its position closest to the Zulu breakthrough on the right, and had little opportunity to rally.

Chapter 7

Sunset

Lord Chelmsford's Rude Awakening, p.m. 22 January

By 10.30 a.m. it was blisteringly hot on the open plain. A powerful heat haze shimmered between Maori Browne's column and the distant Sphinx. Browne was plodding along in company with his adjutant, Lieutenant Campbell, at the head of around fifty whites and 800 or so levies, in no real position to resist the onset of a strong enemy force. The events of the past thirty-six hours had done little to enhance the fragile fighting spirit of 1st/3rd NNC, but at least now they were marching in the direction of a decent meal. Browne himself was in a foul mood, firmly convinced that the general and his staff were mad, incompetent or both. Just ahead of the toiling column, two Zulus suddenly jumped out of cover and made a break for it. Browne and Campbell immediately spurred up their horses and gave chase. The adjutant quickly pistolled his man, but Browne took his alive. The young captive was suitably terrified by the fate of his companion and Browne's fierce demeanour. When Captain Duncombe came up to interrogate him, he was more than willing to co-operate. When he was asked where he had come from, the lad pointed in the direction of the Ngedla Heights, where he said there was an *impi* of twelve regiments. This was significant intelligence which immediately prompted Browne to scribble a note to the general:

> I have just captured a Zulu scout who informs me the Zulu army is
> behind the range of hills on the left flank of the camp. Will push on
> as fast as possible. The ground here is good for the rapid advance
> of mounted men and guns.

Calling up one of his best-mounted subalterns, Lieutenant Pohl, Browne instructed him to gallop the message to the staff at Mangeni as quickly as possible. As Pohl dashed away, Browne waved his battalion forward and then rode on ahead to a vantage point, to scan the ground in the direction of the camp. He was hindered by the heat-haze and for the time being could see nothing untoward. In the near distance, he could see two members of the NNC approaching. Between them they carried a small parcel of food which had been sent out by Acting Surgeon Frank Buée, one of the officers Browne had left behind at Isandlwana. The parcel also contained two bottles of whiskey and a note for Browne, which he read immediately. If he had expected it to deal in weighty tactical matters, then he was to be disappointed. Lieutenants Edgar Anstey and Pat Daly of F Company had passed by his tent the previous evening and found his supper spoiling. It had proved far too great a temptation to resist. Anstey and Daly expressed their hope that the whiskey would be a worthy compensation. Browne called a ten-minute halt, during which he shared the liquor around his Europeans to cheer their flagging spirits. The unfortunate levies of course went without.

Over the ensuing ninety minutes the battalion pushed three or four miles closer to the camp. It was about noon when Browne raised his binoculars once more, and this time saw puffs of smoke rising over the escarpment. There was also a huge dark shadow lying on the hills. He knew at once what he was looking at and reached immediately for his pocket book:

> The Zulu army is attacking the left of the camp. The guns were opened on them. The ground here still suitable for guns and mounted men. Will push on so as to support them.

Sergeant Turner was chosen to bear the second despatch and, as he rode away in the direction of Mangeni, Lieutenant Pohl was sighted coming back the other way. Pohl reported that he had duly delivered the first note to a staff officer, who had read it and then told him to return to Browne with instructions to continue on to the camp. The levies, though, were filled with great apprehension at the sight of the distant host and their progress immediately became reluctant, hesitant and slow. Umvubie, the headman of No. 8 Company, an isiGqoza company, suggested to Browne that he move his men to the rear of the column and kill any of the lowly Natal-born natives who failed to keep up. It was an offer Maori Browne was happy to accept.

It is often not appreciated that, over the next three hours, Browne watched parts of the battle and its aftermath. He may have been a long-range witness, and he may have been a cad not above spinning a good yarn from time to time, but witness he was nonetheless. There is little reason to suspect any of the passages in his memoirs describing what he saw through his binoculars that day; they have an air of authenticity and cross-check well with Zulu accounts of the fighting. It will be useful to test our reconstruction against his recollections in his memoir, *A Lost Legionary in South Africa*.

> I was on ahead and looking though my glasses when I saw a puff of smoke rise from the hills on the left of the camp. It was followed by another. They seemed to come from a huge black shadow that lay on the hills. Presently another puff and in a moment I knew they were bursting shells. Not a cloud was in the sky and I knew that the black shadow resting on the hills must be the Zulu army moving down to attack the camp . . . I could now see the troops lying down and firing volleys while the guns kept up a steady fire. The Zulus did not seem able to advance. [The attack is stalled against the firing line]. They were getting it hot and as there was no cover they must have suffered very heavy losses, as they shortly afterwards fell back [or more accurately took cover]. The guns and troops also ceased firing [volleys]. At about midday I was looking back anxiously to see if the mounted men and guns were coming up, when I heard the guns in camp re-open again . . . I saw a cloud of Zulus thrown out from their left and form the left horn of their army. These men swept round and attacked the front of the camp, and I saw the two right companies of the 24th and one gun thrown back to resist them [the wheel back to the rocky ridge by Pope and Wardell]. There was also plenty of independent firing going on within the camp [but how could he tell the source of the noise – probably this was the sound of the Zulu fire] as if all the wagon men, servants and in fact everyone who could use a rifle was firing away to save his life . . . The camp was still holding its own and the Zulus were certainly checked. The guns were firing case and I could see the dense mass of natives writhe, sway and shrink back from the volleys of the gallant old 24th [a second round of volleying – the withdrawal begins] . . . I happened to glance to the right of the camp. Good

God! What a sight it was. By the road that runs between the hill and the koppie came a huge mob of maddened cattle, followed by a dense swarm of Zulus. These poured into the undefended right and rear of the camp, and at the same time the left horn of the enemy and the chest of the army rushed in. Nothing could stand against this combined attack. All formation was broken in a minute, and the camp became a seething pandemonium of men and cattle struggling in dense clouds of dust and smoke [in other words he could not see very much – probably this was gun-smoke from the British squares in the saddle]. The defenders fought desperately and I could see through the mist the flash of bayonet and spear together with the tossing heads and horns of the infuriated cattle, while above the bellowing of the latter and the sharp crack of the rifles could be heard the exulting yells of the savages and the cheers of our men gradually dying away [poetic licence]. Of course I saw in a moment everything was lost . . . I had often looked back and seen that the fighting was over in camp, but that one company in company square was retreating slowly up the hill surrounded by a dense swarm of Zulus [C Company]. This was Captain Younghusband's company. They kept the enemy off as long as their ammunition lasted, then used the bayonet until at last overcome by numbers they fell in a heap as the brave old British Tommy should.

There are two points of note in Browne's account. Many historians have described how the left horn drove a herd of cattle ahead of them. In fact, as can be seen above, the cattle were driven into the camp from the rear, by the right horn, which makes much more sense – the British are certain to have grazed their oxen behind Isandlwana, rather than on the open plain in front of the camp. The second point of note is that Younghusband fell back up the mountain from the saddle at a very late stage – not up the eastern scree slope as soon as the withdrawal began, as the conventional interpretation would have it. This also makes perfect sense; had he withdrawn onto the high ground immediately, he would have left Mostyn's left flank exposed to attack by the uNokhenke.

As the battle unfolded Browne continued to send updates to the staff. His third despatch was sent before the collapse of the perimeter and was worded in similar vein to the first two:

The camp is being attacked on the left and in front and as yet is holding its own. Ground still good for the rapid advance of guns and horses. Am moving forward as fast as I can.

The fourth and most desperate message sent by Browne that day was a verbal one, which he entrusted to Captain Develin, one of his company commanders. It was sent not long after Durnford had abandoned the Nyogane Donga: 'Ride as hard as you can', said Browne to Develin, 'and tell every officer you meet, "For God's sake come back: the camp is surrounded and must be taken."' He then called in the rest of his officers and told them that he intended to retire to a safe distance as quickly as possible. They were to form their companies into rings with the Europeans concealed in the centre. In this way, if they were noticed by the Zulus, they might stand some chance of being taken for some far-flung element of the *impi*. Over the next hour 1st/3rd NNC withdrew to a point about five miles away from the camp, until they came to a position which Browne considered vaguely defensible. There he halted to await developments. Some time later, Captain Develin could be seen galloping back from Mangeni. 'Well – who did you see?' Browne enquired anxiously. Develin described how he had caught up with Major Black and two companies of the 24th, and Colonel Harness with the guns. Both officers had immediately turned their commands and begun marching to join Browne, but then an officer had galloped up and told them in the general's name to turn again and push on as planned to the new campsite at Mangeni.

Not long after Develin's return, the IMI came up and dismounted some distance away. Browne sent an officer across to Russell with a written message to the effect that there was a large body of Zulus between him and the camp, but that if the IMI would support him, he would resume his advance. Russell was not the man for decisive action; he acknowledged the message but made no effort to move forward. A little while later, Russell mounted and rode back with a small escort in the direction of Mangeni, leaving the bulk of his men where they were. His purpose was to find Chelmsford. With the sun beating down on them, 1st/3rd NNC waited some more.

It was around 3.00 p.m. when a column of riders appeared in the distance. Looking through his binoculars, Browne saw that the GOC himself was at the head of the column. There were about eighty men in the escort, half of them police and volunteers, and the other half IMI. Browne described how the general at first refused to believe that things had gone seriously wrong at Isandlwana. Not only would he not believe it, but he bristled aggressively at the very idea. Then came one of the rudest awakenings ever experienced by a British general officer in the field. Browne recalled:

> I at once mounted and rode to meet him. He looked very surprised when he saw me and said, 'What are you doing here, Commandant Browne? You ought to have been in camp hours ago?' I replied, 'The camp has been taken, sir.' He flashed out at once 'How dare you tell me such a falsehood! Get your men into line at once and advance.' I did so and led my 700 miserables supported by the staff against the victorious Zulu army. We moved on about two and a half miles until we had opened out a good view of the camp, when he called me to him and said in a kindly manner, 'On your honour, Commandant Browne is the camp taken?' I answered 'The camp was taken at about 1.30 in the afternoon, and the Zulus are now burning some of the tents.' He said 'That may be the Quartermaster's fatigue burning the debris of the camp.' I replied 'QM's fatigue do not burn tents sir,' and I offered him my glasses. He refused them, but said, 'Halt your men at once,' and leaving me, rode back to the staff and despatched an officer to bring up the remainder of the column.

As Browne and his officers observed in the direction of the camp, they saw large numbers of Zulus retiring over the escarpment. They must have gone up through the notch, as they were pulling a number of wagons, which Browne speculated must have contained their seriously wounded. He was right – the *voorlooper* hidden on Isandlwana later said that he saw forty such wagons being loaded with the wounded and maimed. The *impi* is known to have fallen back to the Ngwebeni Valley for the night.

It was now about 4.00 p.m. Shortly after the halt was ordered, a lone rider was seen to be approaching from the direction of the camp. It proved to be Rupert Lonsdale, who quickly confirmed Browne's dire interpretation of events at Isandlwana. 'The Zulus have the camp,' he cried as he reined in his exhausted pony. 'How do you know?' asked Crealock. 'Because I have been into it,' came the reply. 'But I left a thousand men to guard the camp,' Chelmsford remarked incredulously.* There could be no doubting the urgency of Lonsdale's tone and demeanour, however. With weary resignation, Chelmsford gripped himself and at last faced facts. Turning to the staff he snapped, 'Glyn must return at once.' It was Major Matthew Gosset, who turned away towards Mangeni and kicked his horse into a gallop. Next, the GOC instructed Russell to push forward with a detachment of the IMI, to reconnoitre in the direction of the camp. He returned only a little while later to report that 'all was as bad as it could be', and that he had seen around 7,000 Zulus amongst the tents and wagons.†

Lonsdale had completely lost his head during the morning skirmish in the Phindo Hills, galloping off on his own to chase down some Zulus attempting to slip away from the fight. Eventually, he lost his way. By the time he found some friendly troops, he was feeling groggy from his concussion. In the early afternoon he had sought and was granted, the GOC's permission to return to the camp to rest. Slumped in the saddle, drowsy from the heat and the effects of his injury, he somehow slipped past Maori Browne's battalion on the plain, and was trotted on by his pony, Dot, towards the camp. He claimed to have ridden right up to the tents before he was snapped awake by a shot, and realised that the men in red coats were in fact Zulus. At this he yanked Dot around and galloped away by the skin of his teeth. It was a great story. Though it was accepted at the time, and by historians ever since, at face value, it is clear that it was embellished for dramatic effect. There were a great many Zulu wounded between the Nkengeni Ridge and the tents, who by that time would have been receiving assistance from their uninjured comrades. Lonsdale simply could not have crossed the Nyogane Donga without being spotted. He might have been fired on, and it might have been a close shave, but it must have occurred well over a mile from the camp.

After despatching Gosset to recall the infantry and the guns, Chelmsford had plenty of time on his hands to contemplate the situation. The camp had assuredly fallen; he had seen the tents being burnt with his own eyes. It followed that the stores were likely to have been looted and the transport oxen run off. This meant that for the time being the wagons

* Gosset.

† Crealock's 'Supplementary Statement' to the Isandlwana Board of Enquiry.

were stranded at Isandlwana. It also meant that he would be unable to feed his troops and could no longer count on a resupply of ammunition. In short, his logistic lifeline was cut. He was quite unable to comprehend that the force at the camp had been annihilated. Probably, he comforted himself, Durnford and Pulleine had retired on Rorke's Drift. Whatever the truth of the situation, all he could do now was fall back on his lines of communication to reconstitute and reorganise. His first port of call would be the mission at Rorke's Drift. For a while he clung to the idea that he had merely suffered a reverse, but the more he thought about it, the worse things seemed. Finally, it dawned on him that he was confronting total disaster.

Nearby, the mounted troops fretted at the long delay, convincing themselves amongst other things, that the camp must contain wounded men requiring their assistance. Looking back over their shoulders, they cursed the slowness of the other arms. Only later would they hear from their comrades in the 2nd/24th that Black and Harness had been stopped and sent back by the staff.

Harness and Black – Turn and Turn Again

Lieutenant Mainwaring of F Company, 2nd/24th, was a key witness to what happened with Black and Harness. Around noon he realised that he had left his monocle on a rock near the mouth of the Silutshane Valley and borrowed a horse to go back and look for it. Notwithstanding the fuss about food for the volunteers and the NNC, Clery of course had sent out a wagon-load of rations with the flying column. Unfortunately nobody seems to have known about it – Maori Browne must have marched his men straight past the wagon, presumably at a little distance, without realising what was on board. On the way back from his unsuccessful quest, Mainwaring found the wagon stuck in a donga, some considerable way from succour. A corporal and three men of the 2nd/24th were faithfully standing guard over it. Mainwaring told the corporal he was too exposed and instructed him to leave the wagon where it was, and march on to join Major Black. Just before stepping off, the corporal enquired whether Mainwaring had heard the sound of guns from the direction of the camp. He had not, but immediately rode up onto some nearby high ground to see what was going on. Through the heat-haze he could make out shells landing on the Nyoni escarpment. He galloped back to the floor of the valley to tell Major Black and Captain Church the news. On his way up the track he passed the native pioneers, whose officers pointed out a body of Zulus on the plain.

Riding on, Mainwaring came upon a gaggle of regular officers. Colonel Harness and Lieutenant Parsons of N Battery were both present, as were Major Black, Captains Church and Harvey, and Lieutenants Banister, Dobree and Curll of the 24th. Mainwaring pointed out the Zulus to Black and Harness. Believing both battalions of the NNC to be in front of them, the officers were quite prepared to believe that they were looking at an enemy regiment. In fact, whilst they had been struggling to get the guns up the valley between Magogo and Silutshane, Maori Browne had marched past behind them and it was 1st/3rd NNC that they were now looking at. It was characteristic of Chelmsford's command style that he made little or no effort to keep his subordinate commanders in the picture. It was fortunate for Browne that he was safely outside the range of the 7-pounders.

After a while the 'enemy' force yielded up a lone rider, who began to gallop in the direction of Mangeni. When he was identified as a European, it finally dawned on the huddle of officers that they were actually looking at a friendly battalion. Captain Church sensed that something was amiss and quickly borrowed a horse from an artillery trumpeter, so that he could meet the man halfway. One of the N Battery sergeants went with him. The round trip took half an hour and the pair arrived back in a state of some excitement. Church announced that Captain Develin's message was, 'For God's sake come back: the camp is surrounded and must be taken.' It was unequivocal stuff, which Harness and Black were content to take at face value. They decided to turn immediately. When Black told the men of F and H Companies that the camp was in danger and that they must march back at best speed, they raised a cheer and quickly formed up. They had covered less than a kilometre, when Major Gosset galloped up and asked Harness and Black what they thought they were doing. A fairly heated exchange ensued, as Gosset tried to insist that they continue as planned.[*]

---

[*] Mainwaring presented a rather different version to the polite exchange that Gosset himself later described in his account of these events. Since Gosset's stance proved to be wrong, and he then had something to hide, Mainwaring's version may be regarded as the more candid. Lieutenant Banister, who was also present, endorsed such an interpretation. He wrote that Gosset 'utterly ridiculed the idea of any assistance [to the camp] being necessary.'

Eventually Black agreed to halt, pending the general's personal direction. Lieutenant Parsons of N Battery accompanied Gosset, in order to bring back the GOC's ruling.

Having ridden the ground to site the new camp, Chelmsford, Glyn and the staff had gone to the top of the conical koppie, Mdutshana, to look in the direction of Isandlwana, following the receipt of one of Browne's despatches, and some ardent gesticulating from a NNC man on its summit that they should come up. It was there that Gosset and Parsons caught up with them. The heat haze was troublesome, but the tents at least were still plainly visible. It was a flimsy line of thought, but the staff convinced themselves that Pulleine would have had them dropped in the event of a serious attack. Parsons was told to return to Harness and Black and tell them to move back in the direction of Mangeni.

Not long afterwards, having already disregarded or dismissed all suggestions of alarm, Chelmsford decided he would ride back to the camp in person. He would take forty of Dartnell's men as an escort. It is perhaps no coincidence that it was now far too late in the day for a comfortable camp to be established at Mangeni in the manner he had anticipated. His lordship may have had one eye on obtaining a situation report from Pulleine and the other on his creature comforts. Glyn was to stay at Mangeni in command of the troops where, no doubt, he would have to spend the night on the ground, wrapped in a borrowed blanket. As they rode back up the valley, Chelmsford and the staff ran into Russell coming the other way. He had seemingly taken delivery of a number of messages of alarm during the course of a lengthy halt between Silutshane and Siphezi. He also passed on to the general the contents of the note that Maori Browne had sent him – to the effect that there was a substantial body of Zulus between Isandlwana and Mangeni. Russell was told to accompany the general back to the camp. As the party rode up the valley, they passed Harness and Black marching in the opposite direction. Black probably gave Gosset the evil eye as he rode smugly past behind the GOC. He need not have worried; Lord Chelmsford would have great need of steady old infantry officers before the day was out.

None of the messages of alarm had anything to do with the return of the main body of the troops to Isandlwana. Even Captain Develin's desperate message had no effect. It was only the sight of smoke rising over the camp that finally persuaded Chelmsford that something had gone awry.

Even then, he proffered his feeble explanation for the fires, prompting Browne's supremely ironic response, 'Quartermaster's fatigue do not burn tents, sir.' And so it was that the afternoon was whiled away at Mangeni.

At about 4.30 p.m. the breathless Major Gosset and an escort of two mounted infantrymen galloped in to the new camp site in search of Colonel Glyn. The officers and men of the 2nd/24th were doing their best to make themselves comfortable for a night to be spent under the stars without the benefit of blankets or greatcoats. As ever, the gunners were attending to their horses. Rumours were abroad amongst the men, who were muttering quietly about generals and staff officers. Gosset slowed his horse over the last few hundred yards, so as to avoid causing alarm. It was a wasted thought; Glyn and his staff had been watching him through their binoculars for some time and his furious pace had been noted.* An audience of officers awaited Gosset's arrival with some angst. His horse was blown and his face anxious.

> The general's orders are that you are to saddle up and march towards Isandlwana at once – the Zulus have got into our camp. Lonsdale met the general about five miles from the camp, and has seen the enemy in amongst the tents. The general is waiting for you with the mounted men.

No doubt Harness and Black caught each other's eye and shook their heads in dismay. In a moment, Henry Degacher's bugler had the men on their feet. The gunners raced to get the limber-horses back into harness. Probably in all their accumulated years of training and campaigning, they never achieved a faster time. Nearby, Commandant Cooper's officers and NCOs jostled 2nd/3rd NNC back into formation. Ten minutes later Richard Glyn marched. Of all the men present at Mangeni, he was perhaps the most anxious of all.

Retaking the Camp

It was after 6.00 when the infantry and the guns finally came up. The united force marched quickly on. Just short of the Isandlwana bowl, the order was given to shake out into battle formation. The plan followed Lord

* Hallam-Parr.

Chelmsford's own textbook. Harness's 7-pounders were in the centre, with three companies of the 2nd/24th disposed either side of them. Black took the left wing and Dunbar the right. Lonsdale joined Maori Browne and 1st/3rd NNC on the left of the regulars. The 2nd/3rd NNC under Cooper and Harford was on the right. The mounted troops under Dartnell and Russell were thrown out further afield to protect the flanks of the infantry, volunteers to the left, IMI to the right. When all was ready, Chelmsford rode to the centre and made a short speech to the 2nd/24th and everybody else within earshot. His words have not come down to us in their verbatim form, but Colour-Sergeant Gittins of the 2nd/24th did his best to recall them:

> Now then 24th Regiment, I am sorry to say that during our absence today the enemy has turned our flank, attacked and taken our camp, stores and ammunition and are in possession. Our only course now is to take it back. I know you 24th and can depend on you. Mind you it means hard fighting at the point of the bayonet. We must get to Rorke's Drift and we cannot get there without retaking the camp.

Somebody else remembered an injunction that, 'No man must retire.' Able to draw on an unfathomable inner strength that has always been, and remains, the envy of the world's armies, the British infantry is at its best in a crisis. From amongst the ranks somebody cried aloud, 'All right sir, we'll do it,' and in token of their indomitable spirit, the 24th raised a cheer. Then, with heavy hearts but resolute minds, the remnants of No. 3 Column advanced on the Sphinx. When they were about a mile and a half from the camp great numbers of Zulus were observed to be crossing the escarpment to the right. A Zulu source recalled:

> The portion of the army which had remained to plunder the camp did so thoroughly, carrying off the maize, bread stuffs and stores of all kinds, and drinking such spirits as were in camp. Many were drunk, and all laden with their booty; and towards sunset the whole force moved back to the encampment of the previous night, hastened by having seen another English force approaching from the south.

Seeing that these warriors posed no immediate threat, Lord Chelmsford ordered that the advance should proceed. Crealock recalled the moment of truth when the force crossed the Nkengeni Ridge and descended towards the Nyogane Donga:

> Day waned and the night hung over the hill as we reached the last
> ridge beyond which had been our camp. To the little hill on the left
> we sent Major Black and 3 companies of the 2nd/24th to seize it –
> for the nek between it and the hill we must gain at all hazards. In
> silence we marched down into the gloom below where lay
> shrouded by a merciful pall the horrors of the past day.

Up until sunset the levies seem to have kept their nerve, so much so that even Crealock spoke well of them in a statement he made a fortnight later. The weight of evidence would indicate, however, that they became next to unmanageable as darkness set in. Crealock was probably too preoccupied in the centre of the line to notice the acute difficulty that Browne and Harford experienced on the flanks. Harford wrote that 2nd/3rd NNC refused absolutely to hold its two-deep line. Despite the best efforts of Cooper's officers and NCOs, the levies chose instead to huddle themselves into quailing clusters. Harford rode ceaselessly up and down behind them in order to prevent lagging and desertion. Browne's recollections are quoted just below and show that 1st/3rd NNC became similarly jittery.

After crossing the Nyogane and following the wagon road a little further uphill, Harness unlimbered and prepared to shell the saddle, where a number of fires were seen to be burning. The order rang out for the 24th to fix bayonets. To the right of the road, Major Dunbar and his wing pushed across the ground where their G Company comrades lay butchered in the grass. Men stumbled against what were clearly corpses, and were forced to step carefully around them to continue the advance. It was as well that by now there was next to no visibility. On the left, Chelmsford pushed Maori Browne's battalion towards Mahlabamkhosi, ahead of Black's wing of the 24th. Undoubtedly he did so in order that any surprise attack the enemy might have in store would fall upon the expendable native troops. Browne paints the picture well and in doing so betrays the contempt he himself felt for the martial prowess of his men. Inevitably, disbandment was only days away for 3rd Regiment, NNC:

> I received orders that I was to retake the koppie at all costs being
> at the same time warned that if my men turned tail the party of the

24th under Major Black who supported me, were at once to fire a volley and charge. This was pleasant for me but of course I recognised the necessity. The word was now given to move on. At the same time the guns opened fire so as to clear the ground in front of us of any large bodies of Zulus who might be there. I dismounted and made for the koppie, dragging the principal Natal induna whom I had clawed hold of by his head ring, swearing I would blow his brains out in case his men turned tail. He howled to them not to run away but behind them came the 24th with fixed bayonets so that no matter what funk the natives were in they had to come on. It was as dark as pitch and soon we were stumbling over dead men (black and white), dead horses, cattle, ruined tents and all the debris of the fight. But up and over the koppie we had to go for every now and then Black's voice would ring out, 'Steady the 24th – be ready to fire a volley and charge.' Up and up we went as the shells came screaming over our heads, the burning time-fuses in the dark looking like rockets. Every time one came over us my wretched natives would utter a howl and try to sit down but bayonets in rear of them will make even a Natal African move on and they had to come. At last we arrived at the top, no living man was there and as the shells just passed over us I told my bugler to sound the 'cease fire'. He could not sound a note, so I shouted to Black that we were on the top and asked him to have the cease fire sounded. This was done and up rushed the 24th who when they reached the top of the hill broke out into cheer after cheer. My Zulus to keep them company rattled their shields and assegais, for had not we retaken the camp; or rather perhaps I ought to say, reoccupied it. Anyhow we were there.

Dark Night

Chelmsford gave orders that the force was to bivouac on the saddle. He had last seen it as a flat grassy area, ideal for the purpose. He could not have imagined in the worst of his nightmares what it now looked like. The European troops were disposed in two-deep lines across either mouth of the saddle, Dunbar's wing facing west in the direction of Natal, and the mounted troops back towards the Isandlwana bowl. Black's wing and

Browne's battalion held Mahlabamkhosi. The N Battery guns and Cooper's levies were in the centre of the saddle. Chelmsford paid great personal attention to the security arrangements and visited the pickets throughout the night. He had been taught the most salutary of lessons about the mighty Zulu, but for Lieutenant-Colonel Henry Pulleine and his men the GOC's new-found wisdom had come far too late.

The pitch-black night that followed was one of the worst that troops have ever spent in the field. It was frightening enough to think of a huge and victorious Zulu army lurking somewhere nearby, without contemplating the scene of carnage that lay on all quarters. Rightly, the men were kept in formation and refused permission to scour through the tents in search of mates or property. Even Sergeant-Major Dan Scott of the Carbineers was refused permission to look for his brother Durrant. Unknowingly, he spent the night less than a hundred yards from his corpse. Hope may have lived on for Dan Scott. In due course he would at least have the consolation of knowing that his brother fought and died like a hero of old. Some of the officers were allowed to go forward with small fatigue parties, in search of unspoiled rations for their men. What little there was – mostly tins of bully beef – was duly shared around, though next day Henry Harford noted the selfishness of Lieutenant Newnham-Davies of the Buffs IMI detachment, who kept a whole tin to himself. In a rare moment of levity, one unknown officer, when told to hold out his helmet to receive the rations of the officers he was representing in the queue, turned away in disgust, remarking that he would rather go without than use his hat for such a purpose.

Maori Browne's batman, an Irishman named Quin, slipped down from Mahlabamkhosi, and returned with a good haul of bully beef and biscuits. He had also commandeered a bottle of brandy and a bottle of port from the wreckage of the camp. Browne passed the brandy on to his officers and shared the port with Wilsone Black, with whom he had now become firm friends. Browne was puffing on his pipe after their meagre meal, when he noticed that there were now regular flashes of light around the distant Oscarberg. 'Those flashes must be musketry,' he remarked to Black and Duncombe. As they stared into the blackness of the night, and strained their ears to the distant popping of rifle fire, a series of fires suddenly sprang up in the hills. 'By God, the Zulus are in Natal,' exclaimed Duncombe, 'Lord help the women and children.' Soon there was also a glow in the sky above Shiyane. It seemed certain that the dawn would bring yet more calamity.

Lanterns were amongst the items most eagerly sought in the wrecked encampments. A few were found and lit. Richard Glyn passed through the camp with a lamp held aloft to try and gauge the extent of the loss in his battalion. He cannot have been encouraged by what he saw. Amongst the many men he recognised was Henry Pulleine. Glyn must have thought at once of Pulleine's family: his wife of twelve years, Frances, and their three young children, a son and two daughters. He also found the 25-year-old Lieutenant George Hodson, the Dublin born second son of the Anglo-Irish baronet, Sir George Hodson. In common with the rest of Natal, Sir Bartle Frere would have to come to terms with personal bereavement; Hodson and Coghill had both served in his household as aides-de-camp. Hodson had also been Coghill's predecessor as orderly officer to Glyn. During the campaign in the Transkei, he had spent many long months at the colonel's side. Glyn could punish himself no more; it was time to sleep. With a heavy heart, he gave up his quest and returned to the rough bivouac of his staff.

Sleep, where it came at all, was fitful. Since they could not see the full horrors of the field, the minds of the men blended the immediate realities of their situation with the imagined horrors of the night. The very ground on which they lay was sodden with blood and entrails. Some soldiers would wake in the morning with the appearance of badly wounded men. Many cried themselves to sleep at the thought of lost mates. The left wing companies of the 24th were lucky to spend the night in their commanding position atop the much less gruesome summit of Mahlabamkhosi, which forever after would be better known as 'Black's Koppie'. The saddle below, though, was a hellish place. When Lieutenant Mainwaring came down from the rocks, he found himself standing over the slaughtered body of Private Waterhouse. Waterhouse had been his batman.

In the middle of the night, Lieutenant John Maxwell of 2nd/3rd NNC was roused to show Chelmsford and Clery around his unit's pickets. As the trio made their way over the southern slope of Isandlwana, Maxwell stumbled and fell and, in reaching out to break his fall, put his hands into something extremely unpleasant to the touch. As Clery swung his lantern round, Maxwell realised that his hands were in the entrails of one of Younghusband's dead. The sensation was appalling.

One of the most haunted men on the saddle that night was Henry Degacher, who sensed at once that his brother had fallen. In the morning, he would tell one of the aides-de-camp that he passed the night in dread of stretching out an arm and hitting William's face. He may have been describing a nightmare. The violent death and mutilation of a brother was tragedy enough for a man to have to dwell on, but Degacher had also lost all his old 1st Battalion friends, as well as five of his own officers and around a third of his men. To make matters worse, the evening breeze bore the sounds of distant battle; it looked as if neither Lieutenant Gonville Bromhead, nor Colour-Sergeant Frank Bourne, or any of the other B Company men at Rorke's Drift, would live to see the dawn. Only one man was more distressed than Degacher.

In some quiet corner Richard Glyn wept.

British Order of Battle and Casualties

Force Engaged at the Camp

Unit	Strength (Officers & Men)	Killed	Notes
Column Staff	7 & 11	3 & 10	Cochrane & Shepstone included here.
1st Battalion, 24th Regt *Brevet Lt-Col H. B. Pulleine*	15 & 398	15 & 396	Coghill included with the staff above so 16 1st/24th officers killed in all.
Staff A Company *Capt W. Degacher* C Company *Capt R. Younghusband* E Company *Lt C. W. Cavaye* F Company *Capt W. E. Mostyn* H Company *Capt G. V. Wardell* Band Pioneer Section			
Rocket battery	0 & 8	0 & 5	Privates of 1st/24th serving with the battery.
Party 90th Regiment	0 & 6	0 & 6	
2nd Battalion, 24th Regt	5 & 171	5 & 171	
G Company *Lt C. d'A. Pope* Guard Rear Details Pioneer Section			
Royal Artillery *Maj S. Smith*	2 & 71	1 & 62	
Lt H. T. Curling's Division, N Battery N Battery rear details			2 x 7-pounder RMLs
Rocket battery	1 & 1	1 & 0	3 x 9-pounder troughs. RA personnel only; men of 1st/24th serving with the battery are listed with their regiment.
No. 1 Squadron, IMI	0 & 31	0 & 21	
Detail 2nd/3rd Buffs Detail 1st/13th LI Detail 1st/24th Detail 80th			

Unit	Strength (Officers & Men)	Killed	Notes
Royal Engineers	2 & 5	2 & 5	Durnford included here.
Natal Mounted Police	0 & 34	0 & 25	
Natal Carbineers *Lt F. J. D. Scott*	2 & 27	2 & 20	
Newcastle Mounted Rifles *Capt R. Bradstreet*	2 & 12	2 & 5	
Buffalo Border Guard *QM D. MacPhail*	1 & 7	0 & 3	

Natal Native Contingent

Strength figures for NNC battalions are approximate. Casualty figures show only whites. NNC losses are traditionally estimated at 470–480 levies in all.

1st Bn, 1st Regt NNC	5 & 318	2 & 10	
D Company *Capt C. Nourse*			
E Company *Capt W. H. Stafford*			
1st Bn, 3rd Regt NNC	11 & 231	8 & 28	
No. 6 Company *Capt R. Krohn*			
No. 9 Company *Capt J. F. Lonsdale*			
2nd Bn, 3rd Regt NNC	9 & 328	9 & 28	
No. 1 Company *Capt O. E. Murray*			
No. 4 Company *Capt E. A. Erskine*			
No. 5 Company *Capt A. J. Barry*			
Natal Native Mounted Contingent *Capt W. Barton*	6 & 257	1 & 27	
No. 1 Troop *Lt C. Raw*			
No. 2 Troop *Lt J. A. Roberts*			
No. 3 Troop *Lt W. Vause*			
Basuto Troop *Lt A. F. Henderson*			
Edendale Troop *Lt H. D. Davies*			
Army Service Corps	0 & 4	0 & 4	
Army Hospital Corps *Lt A. Hall*	1 & 10	1 & 10	
Army Medical Dept *Surgeon-Maj P. Shepherd*	1 & 0	1 & 0	
Pioneers *Lt G. F. Andrews*	1 & 10	0 & 10	From No. 1 Company, Natal Native Pioneer Corps

Civilians

No figures available for those present or killed. Probably 200–300 black *voorloopers*, grooms, etc. Maybe two or three dozen miscellaneous whites.

Total	71 & 1,940	53 & 1,316 (approx.)

Totals do not include civilians.

The Force at Mangeni

Unit	Strength (Officers & Men)	Notes
Army & Column Staff	9 & 0	Chelmsford, Glyn, Crealock, Clery, Gosset, Buller, Milne, Hallam-Parr, Drummond
2nd Battalion, 24th Regt *Lt-Col H. J. Degacher*	17 & 485	Wing commanders *Majs W. M. Dunbar & W. Black*
A Company *Capt J. M. G. Tongue* C Company *Lt H. M. Williams* D Company *Capt W. P. Symons* E Company *Lt Q. McK. Logan* F Company *Capt H. B. Church* H Company *Capt J. J. Harvey* Band		
N Battery, 5th Brigade RA *Brevet Lt-Col A. Harness* *Lt C. S. B. Parsons*'s Division *Lt W. J. Fowler*'s Division	3 & 50	4 x 7-pounder RMLs
No. 1 Squadron, IMI *Lt-Col J. C. Russell* Detail 2nd/3rd Buffs *Lt N. Newnham-Davies* Detail 1st/13th Light Infantry *Lt H. A. Walsh* Detail 1st/24th *Lt E. S. Browne* Detail 80th	4 & 80	
Mounted Police & Volunteers *Maj J. Dartnell* Natal Mounted Police *Insp G. Mansel*	2 & 80	Mounted troops operated as a police troop under Mansel and a composite volunteer troop under Shepstone.
Natal Carbineers *Capt T. Shepstone*	2 & 27	
Newcastle Mounted Rifles *Lt C. Jones*	1 & 20	
Buffalo Border Guard *Capt W. C. Smith*	1 & 16	
1st/3rd NNC *Comdt G. H. Browne* Nos. 1, 2, 3, 4, 5, 7, 8, 10 Companies	20 & 848	Companies of 100 black Africans and 6 white NCOs
2nd/3rd NNC *Comdt E. R. Cooper* Nos. 2, 3, 6, 7, 8, 9, 10 Companies	22 & 742	As for 1st/3rd NNC
No. 1 Company, Natal Native Pioneer Corps *Capt W. J. Nolan*	2 & 90	
Total	83 & 2,417	

Appendix 2

Zulu Order of Battle

Regiment	Strength	Notes
uVe	3,500	Left Horn
iNgobamakhosi	6,000	Chest (centre left)
uMbonambi	1,500	Chest
umCijo	2,500	Chest
uNokhenke	2,000	Chest (centre right)
uDududu	1,500	uNodwengu Corps – Right Horn
iMbube	1,500	uNodwengu Corps – Right Horn
iSangqu	1,000	uNodwengu Corps – Right Horn
uThulwana	1,500	Undi Corps – Reserve
iNdluyengwe	1,000	Undi Corps – Reserve
uDloko	1,500	Undi Corps – Reserve
iNdlondlo	900	Undi Corps – Reserve
Total	24,400	

All figures approximate.

Appendix 3

Isandlwana Survivors

Summary
Europeans   18 officers & 58 other ranks; 5 civilians
Black Africans approximately 560 military personnel and an unknown number of civilian *voorloopers* and grooms

Regular Army Officers (5)
Captain Essex, 75th Regiment (Sub-Director of Transport, No. 3 Column)
Captain Gardner, 14th Hussars (Colonel Glyn's Staff)
Lieutenant Cochrane, 32nd Regiment (Transport Staff Officer, No. 2 Column)
Lieutenant Curling, RA (N Battery, 5th Brigade RA)
Lieutenant Smith-Dorrien, 95th Regiment (Transport Staff No. 3 Column)

Volunteer Officers (13)
Captain Barton (NNMC)
Captain Nourse (1st/1st NNC)
Captain Stafford (1st/1st NNC)
Lieutenant Adendorff (1st/3rd NNC)
Lieutenant Andrews (No. 1 Company NNPC)
Lieutenant Davies (NNMC)
Lieutenant Erskine (1st/1st NNC)
Lieutenant Henderson (NNMC)
Lieutenant Higginson (1st/3rd NNC)
Lieutenant Raw (NNMC)
Lieutenant Vaines (1st/3rd NNC)
Lieutenant Vause (NNMC)
Quartermaster MacPhail (BBG)

European Civilians (5)
Mr Hamer (Commissary No. 2 Column)
Mr Brickhill (Interpreter No. 3 Column)
Mr Foley (Wagon conductor)
Mr Hall (Contractor)
Mr Boer (Mule driver)

Regular Army – Other Ranks (26)

Sergeant Costellow (N/5th RA)
Sergeant Naughton (2nd/3rd Buffs – No. 1 Sqn IMI)
Corporal McCann (1st/24th – No. 1 Sqn IMI)
Bombardier Goff (RA – rocket battery)
Private Bickley (Band 1st/24th)
Private Davis (1st/24th – No. 1 Sqn IMI)
Private Evans (2nd/3rd – No. 1 Sqn IMI)
Private Gascoigne (2nd/3rd Buffs – No. 1 Sqn IMI)
Private Grant (1st/24th – rocket battery)
Private Johnson (1st/24th – rocket battery)
Private Parry (1st/24th – No. 1 Sqn IMI)
Private Power (1st/24th – No. 1 Sqn IMI)
Private Trainer (1st/24th – rocket battery)
Private Wassall (80th – No. 1 Sqn IMI) (Awarded VC)
Private Westwood (80th – No. 1 Sqn IMI)
Private Williams (1st/24th – Colonel Glyn's Orderly)
Private Whelan (1st/13th LI – No. 1 Sqn IMI)
Private Wilson (Band 1st/24th)
Driver Baggeley (N/5th RA)
Driver Burchell (N/5th RA)
Gunner Green (N/5th RA)
Trumpeter Martin (N/5th RA)
Driver Price (N/5th RA)
Gunner Steer (N/5th RA)
Gunner Townsend (N/5th RA)
Driver Tucker (N/5th RA)

Volunteers – Other Ranks (32)

Sergeant-Major Sharp (1st/1st NNC)
Sergeant-Major Williams (1st/3rd NNC)
Sergeant Walsh (NMR)
NCO 3rd NNC Name Unknown
NCO 3rd NNC Name Unknown
Trooper Collier (NMP)
Trooper Doig (NMP)
Trooper Dorehill (NMP)
Trooper Eaton (NMP)
Trooper Hayes (NMP)
Trooper Kincaid (NMP)
Trooper Shannon (NMP)

Trooper Sparks (NMP)
Trooper Stevens (NMP)
Trooper Barker (NC)
Trooper Edwards (NC)
Trooper Fletcher (NC)
Trooper Grainger (NC)
Trooper Muirhead (NC)
Trooper Sibthorpe (NC)
Trooper Tarboton (NC)
Trooper Berning (NMR)
Trooper Brown (NMR)
Trooper Burne (NMR)
Trumpeter Horne (NMR)
Trooper Moodie (NMR)
Trooper Parsons (NMR)
Trooper Walsh (NMR)
Trooper Adams (BBG)
Trooper Adams (BBG)
Trooper Lennox (BBG)
Trooper Stretch (BBG)

Native Troops

Durnford's Native Horse   approx 230 other ranks
Natal Native Contingent   approx 330 other ranks
Voorloopers and other black civilians not known

Bibliography

Adams, Jack, *The South Wales Borderers (The 24th Regiment of Foot)*, London, 1968

Bourquin, S., 'Colonel A.W. Durnford', *South African Military History Society Journal*, Vol. 6, No. 5

Bourquin, S., 'The Zulu Military Organization and the Challenge of 1879', *South African Military History Society Journal*, Vol 4, No. 4

Castle, Ian, *British Infantryman in South Africa 1877–81*, Oxford, 2003

Child, Daphne, ed., *The Zulu War Diary of Colonel Henry Harford*, Pietermaritzburg, 1978

Clammer, David, *The Zulu War*, London, 1973

Cope, Richard, *The Origins of the Anglo-Zulu War of 1879*, Pietermaritzburg, 1999

Coupland, Reginald, *Zulu Battle Piece – Isandhlwana*, London, 1948

Cunynghame, Lieutenant-General Sir Arthur, *My Command in South Africa*, London, 1880

Droogleever, R.W.F., *The Road to Isandhlwana: Colonel Anthony Durnford in Natal and Zululand 1873–1879*, London, 1992

Edgerton, Robert B., *Like Lions they Fought: The last Zulu War*, New York & London, 1988

Emery, Frank, *The Red Soldier: Letters from the Zulu War 1879*, London, 1977

Glennie, Farquhar; Paton George; and Symons, William (eds.), *Historical Records of the 24th Regiment*, London, 1892

Gon, Philip, *The Road to Isandhlwana*, Johannesburg, 1979

Greaves, Adrian, and Best, Brian, eds., *The Curling Letters of the Zulu War*, UK, 2001

Greaves, Adrian, ed., *Redcoats and Zulus; Myths, Legends and Explanations*, Barnsley, 2004

Guy, Jeff, *The Destruction of the Zulu Kingdom*, Johannesburg, 1979

Hall, D. D., 'Artillery in the Zulu War – 1879', *South African Military History Society Journal*, Vol 4, No. 4

Hamilton-Browne, Colonel G., *A Lost Legionary in South Africa*, London, 1912

HMSO, *Field Exercises and Evolutions of Infantry*, London, 1877

Holme, Norman, *The Noble 24th: Biographical Records of the 24th Regiment in the Zulu War and the South African Campaigns 1877–79*, London, 1999

Hummel, Chris, ed., *The Frontier War Journal of Major John Crealock 1878*, Cape Town, 1988

Jackson, F. W. D., *Isandhlwana 1879: The Sources Re-examined*, Brecon, 1999

Jackson, F. W. D., *Hill of the Sphinx: The Battle of Isandlwana*, Kent, 2002

Jones, Alan Baynham, and Stevenson, Lee, *Rorke's Drift By Those Who Were There*, Brighton, 2003

Knight, Ian, *Great Zulu Commanders*, London, 1999

Knight, Ian, *Brave Men's Blood; The Epic of the Zulu War, 1879*, London, 1990

Knight, Ian, *Zulu: Isandlwana and Rorke's Drift 22–23 January 1879*, London, 1992

Knight, Ian, *The Anatomy of the Zulu Army from Shaka to Cetshwayo 1818–1879*, London, 1995

Knight, Ian, *Isandlwana 1879: The Great Zulu Victory*, Oxford, 2002

Knight, Ian, *The Zulu War 1879*, Oxford, 2003

Knight Ian, *The National Army Museum Book of the Zulu War*, London, 2003

Laband, J. P., *Rope of Sand: South Africa 1995.* Reprinted as *The Rise and Fall of the Zulu Nation*, London, 1997

Laband, John, and Mathews, Jeff, *Isandlwana*, Pietermaritzburg, 1992

Laband, J. P., and Thompson, P. S., *Field Guide to the War in Zululand*, Pietermaritzburg, 1979

Laband, J. P., and Thompson, P. S., *Kingdom and Colony at War*, Pietermaritzburg, 1990

Lock, Ron, and Quantrill, Peter, eds., *The Red Book: Natal newspaper reports on the Anglo-Zulu War, 1879*, Pinetown, KZN, 2000

Lock, Ron, and Quantrill, Peter, *Zulu Victory: The Epic of Isandlwana and the Cover-up*, London, 2002

Mackinnon, J. P., and Shadbolt, Sydney, *The South African Campaign 1879*, London, 1880; reprinted London, 1995

Mitford, Bertram, *Through the Zulu Country*, London, 1883; reprinted London, 1995

Morris, Donald R., *The Washing of the Spears*, London, 1966

Myatt, Frederick, *The British Infantry 1660–1945: The Evolution of a Fighting Force*, Poole, 1983

Norris-Newman, Charles L., *In Zululand with the British Throughout the War of 1879*, London, 1889; reprinted London, 1988

Rattray, David, and Greaves, Adrian, *David Rattray's Guidebook to the Anglo-Zulu War Battlefields*, UK, 2003

RHQ RRW, *A Short History of the Royal Regiment of Wales (24th/41st Foot)*, Cardiff, 1993

Smith-Dorrien, Horace, *Memories of Forty-Eight Years Service*, London, 1925

Spiers, Edward M., *The Late Victorian Army 1868–1902*, Manchester, 1992

Stalker, Reverend John, *The Natal Carbineers 1855–1911*, Pietermaritzburg and Durham, 1912

Sutherland, Jonathan, and Canwell, Diane, *Zulu Kings and their Armies*, Barnsley, 2004

Thompson, P. S., *The Natal Native Contingent in the Anglo-Zulu War, 1879*, Pietermaritzburg, 1997

War Office (compiled by J. S. Rothwell), *Narrative of Field Operations Connected with the Zulu War of 1879*, London, 1881; reprinted London, 1907 & 1989

Webb, C. de B., and Wright, J. B., *A Zulu King Speaks: Statements made by Cetshwayo kaMpande on the history and customs of his people*, Pietermaritzburg, 1978

Whybra, Julian, *England's Sons: A Casualty and Survivors' Roll of British Combatants for Isandlwana and Rorke's Drift*, UK, 2004

Wood, Evelyn, *From Midshipman to Field Marshal*, London, 1906

Yorke, Edmund, *Rorke's Drift 1879: Anatomy of a Zulu War Siege*, Stroud and Charleston SC, 2001

Young, John, *They Fell Like Stones: Battles and Casualties of the Zulu War, 1879*, London, 1991

Glossary

amaChunu: one of the native clans of Natal which provided levied warriors to the British. The amaChunu found Nos. 4 and 5 Companies of 2nd/3rd NNC.

amaNgwane: another of the native clans of Natal which provided levies for the British force. The clan was led by the chief Zikhali, and found D and E Companies of 1st/1st NNC, and Nos. 1, 2 and 3 Troops (known collectively as Zikhali's Horse) of the NNMC.

assegai: not actually a Zulu word but now synonymous in common English-language usage with the short stabbing spear more properly known as the *iklwa*. Also used to mean spear in the wider sense; for example 'throwing assegai'.

BBG: Buffalo Border Guard. A small part-time unit of mounted volunteers from the remote farms along Natal's Buffalo River frontier with Zululand.

boy: rank by which those under the age of eighteen serving in the British Army as drummers or bandsmen were known. Many of them were the orphaned sons of army families.

brevet rank: An officer's paid rank is known as his substantive rank. It was the practice in the Victorian era to grant an officer a brevet promotion to the next higher rank in recognition of distinguished service. He would wear the insignia of the higher rank and be addressed by it, but he would not be paid in that rank until he received substantive promotion into an appropriate vacancy on the establishment. Down to the modern day, a unit's establishment regulates what the taxpayer is prepared to pay for; the establishment may not be exceeded.

colour-sergeant: the equivalent in 1879 of a company sergeant-major today. He was the senior non-commissioned man in his company and was responsible to the company commander for its discipline, drill, turnout and administration.

division: a tactical subdivision of a British artillery battery. A battery had three divisions each of two guns. A division was commanded by a lieutenant and consisted of around 20 men, including two sergeants who each commanded one of the gun-crews.

drift: natural river crossing, ford.

GOC: general officer commanding. In this case GOC South Africa – the senior British officer in the colony.

hlomula: Zulu ritual practice associated with the hunt for dangerous game. It was normal for all the warriors who had participated in the chase to bloody their spears in the corpse of the prey by way of tribute to its courage. The British dead at Isandlwana were subjected to *hlomula*.

horns of the buffalo: the Zulu battle formation aimed at achieving the rapid double envelopment, encirclement and consequent destruction of an enemy. In Zulu *impondo zankomo*, or 'the beast's horns'.

ibutho (plural amabutho): a Zulu regiment formed by mustering the youth of a new generation into a formed and disciplined body of troops. Hence a Zulu army consisted of a number of *amabutho* in or approaching middle age (typically kept in reserve), *amabutho* in their early twenties (which were usually assigned to the horns), and *amabutho* in the prime of life (normally assigned to the 'chest' or centre).

iklwa: the short stabbing *assegai* designed and introduced by King Shaka.

IMI: Imperial Mounted Infantry. Detachments of regular infantrymen mounted on African ponies. Although such units were formed in lieu of regular cavalry, they were incapable of shock action and customarily dismounted to fight on foot.

impi: a Zulu army consisting of a number of *amabutho*.

indaba: a meeting or parley.

induna (plural izinduna): a Zulu headman or officer-grade leader in an *ibutho*.

isiGqoza: a Zulu faction forced to flee to Natal after the war of succession fought to determine King Mpande's successor; they had opposed Cetshwayo and thus found themselves on the losing side. When the NNC was levied, they found Nos. 8, 9 and 10 Companies in 1st/3rd NNC.

ka: used in Zulu as a prefix to mean 'son of', hence Cetshwayo kaMpande.

kloof: Afrikaans word for a steep-sided wooded valley, gorge or ravine.

knobkerrie: African hardwood club; a crude round-headed cudgel.

koppie: Afrikaans name for a low hill or ridge, typically covered in sandstone scree-boulders.

kraal: Though this is not a Zulu word, it was in common usage amongst the European population of 19th-century South Africa to describe an African homestead, village, or barracks. It survives in many modern place-names in modern South Africa. Typically a 'kraal' consisted of a ring of beehive huts arrayed around a central stock pen or arena and inside an outer enclosure fence. Royal or military kraals could consist of hundreds of huts.

NC: Natal Carbineers. Fashionable, part-time unit of mounted volunteers, recruited from the well-to-do families of Pietermaritzburg. Formed 1855.

nek: geographical term – in more common usage, a 'saddle'. The lower ground lying between two adjacent high points.

NMP: Natal Mounted Police. The professional quasi-military constabulary of Natal. Formed in 1874.

NMR: Newcastle Mounted Rifles. Small part-time unit of mounted volunteers from the frontier town of the same name.

NNC: Natal Native Contingent. Temporary native infantry battalions levied from the black population of Natal. NNC battalions had European officers and NCOs recruited from the settler communities of Natal or the Ciskei (in particular King William's Town).

NNMC: Natal Native Mounted Contingent. Troops of irregular horse raised from the black population of Natal by Colonel Anthony Durnford, RE.

NNPC: Natal Native Pioneer Corps. Corps of uniformed native pioneers raised by Colonel Durnford in the absence of any formed bodies of Royal Engineers.

picket (plural pickets): also 'picquet'. A picket is a group of soldiers thrown out at a distance from a position to give early warning of an approaching enemy. It was the practice for a picket company to deploy its men across a wide frontage in groups of four. Pickets withdraw closer to the main position by night. Also used as a verb: 'It was decided to picket the heights.'

qaqa: Zulu ritual practice of slashing open the abdomen of a fallen enemy for superstitious reasons.

Special Service Officer: A regular army officer seconded from his regiment to detached duty in an operational theatre. The GOC could employ such officers in whatever way he felt best. Typically they were employed as staff officers or as commanders of irregular troops.

vedette: the cavalry equivalent of a picket – mounted soldiers thrown out even further afield than the outlying infantry pickets, in order to provide early warning.

veldt (or veld): pronounced 'felt'. Afrikaans word for grasslands or the open field. Also used in a wider sense to mean 'countryside'.

voorlooper: literally 'one who goes ahead'. Used to mean an assistant to a wagon driver (and in 1879 thus usually a black employee of a white man) who walked at the head of the trek-oxen to set direction, to prevent the animals becoming entangled and to keep them on the move.

umnyama: the evil forces or spirits of which all Zulus lived in superstitious dread.

uSuthu: the name of King Cetshwayo's faction in the Zulu civil war that brought him to power; also a battle cry of the Zulu *amabutho* of 1879.

Index